EDITH'S WAR

NUMBER 159

Williams-Ford Texas A&M University

Military History Series

EDITH'S WAR

Writings of a Red Cross Worker and Lifelong Champion of Social Justice

Peter A. Witt

Foreword by Kara Dixon Vuic

TEXAS A&M UNIVERSITY PRESS • College Station

First edition

This paper meets the requirements
of ANSI/NISO Z39.48–1992 (Permanence of Paper).
Binding materials have been chosen for durability.
Manufactured in the United States of America

LIBRARY OF CONGRESS CATALOGING-IN-PUBLICATION DATA

Names: Witt, Peter A., 1943– author, editor. | Witt, Edith, 1911–2000, author.
Title: Edith's war : writings of a Red Cross worker and lifelong champion of social justice / Peter A. Witt.
Other titles: Williams-Ford Texas A&M University military history series ; no. 159.
Description: First edition. | College Station : Texas A&M University Press, [2018] | Series: Williams-Ford Texas A&M University military history series ; Number 159 | Includes bibliographical references and index.
Identifiers: LCCN 2017045890| ISBN 9781623496258 (book / cloth : alk. paper) | ISBN 9781623496265 (e-book)
Subjects: LCSH: Witt, Edith, 19112000. | World War, 1939–1945—Women—United
States—Biography. | World War, 1939–1945—War work—Red Cross. | World War, 1939-1945—Personal narratives, American. | Social reformers—United States—Biography. | Political activists—United States—Biography. | Women social reformers—United States—Biography. | Women political activists—United States—Biography. | Lesbians—United States—Biography. | LCGFT: Biographies.
Classification: LCC D811.5 .E35 2018 | DDC 940.53/1 [B] —dc23 LC record available at https://lccn.loc.gov/2017045890

Contents

Foreword

Not long after Red Cross worker Edith Witt arrived in the Algerian coastal city of Oran in early 1944, an American GI asked her where she got her freckles. "They look awfully pretty with the sun on them now," he commented before explaining that he had been reminded of the sunshine in his native Kansas and his sister, who had freckles too. The brief interaction resonated with Edith, who wrote to her mother that she had finally "discovered the raison d'etre of my freckles." In her wartime role as a recreation worker whose job it was to entertain, comfort, and reassure homesick and embattled American soldiers, Edith realized that she had become "the living symbol of all the freckled-face gals that ever saw the sun from coast to coast back home." Even without freckles, Edith would have reminded GIs of girls from home, but as her encounter with the GI from Kansas hints, Edith was unique.

Edith both embodied many of the characteristics of women of her generation and defied them. She grew up at a time in US history when women's access to education, political participation, and the workforce was slowly expanding. Yet obstacles remained. When, as a young girl, Edith encountered the limitations all women faced, she resolved to resist them nonetheless. Despite her occasional wish to have been born a boy who would have enjoyed opportunities that she did not have, she forged ahead, earned a college degree, and took an active role in the pressing political issues of the 1930s and early 1940s. When the United States entered World War II, avenues for women's civic participation widened, even as prevailing notions of white, middle-class womanhood continued to constrain women's lives. Hundreds of thousands of women entered factory work, joined the military, and rushed through nursing school, for example, but media consistently presented the public with reassuring images of well-coiffed and manicured women who had only temporarily and out of necessity joined the war effort. Edith was a part of this. In some ways working in a Red Cross service club fit nicely with contemporary images of women as cheerful companions for soldiers. However, this work also took Edith far beyond the typical experience of women in her generation and enabled her to venture much closer to the war itself than most.

Edith's account of her Red Cross work illuminates the nuances and contradictions that women faced during World War II and draws our attention to a little-known but essential part of the American experience in the war. Picking up the mantle of civilian service to the military that had been established in World War I, the Red Cross offered an extensive array of assistance to military personnel stationed across all of the war's theaters. Women like Edith established clubs where soldiers could find a bit of home. Stocked with newspapers and magazines, popular music, doughnuts and coffee, and, best of all, young women from home, Red Cross service clubs offered GIs a place where they could escape the stresses and the boredom of war. Military and Red Cross officials maintained that women like Edith were the most essential part of the clubs, antidotes to the temptations that awaited young men stationed far from the moralizing influence of home. Thus, Red Cross officials recruited women like Edith who embodied conventional notions of respectable femininity and who, they believed, would remind the men of women from home. Women needed to be attractive and enticing enough to draw soldiers off the streets and into the clubs, then be sufficiently warm and friendly to make the men feel welcome. Yet the women had to be careful that their interactions with soldiers did not become so friendly that they opened the women to questions about their reputations. Several of Edith's colleagues likened this constant attention to living in a goldfish bowl, and it proved wearing on women charged with maintaining a proper balance between friendliness and flirtation.

Edith understood the many expectations placed on her by Red Cross and military officials as well as the soldiers she entertained in her club. As she later explained, men attributed great significance to something as simple as a game of Ping-Pong, a dance, or a conversation with a woman like herself. It was moments like these, Edith knew, that allowed a homesick man to forget "the burden of his thoughts for a moment." Even sharing a cup of coffee symbolized something much more profound than refreshment. While sitting with "an American girl," she reflected, a man could "have someone to say hello to and good-bye to, someone to be remembered by."

As Edith's writings reveal, being open to and caring for the men with whom she worked made her vulnerable to their loss. Indeed, her war stories offer a counter-narrative to more common and well-known narratives that privilege combat and heroics. Edith's war was personal and intimate, shaped by the constant rotation of men who came into her club, left, and sometimes never returned. As she confessed when asked to attend a memorial service, she did not want to go because she feared hearing the names of men she had known. Despite her reluctance, Edith felt a deep responsibility to remember the men who had died in the war that she hoped would eventually pave the way for a better world. Characteristic of what would become a lifetime of commitment to causes she believed in, she summoned the strength to mourn their loss and work toward a brighter future.

In fact, Edith's wartime work constitutes only a small portion of a lifetime of fighting to create a more just and humane world. The stalwart attitude she displayed during the war reflected the young woman who had grown up in Brooklyn and worked for progressive causes. And it foreshadowed the postwar woman who refused to sign a Cold War–era loyalty oath, marched alongside civil rights protesters in Selma, earned a graduate degree, and fought for environmental causes and human rights in San Francisco. Edith Witt was anything but ordinary. Relatively few American women participated in such extensive political activities, and even fewer preserved their experiences for posterity. *Edith's War* thus provides a rare and remarkable picture of the life of a unique American woman. In the end, it was not her freckles but instead the broader contours of her life that made her unique.

—Kara Dixon Vuic
Texas Christian University

Preface

Edith Witt was a passionate participant in history, from her childhood in the early 1900s through the Depression, World War II, the McCarthy era, the civil rights movement, and events that transformed American cities in the 1960s and 1970s. Through her autobiography and writings about World War II, this strong and insightful woman provides us with fascinating, provocative, and eyewitness accounts and stories about many of the historic changes that took place in the United States in the twentieth century.

Edith was an advocate for social justice and equal rights years before the women's movement of the 1960s. Edith was eighteen when the stock market crashed in 1929, leading to the Great Depression with its decade of massive unemployment and labor unrest. Along with her older brother, Arthur, and younger brother, Bert, Edith became an activist concerned with the plight of workers, racial and economic justice, and the threat of another world war. Arthur's passion took him to fight as a member of the Abraham Lincoln Brigade for the Republic in Spain. In the United States, Bert joined a number of student groups that struggled for workers' rights and peace.

Edith started her undergraduate education at Barnard College in New York and gained her bachelor's degree ten years later at the University of Chicago. During the 1930s, Edith helped organize a biracial sit-in that stopped a restaurant from refusing to serve black patrons. She worked to organize steelworkers' wives as millions of industrial workers were seeking better working conditions and pay during the Depression. She helped organize rallies protesting cutbacks in Works Progress Administration (WPA) funding when the Franklin Roosevelt administration began to curtail support for the unemployed. She participated in student and worker protests for civil liberties and against war and fascism. Then, in 1943, Edith joined the American Red Cross Club Service and for three years, first in North Africa and then in Italy, provided assistance to off-duty or injured soldiers returning from the front.

After the war, Edith was one of California's first casualties of the McCarthy era when public servants were fired not for job performance shortcomings but for their personal beliefs. In 1965 she marched with Martin Luther King Jr. and thousands of other protesters during the final days of the Selma–Montgomery march, facing down the Alabama governor, the KKK, and the very real threat of violence along the way.

In the 1960s and 1970s, Edith helped build community organizations in San Francisco to advocate for decent and affordable alternative housing when cities were evicting low-income residents, families with children, and seniors to make room for corporate convention centers, headquarters for financial institutions, and sports arenas. When a new ferry service for the convenience of commuters to San Francisco threatened to destroy essential marshlands and homes, Edith organized efforts to mitigate the impact and gain property and environmental protections.

Edith May Witkowsky came from a humble background. She was born on May 11, 1911, in Brooklyn, New York. Her father, Herman, came from a poor immigrant family, and he and his siblings had gone to work as soon as they were able (Herman as a law clerk by age sixteen). Edith's mother, Ida, also born to an immigrant family, was employed as a secretary-stenographer by the time she was sixteen. She wanted to continue her schooling and become a teacher, but her father told her she had to go to work. Herman and Ida married in 1905, when Herman was twenty-three and Ida twenty-one. Edith was the middle child of their three, with Arthur born in 1907 and Bert in 1916. Shortly before Bert was born, the family changed its name to Witt, most likely in an effort to avoid discrimination commonly experienced by first- and second-generation immigrants.

While Edith's parents had humble beginnings and were not of substantial means, they did provide her and her brothers with a solid upbringing and an appreciation for education. And oldest sibling Arthur would serve as a model to Edith and Bert with his social justice activism. For example, Arthur worked in a Cleveland settlement house, organized workers in Chicago, and in 1937 went to Spain to join the international brigades that were aiding Spanish government forces in their fight against the fascists. We are fortunate that Edith not only participated in social movements herself but also wrote about them over her life. She started writing when she was very young and never stopped. In her youth she wrote poems and stories, and she later wrote letters to her mother and other relatives during her World War II Red Cross service in North Africa and Italy. After the war she wrote more detailed accounts of those experiences based on her letters and the copious notes she made during the war. And finally, near the end of her life, Edith wrote a vivid and engaging autobiography. Combined, these materials provide us with a compelling look into the life of a woman who was ultimately honored by her community for her many contributions through the naming of the Edith Witt Senior Living Community housing project in San Francisco.

Edith's story takes us on a journey from the second decade of the twentieth century to near its end. Her writings provide a window through which we can view and better understand some of the issues and events that helped shape the country.

Organization of the Book

In part 1, Edith tells about the first thirty-two years of her life, the years before she joined the Red Cross in 1943. Supplemental material is provided to aid understanding of the context of events Edith describes.

Part 2 contains accounts that Edith wrote detailing her first four months with the Red Cross Club Service in North Africa in the spring of 1943. Edith tells about her passage by troop transport to Algeria, her efforts to open the first Red Cross club for officers in Oran, and daily life at the club. She conveys the excitement generated by the troops of the First and Fifth Army units returning to Oran in May 1943 after the Allies have defeated Hitler's forces in North Africa. Her rich descriptions and compelling dialogue enable us to share her experience of interacting with the soldiers and other Red Cross workers. Edith's accounts raise questions about the status of the "girls" who undertook wartime service through organizations like the Red Cross to support "our boys" overseas. The section includes a discussion of the training that club staff received before they were assigned overseas and the various roles the women played in maintaining troop morale.

Part 3 begins with Edith's letters reflecting on the end of the war in 1945 and her preparations to go home. Next, a story she wrote after the war reflects on its impact on the soldiers and their thoughts about the future. This part concludes with another story she wrote after the war, reflecting on racial discrimination and the problems some soldiers faced on returning home.

The book's final part provides Edith's account of the events and issues that shaped her life after World War II, including her refusal to sign a mandated California loyalty oath, her participation in the Selma–Montgomery march, her work with the San Francisco Human Rights Commission, and her daily life and environmental activism along the Greenbrae Boardwalk, a unique community of forty-eight houses north of San Francisco in San Rafael.

Throughout the book, I have supplied some context and background to events in which Edith participated. I hope that this material will enrich what the reader takes away from reading Edith's accounts of her life.

A missing piece in all of Edith's accounts about her life is a discussion of her sexual orientation. Edith was a lesbian who, like many women of her time, did not discuss her sexual orientation with friends or family. It was known within the family that she had at least two romantic partners after World War II, the first in the late 1940s and early 1950s, and the second beginning in the mid-1960s. For years she lived in a house owned by that second partner, and she would continue living there even after that relationship ended, until Edith moved to an assisted living facility in 1994.

In conducting interviews with some of the people Edith worked with during her time with the San Francisco Human Rights Commission, the issue of Edith's sexual orientation never came up. In fact, when a man who had worked with her and kept contact with her after she retired read an early draft of this introduction, his reaction was, "I never knew."

Consequently, an important piece of Edith's story is hidden. We are not able to interpret choices she made, causes she got involved with, or anything regarding her romantic or social life through the lens of Edith being a lesbian. And perhaps that is a story in itself.

How this Book Came About

Edith knew about me before I ever learned about her. During her service in the Red Cross, she wrote her mother from Oran asking if there was any news from my parents about my birth. In late August 1943, word reached her that I had been born. However, we would not meet formally until early 1946, when Edith had returned from her Red Cross service and moved to California, where I was living with my parents in Los Angeles.

After a brief period in Los Angeles, Edith moved to the San Francisco area, which was to be her home for the rest of her life. Over the years, I saw her when she came to Los Angeles to visit over the Christmas holidays or to visit her mother while she was still alive, or when I visited her in San Francisco. I did spend a memorable five days with Edith and her partner in San Francisco when I was almost six years old. What I cannot recall directly about that is made up for by having copies of letters Edith sent to my parents about my visit. Over the years I learned other things about Edith's life from my father, but in general we were not a family that interacted a lot with relatives or shared a lot of family information, especially about out-of-town family members. And, unfortunately, during the few times I visited Edith in San Francisco, somehow the discussion was more about my life than hers.

I came to know a lot more about Edith when in 1990 my parents completed a ten-year project to create both a written and pictorial family history. Besides constructing an extensive family tree and doing historical research on deceased members of the family, they cajoled their sons, daughters-in-law, grandchildren, Edith, and another aunt to provide a written history of their lives to that point, a considerable undertaking for everyone involved. Ultimately my parents presented five resultant leather-bound volumes of narrative and pictures to each family member. I was enthralled to read about distant, now-deceased relatives, and the life stories of my brothers, my parents, and my aunts, including Edith. Reading about our family led to a deep desire to learn more on the part of many of us. However, because of distance—I lived in Texas and my family largely lived on the West Coast—discussions and follow-ups, at least with me, did not occur.

For me, this was particularly true with Edith. Then, in 1994, Edith moved into an assisted living facility where she lived until her death in

2000. The door to knowing more about her seemed to be closed. We all learned more about her in 2010, when she was honored with the dedication of the Edith Witt Senior Living Community, but this only provided a small amount of additional information about her many contributions while working for the San Francisco Human Rights Commission. Given Edith's modesty, she had not included in her autobiography many details about the significance of her work with the commission.

In the spring of 2015, the door to Edith's life opened again. The wife of one of Edith's cousins contacted one of my brothers and asked if we had any interest in having some notes, writings, and other materials that Edith had saved concerning her World War II experiences. The cousin had helped Edith move in 1994 and had "cleaned out" her remaining belongings after she died in 2000 but had saved these papers. After that cousin died in 2014, his wife had come across Edith's "stuff" and made an effort to get the papers into the hands of family members.

My brothers and I hadn't known these materials existed. Our father passed away in 2013, and we are not sure that he knew about them. After receiving the box sent to us, my brothers and I read them and were delighted to find that Edith had saved some of the letters she'd written home to her mother about her World War II overseas experiences. She also had saved a typed chronological record of important paragraphs from her letters and had written some extended accounts about her time with the Red Cross after she had returned to the States. My brothers and I were amazed that these papers had survived all these years and only now were being made known to our family.

What followed was a decision on my part to see if, together with Edith's autobiography, there was enough material worth sharing beyond our family about the life and times of this truly remarkable woman. Having retired in 2013 from a university teaching and research career, I set about, with the permission of my brothers, organizing Edith's papers into a format that would be of interest to others. This process led to reading books of letters and accounts compiled by several other women who had served with the Red Cross during World War II and subsequent wars. It also enabled me to increase my knowledge of many of the other events and time periods in which Edith had participated.

In doing research I came across further documentation, writings, and other material directly related to Edith. For example, I found her poems and short stories published in a Brooklyn newspaper when she was just nine to eleven years old. I found poems and stories that she wrote during high school and stories she had published in several literary magazines in the 1940s and 1950s. A search through the *New York Times* and several San Francisco newspapers also revealed information about Edith's life, and minutes and annual reports from the San Francisco Human Rights Commission yielded a much better understanding of her many contributions during her ten years of service with the commission. Finally, interviews with several people who had worked with Edith during her days on the commission and people who knew her during the years she lived in San Francisco provided further insights and valuable information.

As Edith's life became more known beyond information in the autobiography she had provided the family in 1990, I became convinced that it was worth sharing her story more broadly. In addition, reading accounts of other Red Cross "girls" about their World War II experiences led me to conclude that Edith's accounts of the war provided a unique perspective that would add substantially to the existing literature.

Edith's story is one of independence, social concern, activism, service to others, and a deep commitment to protecting the quality of life for all who live in a community. Edith was a humble and reserved woman, but her contributions made a difference. It is my hope that others will be enriched by her life story and inspired to action in their own communities.

—Peter A. Witt
Bryan, Texas

Note: In what follows, the text in italics is the voice of Peter Witt or another source. All other writing is from Edith Witt.

Acknowledgments

Many individuals contributed to making this book a reality. First, I want to thank my parents, Ellen and Bert Witt, who started a family history project in the 1980s and persuaded family members to contribute autobiographical material. Edith Witt was one of the contributors, and her autobiography provided the initial outline of her life story.

Edith's cousin Charles Brandes was also critical to this effort. When Edith died in 2000, he saved her wartime Red Cross letters and writings, along with some other materials, that were critical to producing this volume. His wife, Linda Lee Boyd, made sure that the materials were passed on to my brothers and me after Charles passed away in 2014.

I am also grateful to my brothers, Paul, Matt, and Tony Witt, who entrusted me with editing Edith's materials and producing this book. They also provided helpful feedback regarding some of the chapter drafts. Matt, in particular, helped me keep the story focused on the important elements of Edith's life and story and prevented me from wandering down too many rabbit holes. Family members Paul Brandes, Sandy Hanson, and Vera Cousins also shared some remembrances about Edith and provided encouragement for the project.

Several other people provided critical advice and valuable comments, including Teri Metcalf and Arnold Krammer. Teri inspired me through her efforts to document important aspects of her own family history, and Arnie was a good touchstone on questions related to World War II history.

Kara Vuic, a history professor at Texas Christian University, was also critical to completing the book. She supplied encouragement, a useful and informative review of an early draft, copies of needed documents, and, most importantly, access to four chapters from a book tentatively titled *The Girls Next Door: American Women and Military Entertainment*, which is under contract with Harvard University Press. Discussion of many of the contextual issues involving women serving with the American Red Cross would not have been possible without Kara's assistance.

The book could not have been completed without the willingness of several people from the San Francisco area to talk with me about their remembrances of working with or living near Edith. In particular I want to thank Calvin Welch, David Prowler, Chester Hartman, Faye D'Opal, Wandine Treanor, Claudette Josephson, and Martha Jaroski for their thoughtful comments and background information.

I want to acknowledge the critical role played by my wife, Joyce Nies, in the completion of this project. She provided thoughtful comments throughout the process of developing a readable manuscript, undertook much-needed proofreading, and made editorial suggestions. More importantly, her interest in family history and positive outlook on life provided the encouragement that helped me to see the project through to completion. I am sure we missed some joint endeavors because of my determination to finish this book. I appreciate her understanding and support.

The library staff at Texas A&M University were also most helpful in identifying materials for this book. In particular I would like to thank Stephen Bales, who found several of Edith's writings, provided access to the *San Francisco Chronicle,* and helped gather other materials critical to background research. Interlibrary loan staff were also helpful, tracking down articles, books, and other documents not held by the A&M library.

I also want to express my gratitude to the staff at the Texas A&M University Press and in particular editor-in-chief and acquisitions editor Jay Dew, who believed in this project from the beginning and patiently guided me through the review, institutional approval, and manuscript revision processes. Appreciation also is extended to the excellent staff at the Press who helped process the book, including Patricia Clabaugh, project editor; Emily Seyl, editorial assistant; Mary Ann Jacobs, book designer; and Gayla Christiansen, marketing director, and her team.

In addition, Chris Dodge, copyeditor and indexer, was invaluable to creating a readable final product. Chris was responsive and helpful in guiding me through needed edits and worked diligently to preserve Edith's voice.The work and advice of cartographer Anne Boykin is also appreciated.

Last, but most importantly, I want to thank Edith Witt herself. Edith led a rich and interesting life. She left enough documentation through her autobiography and World War II writings to enable me to share in her story and commitment to social justice. It has been an honor to be the steward of her legacy in the process of preparing this book. However, it has also been a heavy responsibility to represent properly Edith's ideas and the quality of her experiences.

While I am indebted to all of the above individuals, all factual and interpretative errors in the book are solely my responsibility.

Edith Witt Timeline

May 11, 1911	Edith May Witkowsky born in Brooklyn, New York
1916	Family name changed to Witt
1920s	Attended P.S. 128 in Brooklyn
1927	Valedictorian, New Utrecht High School, Brooklyn
1928	Attended Barnard College, New York City
1929	Volunteered at a mental health clinic in New York City
Early 1930s	Lived in Croton-on-Hudson, New York, selling firewood
1933	Father died
1935	Worked in a bookstore
1936–37	Employed as recreation worker, Works Progress Administration
1937	Brother Arthur Witt killed fighting Franco's fascists on February 27 at the Battle of Jarma during the Spanish Civil War
1937	Helped organize protests against cuts of WPA jobs and wages
1938	Attended University of Chicago while living with Arthur's widow and young daughter
1939	Received bachelor's degree in sociology from the University of Chicago
1940	Moved back to New York and lived with her mother
1941–42	Employed as a counselor, Brandes School, Phoenix, Arizona

1943–45	Worked for Red Cross Club Service, North Africa and Italy
1946	Moved to Los Angeles to be near her mother
1946	Moved to San Francisco
1948	Junior probation officer, City of San Francisco
1950	Refused to sign loyalty oath and fired from probation officer position
1950s	Worked for survey and consulting firms, including Kellogg and Associates and Hal Dunleavy and Associates, and undertook private consulting work
1960	Conducted feasibility study for St. Francis Square development in San Francisco
1962	Earned master's degree in social science, specializing in housing, from San Francisco State University
1963	Mother died
1965	Participated in Selma–Montgomery civil rights march in Alabama
1966	Employed as housing representative, San Francisco Human Rights Commission
1970	Moved to home on Greenbrae Boardwalk, San Rafael, California
1975	Retired from job with Human Rights Commission
1994	Moved to assisted living facility
Feb. 23, 2000	Died; funds raised to name an internship in her honor at the Poverty and Race Research Action Council
2010	San Francisco's Edith Witt Senior Living Community named in her honor

PART ONE
Early Life

1
Growing Up in Brooklyn

The Early Years

As a child I loved to write, "Edith May Witt, 1943 Benson Avenue, Brooklyn, New York City, New York State, USA., Western Hemisphere, The Earth, The Galaxy, The Universe." That's who I was. That's where I lived.

In summer I helped pick cherries off the trees in the backyard. With the neighborhood kids, I swam in Gravesend Bay. We played Follow-the-Leader around the stable fence where the peddlers kept their horses. The peddlers brought excitement to the street. We sucked slivers of ice snatched from the ice wagon and chewed little balls of tar from the roofing wagon. We rode the rooster or the tiger on the merry-go-round for a penny a ride as the man turned it around with the hand crank and the calliope music played. Fish, fruit, and vegetable wagons blew their horns or whistles, and the mothers came out and talked to one another. The junk man and the ragman were collecting. "Old clothes! Rags! I buy junk!" At night, the milkman—clop, clop of the horse. We played games outdoors: jacks, jump rope, 1–2–3 Alairy, potsy, stoopball.[1] At dusk I waited on the front stoop for the lamplighter to light the gas lamp on our corner with his pole.

In winter we skated on the bumpy, frozen golf course, played Snap-the-Whip, and built small fires, trying to get warm. We played games

1 Alairy (also known as O'Leary) is a game that involves bouncing a ball on the ground and catching it with one hand. Each time "alairy" is said, the player does a circular swing with one of her legs. "Potsy" is the name of the object thrown in a game of hopscotch. Stoopball is a game resembling baseball, where a ball is thrown against a building or stoop rather than to a batter.

indoors: crokinole, tiddlywinks, Parcheesi, checkers, cards, and word games such as ghost, little words out of big, and anagrams.[2] My mother played the piano and sang, and we sang along with her; later we sang Negro spirituals and folksongs my older brother, Arthur, brought home and played on his guitar. After we got a Victrola, we listened to records. When we got a radio, my father would wake us up late at night. We sat together in the living room and listened to Fred Allen, Jack Benny, dramas, mysteries, news, election returns.

We went on vacations to a farm or to small places in the Adirondacks or the Ranger Lakes in Maine and hiked and rowed and swam and read and played billiards and word games. We went on trips and tours to see historic sites.

Summer and winter, I read a lot and wrote stories and poems. Some even got published in our local newspaper.

In 1921, at age ten, Edith applied to become a member of the Junior Eagle Club *sponsored by the local paper, the* Brooklyn Daily Eagle. *The club was run by an "Aunt Jean," who referred to all the young readers as her nieces and nephews. News about the club appeared in the Sunday edition. Aunt Jean sponsored four interest groups: Art Club, Humane Club, Literary Club, and Puzzle Club. Children could earn credits or points for solving a weekly puzzle or participating in other activities. What they could do with the credits is unclear.*

The following is Edith's letter to Aunt Jean applying for membership in the club.

Dear Aunt Jean—

I love to read the stories and poems written by your nieces and nephews. I hope to become an author when I grow up, and writing stories for The Junior Eagle will help me; therefore, I would like to belong to the Literary Club. I also enjoy solving the puzzles. It is so interesting. When you solve a puzzle it gives your brain a chance to work real hard. I would like to belong to the Puzzle Club also. The answer to the caprice puzzle is Robert E. Lee. I would also like to belong to the Humane Club.

I have a puppy Buster. He is 3 weeks old. Buster is a terrier. If I tell him to lie down, sit up, stay still, come here, he will do so.

2 Crokinole: a game where players take turns flicking disks on a board.

He learned to understand very quickly. He is very playful during the day. I will be very kind to him and to all dumb creatures. Sometimes a squirrel comes around and my brother and I feed him nuts. He will come to our hands for them. It is very interesting to watch how he buries some and then covers the earth up so no one would think anything was buried there. Some he eats. He sits on his hind legs and puts his tail up very straight and eats the nut, using his front paws for hands. It is wonderful how Mother Nature gave all animals their peculiarities, but it is too bad we cannot understand their language. When I grow up I would like to live on a farm and have all the domestic animals I could.

Please send me my buttons and certificate as soon as possible, for I am anxious to wear them and be proud because I belong to Aunt Jean's clubs.

Your niece-to-be—
Edith Witt (age 10), 1943 Benson Ave.[3]

Beginning in 1921, several of Edith's poems appeared in the club section of the paper.[4]

Interrupted Fun

"I betcha a dime, I can climb"
Said Bob to his brother Bill.
"I betcha you can't"—then along came his aunt,
Said: "what are you saying?"
"Aw, we're just playing," said they together.
"And why are you out in this rainy weather?"
They looked at each other, and thought of their mother!
Their faces fell, they couldn't tell.
So they scampered home, pell-mell.

—Edith Witt (age 9), 1943 Benson Ave.

3 Edith Witt, "A Newsy Letter," *Brooklyn Daily Eagle*, September 25, 1921.

4 Edith Witt, "Interrupted Fun," *Brooklyn Daily Eagle*, January 30, 1921; Edith Witt, "Two Points of View," *Brooklyn Daily Eagle*, January 30, 1921; Edith Witt, "Nature," *Brooklyn Daily Eagle*, November 19, 1922; Edith Witt, "The Pencil," Brooklyn Daily Eagle, March 25, 1923.

Two Points of View

Says Jerry:
"Why does it rain? It gives me a pain,
Yuh can't go out, an' hafta sit about,
Yuh can't play and run an' have some fun;
I can't read now—I've got goggles, anyhow."
Says Jack:
"I love a rainy day to come, 'cause I have lots of indoor fun.
I play with my soldiers, and read my book,
I draw pictures of kings and cooks.
But I don't play with my brother Jerry,
For on rainy days he isn't merry."

—Edith Witt (age 9), 1943 Benson Ave.

Nature

I ne'er have seen a more wondrous sight
Than that of the sun's reflecting light,
O'er purple mountains just at dusk,
With the clouds as white as an elephant's tusk
'Twas after a shower I saw this scene,
A rainbow arched above the green,
And still more wondrous to behold
The mountain seemed like a hill of gold,
As I watched the colors fade
From the beautiful scene the sun had made.

—Edith Witt (age 11), 1943 Benson Ave.

The Pencil

An old pencil am I.
Quite ready to die;
Scratched and bitten on.
In many places I have gone:

I have fallen on the ground,
I've been lost and found;
All 'round I've been tossed.
My eraser is lost:
I'll be thrown away for good.
This is a cruel world, I wish I would.

—Edith Witt (age 12), 2328 Bay.

Sometimes I wished I were a boy because in those days boys were allowed to do things girls couldn't do, and girls had to do lots of things boys didn't have to do. My mother told me that when she finished high school she wanted to go to normal school and become a teacher, but her father said no. Luckily for me, my parents accepted my doing many things girls were not supposed to do, and my parents and I took it for granted that I would go to college. Gradually I learned that girls and women could do all kinds of things if they just did them.

Still, I saw that the only thing my father did around the house to help was to shovel coal into the furnace. True, he worked hard and long to provide for us. But my mother worked long and hard too, but at duller, more repetitive things, and then had to do the household work when she got home. She had little chance for a life of her own. I didn't want to live like that when I grew up. Instead of sympathizing with my mother, I was angry with her for accepting the inequality. After I grew up, I wished I had talked to her then about it and to my father too.

I liked school tremendously. I loved to learn new things, in school and out of school. Almost all of the children who started out in kindergarten stayed together as a class all the way through eighth grade. I felt very much at home in school. We liked to present plays to other classes. We always had a girls' club going, and we had lots of birthday and holiday parties with the boys. Although I was shy and could not ask for anything for myself, when there was something our class wanted changed, I had no hesitation going into the principal's office as spokesperson. In 1924, I spoke as valedictorian at our P.S. 128 graduation on "Service Not Self," which was our school motto. When I grew up I decided that service to others also served one's self, thus, "Service and Self."

My younger brother, Bert, and I went to the reform Temple Beth

Shalom (House of Peace) for Saturday morning services and to Sunday school until I was confirmed at fourteen. I enjoyed seeing the other kids every week and the Bible stories, but I did not believe the stories and by fourteen I did not believe a god had created the universe with drought, flood, fires, tornadoes, hurricanes, and earthquakes in it. I did not believe a god had created an earth where the big ones ate the small ones. I did not believe that poverty, hunger, cruelty, greed, selfishness, hatred, injustice, prejudice, and war would exist in a universe where there was a god. When I mentioned this to my mother, she told me that she and my father were agnostics, but it was up to me to decide my own beliefs. She thought I should talk to the rabbi and made an appointment for me. That conversation confirmed my conclusions. It was up to us to take care of the earth and one another.

My mother and father had a lot of sisters and brothers so there were lots of aunts and uncles, and my parents' grown cousins, coming to visit, bringing us presents and playing games with us.[5] And my own cousins also kept arriving on the scene as aunts and uncles married and had children of their own.

Many Sundays, my mother's family gathered at their mother's house for dinner. I made a beeline for the heavy top drawer of the china closet. This was the children's drawer, and we could play with anything in it. The house was full of accumulating children and adults. My grandmother was sweet and gentle and cooked a wonderful meal. I was surprised to learn how these grown people confided in their mother and asked her advice. We children had prickly ears. The aunts spelled out certain words, and we pretended not to understand or care. They also spoke rapidly to one another in a made-up language called pig Latin, but we finally broke the code.

Once when I was little, my mother woke me during the night, and my father carried me, bundled up, to the attic from where I could see the northern lights. And once on a freezing early morning my mother took my Girl Scout troop on the long subway ride to Columbia University where, bone-cold on the steps of the library, we looked through black film at a total eclipse of the sun. And who was I to be present at such great events?[6]

5 Edith's mother, Ida, was one of nine children, and her father, Herman, was one of ten.

6 Given that Edith says it was cold, the eclipse was total, and she was in the Girl Scouts, the date was probably January 24, 1925. "January 24, 1925—Total Solar Eclipse," Timeanddate.com, http://www.timeanddate.com/eclipse/solar/1925-january-24.

High School

The first years of high school were a time of confusion for me. The kids with whom I had gone through P.S. 128 were scattered or lost in the much larger New Utrecht High School. The procedures of high school were very different, and we had much more homework. I rode to school by bus, which made a long day.

Most of all, I was confused about myself. I was a child, trying to grow up and become independent and self-reliant. I was growing, and my body was changing; there were so many new kinds of feelings and relationships, and expectations and desires, and ambitions and information about the world to be figured out. I was very self-conscious and awkward. I had only a few friends although I was a leader in school events.

I wrote some stories for the literary magazine [see below], and joined the horseback riding club, riding Fridays in Prospect Park, and served as president of the Girls Arista Society [National Honor Society]. I helped organize the class variety show, given before graduation, and in a bright red dress was master of ceremonies. We thought the show was the most glorious entertainment ever presented, even when our fellow students threw pennies onto the stage [to show their disapproval for a particular act]. I was vice president of the senior class (only a boy could be president). In the class yearbook my photograph was labeled "Class Genius" and "Class Poet," which I liked. I was awarded a medal by the chamber of commerce for Excellence in Economics, which I thought was funny because nobody seemed to understand economics.

In 1927 I spoke as valedictorian at graduation, "As We Go Forth into the Future," but I had laryngitis and only the first few rows could hear me. I was very happy as I met my mother, father, big brother, and little brother afterward. I felt grown up and ready for the world and college. As arranged, my big brother, Art, took two of my close friends, (twins) Louis and Henry, and me up to a nightclub in Harlem, where we drank ginger ale and were excited about the atmosphere.

THE ARTIST BY EDITH WITT

Once the Artist was lying under a willow tree on a mound of grass near a brook. The ground was soft and cool. The willow whispered strange secrets of Beauty to the Artist. And the stream frolicked with its song into the Artist's heart. He stared into the Heavens and thought, "God is good, for He is the God of Beauty and all that He created is beautiful." And just then the Artist's arm twitched and jerked, and onto his face came a look of disgust, and he shrank back as he looked at the Ant on his arm. It was ugly and crawling and helpless. Yes, God had made it. But He had created the sunbeams flashing in the pebbles. And the Artist brushed away this horrible black spot from his arm.

He breathed deeply and sighed with the joy of life. The sounds about him were soothing—the trilling of water, the swishing of reeds, the swaying of trees. Then suddenly, he clicked his teeth together and shut his eyes tightly. He had heard the discordant, coarse buzzing of a Bee that buzzed around his head. The Bee was as ugly as the discord it made, and as coarse. And then a robin flew into the willow tree, and it was sweet to hear his chirp. Yes, it was good to think that God had created all the beauty in the kingdom of birds.

And then he shuddered and dug his fingernails into the palms of his hands. Into his trouser-leg there had sidled a Caterpillar. As he drew it out he saw that it was the most miserable creature—slimy, awkward, and bound always to the earth. It, too, belonged to God. But the rainbow-colored maple leaves were God's, too. And the wisps of goldenrod. And the purity of the clouds. And the pale moon that could be seen in daylight. The Artist wondered how one God could create Beauty and Ugliness—how He could give breathe to the Ant, the Bee, and the Caterpillar. And as he left his haven, he said, "I will come back again next year. Perhaps things will be changed?" And he went away.

The three insects had all heard his words, and they began to prepare themselves for his next visit. Each one was determined to satisfy the Artist's longing for Beauty.

The Ant heavily burdened with his secret, plodded back to the ant hill; he would slave and labor for the Artist. There would be no frivolity nor laziness. None should know, but he would be a martyr. He worked steadily and solidly. He performed his tasks and bore the burdens of those around him. He had no pleasure but pride in his pain.

The Bee thought that to gain Beauty, one must seek it. And so he did not tarry at the hive. There was no beauty there—only more of himself. Out into the world! Out into parts unknown! He wandered aimlessly here and there. Always he was alert for Beauty. He passed by sordid things without seeing them. But let him catch light of a delicate sweet-scented flower. Then he would drink to overflowing. He would suck the pollen pouch dry. And day by day, he imagined that his buzz was becoming honeyed. He imagined that the flowers bestowed their colors upon him. And so he grew vain and reckless. He wandered far and pilfered as he went.

The Caterpillar had heard the words of the Artist too. But what could he do? He had no friends with whom to work. He had no wings with which to travel. Why work? Why strive to help others? They said he was slow and sluggish, but he was merely tired. Tired of everything. And so he wove a soft bed for himself on a willow twig, and shut himself off from the things he was tired of. And he went to sleep. And he slept for the whole year.

And then the Artist came from over the hills. His heart beat fast and his eyes glowed. The breeze was in his hair and the sun on his cheeks and he trod lightly on the grass. When he heard the welcome of the brook, he began to tremble, for he loved his God of Beauty, and dreaded that he might lose his faith. And as he walked on, he chanced to look down at the path directly in front of him. And when he saw that he had stepped on the Ant, had crushed the ugly crawling helpless Ant, his whole body twitched and jerked and onto his face came a look of disgust. His steps became slower and there was no longer a gleam in his eye. Suddenly he shut his eyes tightly and clicked his teeth together. His ears were filled with the discordant coarse buzz of the Bee. A sharp pain shot through his hand, and when he looked at it, he saw a huge swelling, but his heart ached more than that.

And in his pain, in his despair, he lay down under that same willow tree, on the mound of grass near the brook. And as he lay there despondently, with no faith in God, there was a soft, hushed flutter from above, and a delicate speck of Beauty, a bit of his God—a Butterfly glided through the air and alighted on the Artist's soul.[7]

■ ■ ■

The Roaring Twenties was a decade of getting rich, nightclubs, the Follies, of men's silk shirts and women's silk stockings. When I was sixteen,

7 Edith Witt, "The Artist," *The Comet* 9, no. 2 (June 1927): 54.

Sacco and Vanzetti were framed and executed because they were anarchists. American newspapers and magazines had cartoons of ferocious Bolsheviks, with bombs in their hands, who were going to take over the United States and the world.[8]

College, So Much More to Learn

In 1928 I took the long subway ride up to Barnard College, the small girls' school protected by a high green wooden fence, across the street from Columbia University. Here I would find the answers to the world and to life. In those days, one went to college to learn to become an educated citizen and a thinking person, not to be trained to make money. I was thrilled with the catalogue of courses: anthropology, archaeology, art, astronomy. Every day I went down the list. I wanted to learn all about all of them, although my major was psychology. The handsome, shy philosophy instructor slapped his hand on the worn desk and said, "Atoms, everything is made of atoms." The psychology prof told us that cats saw only grays (which scientists have recently learned is not true). When we dissected a dead fish in zoology, I discovered the pearly eyeball bounced on the table, but I couldn't find out what it was made of or why it bounced.

I walked a lot along the Hudson in Riverside Park and talked to people. Once, in one of the coffee shops with a friend, out of the tapestry of intense discussions, we heard the shining thread, "The good, the true and the beautiful."[9] Ah, that was it. We walked back to the voice, a dwarf philosophy student with dark burning eyes. He told us to look up a friend of his at Barnard. She was black, the only black person we

8 Nicola Sacco and Bartolomeo Vanzetti were Italian-born immigrants, who along with unions and other labor representatives were concerned about the extreme pay inequality, worker rights, and government and corporate power during that time. Sacco and Vanzetti were convicted of murdering a guard and a paymaster during a 1920 armed robbery of the Slater and Morrill Shoe Company in South Braintree, Massachusetts. Despite years of appeals and organized protests in almost every major American city and worldwide, they were executed via electric chair in 1927. Protests and appeals had focused on the judge's handling of the case, recanted testimony, conflicting ballistics evidence, a prejudicial pretrial statement by the jury foreman, and a confession by an alleged participant in the robbery. Felix Frankfurter, "The Case of Sacco and Vanzetti," *Atlantic Monthly*, March 1927, http://www.theatlantic.com/past/unbound/flashbks/oj/frankff.htm.

9 The good, the true, and the beautiful are said to be three of the transcendental attributes of being. They are often attributed to the Greek philosophers but may have had an earlier origin in the Bhagavad Gita.

knew, the only black student at Barnard, charming and brilliant. Two billion people in the world, essentially the same but different from one another. If only I could know them all.

Barnard's athletics centered around the Greek Games, in which the freshman class challenged the sophomore class in a series of competitions. Chariots were pulled by teams of four students, and there was a torch race. I chose archery and loved the feel of the arrow as it left the bow and the sound as it hit the target.

With another New York Barnard girl, I went to Harvard summer school (the only time girls could attend that school at that time). A wonderful six weeks. We lived in a dormitory suite facing the Charles River, played tennis in 96 degree heat, explored the exciting historic sites of Boston (as I had done with my family as a child), walked along the river, and spent time in the Widener Library. The psychology instructor was working on experiments with baby chicks running up and down his runway; they were cute but didn't throw much light on why human beings had gotten the world into the mess it was in. The philosophy instructor kept asking, "If no one was thinking about the Widener Library at midnight last night, was it there?"

After the spring semester of 1929, school no longer seemed like the right thing to be doing at the moment. I told my parents, "I want to get a job. I want to live." I looked up mental health clinics in the phone book. I started with one I'd heard of, and I was lucky. The hospital administrator said he couldn't give me a job, but I could volunteer under the supervision of the psychiatric social worker. For six months it was an intensive independent self-directed study course. I wasn't asked to do anything for them, probably because I didn't know how. I observed in the waiting room. I read case studies. I attended some of the case conferences. I attended the course in psychoanalysis for doctors and some of the psychological testing. What I saw was that the patients went back to the same impoverished conditions they had originally come from, conditions that did not nurture human beings. I saw that while the professionals could treat each person in the world one by one, together we could change the context of society so people could be human.

2

The Great Depression

President Hoover had promised "a car in every garage and a chicken in every pot," but after the stock market crash of 1929 we were sliding into the Great Depression. It was a crazy time. I was living in a Hell's Kitchen apartment with a friend, splitting the $16 monthly rent.[1] The bathtub was in the kitchen. Inhabitants of two apartments on our floor shared the hall toilet. One day I went around the corner to the grocery store. A man who had lost his money in the stock market had just jumped out a window. His body lay covered with wrapping paper on the street, and there was a thick red substance that looked like ketchup along the gutter. When I got home people were talking about it, and our neighbor, whose longshoreman husband had been killed on the docks, was singing to her two little kids, "Life is just a bowl of cherries."[2]

We went up to my friend's summer cabin in Croton-on-Hudson and earned money for our food by charging more affluent friends $3 a weekend for room and board. Then my friend rented out her cabin for the summer. A neighbor built us a wooden floor on which to put up a tent on some land he had. That was the first time I made a vegetable garden, breaking the ground with a pickaxe, removing rocks, et cetera. What hard work and what a joy! It was a wonderful summer. I used to lie deep in the grass to get an insect's view of the world. All our neighbors were about in the same boat. We lived mainly on bread, cornmeal, and onions, and, later on, whatever grew in the garden. Nothing tasted better than two slices of rye bread with a slice of onion between them when I couldn't sleep for hunger.

That winter we moved back into the cabin. The only resources we

1 Hell's Kitchen, a Manhattan neighborhood adjacent to the West Side docks, was once home to many poor and working-class Irish Americans.

2 This mother may have been trying to reassure her kids with a popular song of the day or reflecting ironically on the current situation.

had were some dead trees and dead ground wood on the land. We figured we could cut this up and deliver it to Greenwich Village fireplaces. A neighbor appeared, said he had to go into the city to survive, and gave us his station wagon. We started our "business" with people we knew and added to our customers. We earned $9 a week: $3 for each of us—and $3 for the car. That winter it got down to twenty below in Croton. When we had the wood small enough to fit in the house, we dragged it inside and continued sawing it indoors. I got chilblains.[3] We had to give up and go to my family's house back in Brooklyn.

While I was in Croton I got a message that my father was in the hospital with a ruptured appendix. I went into the city. My father died on November 13, 1933. I was only twenty-one years old. His strong handclasp, when I saw him first in the hospital, is still on my palm.[4]

In the spring of 1933, I rode a rickety-rackety Greyhound bus three days to Chicago to see my older brother's first child, Syreia.[5] Art held his daughter in his hands to show her to me and said, "What kind of world will it be when she grows up?" He put her back in the crib and played his guitar and sang her a song.

People he knew were working on the campaign to free the Scottsboro Boys.[6] Some of those people were Communists. When I met them they were turning the handle of a mimeograph to run off leaflets about

3 Chilblains are inflammations of the small blood vessels in the skin in response to sudden warming from cold temperatures.

4 Today the rupture of an appendix is highly treatable and usually not fatal.

5 Arthur had first attended the College of the City of New York (CCNY) but later transferred to the journalism program at the University of Missouri. With the stock market crash in 1929, Art looked for ways, beyond journalism, to make a difference. This led him to Cleveland, where he worked at two different settlement houses. At a conference of community activists, he met Ruth Cizon. They married in 1930 and moved to Chicago where Ruth was a social worker and Art a union organizer and activist trying to help workers who had been evicted from their apartments.

6 The "Scottsboro Boys" were nine unemployed African American teenagers falsely accused of raping two white women on a train in Alabama in 1931. Eight of the nine were convicted, although medical evidence suggested they had not committed the crime and one of the two women recanted her story. Despite these factors, and after repeated trials and appeals (as high as the Supreme Court), several of the defendants served prison time. The case resulted in a Supreme Court ruling against the use of all-white juries and for the right to adequate legal representation. The last four of the defendants were not fully pardoned until 2013. Dan T. Carter, *Scottsboro: A Tragedy of the American South*, rev. ed. (Baton Rouge: Louisiana State University Press, 1984); James R. Acker, *Scottsboro and Its Legacy: The Cases that Challenged American Legal and Social Justice* (Westport, CT: Praeger, 2008).

the case. They were singing and joking and laughing. They were the only happy people I had met for a long time. I thought it was because they had found a way to do something about the way the world was.

When I returned to Croton, I got in touch with the Negro church and told them I wanted to speak to them about the campaign to free the Scottsboro Boys. They did not know about the case, and they invited me to come on Sunday. They were interested and friendly.

The city was full of soup lines, men selling apples on the street, men huddled in doorways or on grates where the heat came up from furnaces, people searching for food in garbage cans. There were meetings, rallies, demonstrations, marches, mostly led by the Communist Party, for jobs, unemployment insurance, social security, for the organization of CIO [Congress of Industrial Organizations] unions, against the rise of Hitler and Nazism, for world peace, against war, against lynchings and the poll tax, for workers' rights, for Negro rights, for the First Amendment, for the Spanish Republic.

My friend got a job as a bookkeeper. I got a job in a bookstore for $6 a week. I learned to dust books by banging them together. Then I got a job for $6 in a place that wrapped small jars of gourmet foods in fancy packages (while people starved). When I quit there, I walked out into a large parade for jobs. The marchers were chanting, "Fellow workers, join our ranks! Fellow workers, join our ranks!" I walked alongside on the sidewalk. It was stirring, exciting. "We want jobs!" A lot of the marchers were singing. "Solidarity forever, for the union makes us strong!"

WPA Saves Lives; We Try to Save the WPA

After Franklin D. Roosevelt was elected president in 1932, a host of federal programs were enacted by Congress to try to save the economic system of the country. One day a friend phoned me. "They're hiring for the WPA [Works Progress Administration] Puppet Project. Go right down. On the subway, make up your puppet experience." It was a long enough subway ride, and I was hired. I learned that the Bunins, one of the very best puppet groups in the city, let anyone come down to their studio and practice with their wonderful marionettes.[7] Remo Bufano headed the

7 In the 1930s Hope and Morey Bunin were at the beginning of their outstanding careers

project. He was director of the New York marionette unit of the Federal Theatre Project [1934–39] and considered to be the best puppeteer in the country. He asked each of us to walk a marionette across the stage and then assigned me, with three professional puppeteers, to the story of the Princess and the Frog. I was the curtain puller and understudy for the Princess. Gradually I learned to operate and make marionettes and hand puppets. It was an idyllic year. A crew brought our stage out to the park, playground, school, or hospital ward and set it up. We had large audiences. The children loved our show, and we loved them. We traveled mainly by subway or to Staten Island, which I liked best of all, by ferry and train. We grew very close; our lives were saved.

After a year, I was transferred to the WPA Recreation Project to teach arts and crafts to children at Christadora House, a community recreation center on the Lower East Side.[8] I loved that job too, and I learned from the children. One cold day I took my wool gloves from my coat pockets as I was getting ready to go home. Anna exclaimed, "Oh, you have gloves and pockets too!" Another worker, Leah, told me her sister had gotten married. "Now I have the bed to myself," she said, "and now it's my turn to throw the rats out the window." After our shift we went bowling together to drive the helplessness from our bodies.

Congress kept trying to cut WPA funds. We organized the WPA Recreation Workers Association, about a thousand people, to keep our jobs and expand the projects, to try to get people hired or reinstated when they were laid off. Sometimes on our own, sometimes with other WPA workers, we sent delegations or large marches to the local WPA headquarters. Once, as we reached the intersection of many streets near Wanamaker's, a phalanx of mounted police, clubs ready, advanced

that would eventually lead to their performing with their puppets in vaudeville shows after World War II, a children's television show, and collaboration with David Seville to create the puppets for Alvin and the Chipmunks. During the thirties they worked for the WPA Children's Project, built puppets, and performed free shows in schools and parks. During the war they spent a year entertaining troops as part of the Army USO. Rhett Bryson, "The Bunins: Meet the Bunins, Hope and Morey," *Great Foodini*, http://drama2014.furman.edu/FoodiniWeb/FoodiniBunins.html.

8 Christadora House was constructed in 1928 as a settlement house for low-income and immigrant residents. The million-dollar sixteen-story building included a gym, swimming pool, music school, and theater on the first five floors. Another floor housed the settlement workers. Apartments on the top nine floors were rented out to provide income for the work of the settlement. "Christadora House," https://en.wikipedia.org/wiki/Christodora_House.

toward us. Many of us had been pressed up against buildings by graceful dancing horses. Many of us had heard the doom of wooden club on skull. We continued walking slowly, and the horses continued toward us slowly. Suddenly one of us cried, "Sit down! Sit down!" Another and another took up the cry. We sat down. The police and horses stopped. They might not have, but they did. What a demonstration of nonviolent action to remember all my life!

A woman comes into the union office. She has been laid off. She has two little children. They have no more food. She hasn't been able to get any help. We get her something to eat. Then she and I go to the relief office. She explains her situation. "Fill out this form." "Come back in the morning." "Bring in your documents." "Come back next week." "Bring in the children's birth certificates." We sit there. We are passed on from one person to another, to the supervisor, to the supervisor's supervisor. It's not their fault. There are too many hungry people and not enough money. "Well, we'll just sit here," I say, "until you find some milk and food for the kids and some food for this woman." Just before five o'clock they give her an emergency voucher for food.

The Works Progress Administration was created on May 6, 1935, to provide direct government employment for some of the 20 percent of the workforce who were jobless in the United States. Between 1935 and 1943, a total of over 8.5 million Americans were employed by the WPA, with an annual peak of 3.3 million in 1938. The WPA spent a total of $11 billion. WPA workers were typically paid $15 to $90 a month. Wages differed from region to region and state to state, with adjustment due to differing costs of living in each region or state.

Over the eight years of the WPA's existence its workers built and repaired a huge amount of the country's transportation infrastructure, including airports, seaports, and bridges. The projects put people to work and significantly improved commerce for decades. Workers paved 650,000 miles of roads, built or improved 124,000 bridges and 8,000 state and national parks, and built, improved, or repaired 950 airports and airfields. The WPA also funded programs in the humanities, including the Federal Arts Project, Federal Writers' Project, Federal Theatre Project, National Health Survey, and Historical Records Survey.

Some government officials were critical of the WPA, arguing that money was being spent to fund things that people did not need, such as tap dancing lessons and murals in post offices. However, Harry Hopkins, the WPA's administrator, thought that work provided by the WPA should match the skills of the unemployed. Thus he supported hiring artists to paint murals, sculptors to create park and battlefield monuments, and actors and musicians to create and perform cultural works. President Roosevelt claimed that the high morale of the workers was well worth the money.

WPA funding was cut, especially after the 1936 elections, resulting in reductions in both wages and the number of slots for workers. Workers were also more carefully screened to determine if they had a true economic need, and the rule that workers were only to have WPA positions for eighteen months was more strictly enforced.

As a result, WPA workers began organizing sit-down strikes, occupying state or federal WPA offices, organizing marches in major cities across the country, and marching and lobbying in Washington, DC. Many of the WPA workers joined unions or workers' associations to represent their interests. The Workers Alliance of America, headed by David Lasser, was the major organization representing the WPA workers.[9]

All Men are Created Equal

We went to Washington in six buses to see that the WPA got the money it needed for jobs.[10] In a small town in Maryland five of our people from the first bus were put in jail. Their bus had stopped for breakfast. The restaurant served the whites but would not serve the blacks. The whites would not pay for their food if the blacks were not served. The four other buses pulled up in line. We all got out. "We'll all just stand here until you release our brothers from jail." It was early morning, quiet, just getting light. We stood and stood. Here and there someone looked out the

9 John E. Hansan, "The Works Progress Administration," Social Welfare History Project, Virginia Commonwealth University Libraries, http://www.socialwelfarehistory.com/eras/great-depression/wpa-the-works-progress-administration; *Final Report on the WPA Program, 1935–1943* (Washington, DC: Government Printing Office, 1946), 134–36, http://lccn.loc.gov/47032199; Nick Taylor, *American-Made: The Enduring Legacy of the WPA, When FDR Put the Nation to Work* (New York: Bantam Books, 2009).

10 The *New York Times* reported the departure of six buses for Washington, DC, with 190 members of the Workers Alliance. There they were to join with WPA workers from around the country to protest the Schwellenbach-Allen resolution in Congress that would lead to cuts in WPA funding. "WPA Protest Trip Starts—Six Busloads of Workers Alliance Members Start for Washington," *New York Times*, August 17, 1937.

corner of a curtain. After a while some people in the town began dragging out heavy fire hoses. We braced ourselves. We had seen pictures of that. We stood quietly, sometimes speaking or singing softly. No one came out of the houses. It was a pleasant little town. What were they afraid of? Were they afraid of me? What was happening to my country? Why were people hungry in such a bountiful land? Why were we wasting people by throwing them out of jobs? Why didn't we care for one another? After a couple of hours the word was passed, "They're out!"

When we got to Washington, we broke up into groups of eight or ten and went looking for breakfast. In one restaurant and out, and in and out of another. "We don't serve Negroes here." We came to a cafeteria. This is it, we decided. We're going to eat here, all of us. The four white people behind the counter grew very agitated. Two black workers stood smiling in the kitchen door, watching. Finally we asked for the manager. He came out. He was very agitated. "Serve them," he told his workers. One of the woman workers took off her apron and walked out of the restaurant. The other women started serving us, one after another, black or white. In the capital of my country. A few blocks from the Capitol.

As the thirties went on, I was picketing, marching, meeting, singing, giving out leaflets, turning the mimeograph, more and more, not only for jobs, but to stop fascism, to stop war, to build peace, to support the Spanish Republic, to improve civil rights.

Brother Art and the Spanish Civil War

One day in January 1937 my older brother Art appeared from Chicago. We walked the streets, talking. He said, "I want to tell you something, but you can't tell anyone else, not even your friends, not even your roommate. I'm on my way to Spain to join the Abraham Lincoln Brigade." Oh, how thrilling that was. How romantic we were. How I envied him. It was always like that. He was older. He was a man. He could do things I couldn't do. "If you have any money you can spare, I'd appreciate it," he said. "I have a little shopping to do." I reached into my purse. I had twelve dollars. I gave them to him. "That's great," he said, "I can buy a pair of boots. By the way, there are a few other fellows with me. Could you get some of your friends over tonight and have a party?" We had spaghetti with meat sauce, French bread and salad, and red wine, our special, deluxe, gourmet, haute cuisine during the Depression. It was the last time I saw him.[11]

University of Chicago, Haven of Sanity

By the fall of 1938 I wanted to go back to school. I had saved some money. I learned to live below my income so I'd always have a reserve if I wanted to change what I was doing. My mother offered me $50 a month for school. I'd read that at the University of Chicago you didn't have to attend classes. To get a B.A. you had to pass two daylong exams, one in your division and one in your department. You could take them whenever you were ready. I'd also read that the University of Chicago had a good social science division and a fine sociology department headed by Louis Wirth and specializing in the life of cities.[12] Art's wife Ruth told me that I could live with her and their daughter Syreia. I enrolled ten years after my first college stint.

I thought it would be something just to get through so I could get the kind of job I wanted, to do the kind of work I wanted to do. But in the first week I discovered I was in wonderland. The library had more books than I knew existed. The instructors had long lists of books they

11 Arthur Witt left his wife and four-year-old daughter in Chicago to join one of the early groups that sailed for France, to be smuggled into Spain, to join the Abraham Lincoln Brigade. The brigade was trying to support the duly elected worker-backed leftist government that had come to power in Spain in 1931 as the Second Spanish Republic. Supported by personnel and armaments from Italy and Germany, General Franco had led a coup against the government. Russia supported the Spanish government forces. The almost three thousand Americans who joined the struggle fought alongside the government forces, along with forty thousand volunteers from all over the world who made up the international brigades. Arthur arrived in Spain in early February 1937. He died on his first day in battle, February 27, 1937, at Jarama, just outside of Madrid. His family, including Edith, did not learn of his death until early summer. Half of the Americans did not make it home. Franco's fascist forces won the war, and Franco ruled Spain until his death in 1975.

12 Louis Wirth joined the faculty at the University of Chicago in 1931. In 1938 he published a landmark article, "Urbanism as a Way of Life" (*American Journal of Sociology* 64, no. 1: 1–24), that outlined the way that the size and density of urban environments had made relationships between people less connected, more superficial, and transitory, leading in turn to the segmentation of cities into a variety of disconnected social worlds. Wirth also made significant contributions to the study of housing, race relations, human ecology, and social organization. It would appear that Wirth's ideas had a significant influence on Edith's later work in the area of housing and urban development. "Louis Wirth," American Sociological Association, http://www.asanet.org/about/presidents/Louis_Wirth.cfm.

recommended for each course. I read those and twice as many more that I discovered from them. I tried all the classes and then went to some and not to others. I bought a secondhand bike and took my books down to the lake and read. I turned in papers because they were fun to do. I sat on the lawns with fellow students and discussed life. Louis Wirth was great and ran a small seminar. Paul Douglas, later mayor of Chicago and US senator, strode up and down the aisles of the auditorium where he lectured on labor economics to a hundred students. He declaimed about free enterprise and competition. One day I asked, "What about monopoly?" He answered, with gestures, "Lead, kindly light . . . one step enough for me."[13]

During the summer of 1939 I did seven classes, saving money and time, and took the two exams and was awarded my B.A. in sociology in December. It was a wonderful school at the right time for me. I had had enough life experience and enough time to think. I was ready to be excited about books again. I felt very privileged to have worked out going to school with the great help of my sister-in-law and my mother.

I led a discussion class of steel workers' wives in South Chicago. It was held in various homes. It was the only sort of place their husbands would let them go to at night, and they called for them after class to take them home (and to see what we were doing). I went to the end of the line on the train. I walked along a chain link fence that bordered the dark gigantic body of the lifeless steel mill. The class was about why the mill closed down. They started out thinking it was their fault, theirs and their husbands. It wasn't on the comprehensive exam at the university, but I learned a lot. When I had first come, I had gone out to Republic Steel, where workers had been shot to death. We went round and round on the small picket line while the police played horseshoes nearby.[14]

As much as I joined in student actions for civil liberties and against

13 Words to a hymn attributed to John Henry Newman, 1801–1890.

14 In 1937 what was later referred to as the Little Steel Strike was called by workers at Republic Steel in Chicago after the anti-union company refused to follow the lead of giant US Steel and sign a new labor contract. During a Memorial Day demonstration, police fired into the crowd, killing two, which led to further protests and picketing. It was not until 1941 that Republic Steel and several other smaller steel companies signed their first contracts with the United Steelworkers. William Bork, "Massacre at Republic Steel," *Chicago Labor & Arts Festival Blog*, https://chilaborarts.wordpress.com/2007/05/18/background-on-memorial-day-massacre-527-event.

war and fascism, the future grew darker.[15] The university had been a haven of sanity. I stood on a bridge over the Chicago River with the scroll of my diploma in my hand, looking over the myriad buildings of the city. *Hey!* I thought. *Who's looking to give me a job?* I went in door after door. They would have cared if I didn't have a degree, but they didn't care that I had one, and they certainly didn't care what my grades had been. I was full of new knowledge and wisdom and raring to use it for the benefit of the world. However, after two puny jobs I headed back to my New York City home.

Where Edith spent her time during 1940 is not known. However, she did spend some time during 1941 and 1942 working as a counselor at the Brandes School in Tucson, Arizona. The Brandes School was owned by her aunt and uncle, Ray and Elsie Brandes, and served primarily elementary through high school Jewish boys and girls from the Midwest and East. Many of the children who attended the school suffered from asthma.[16] Pictures exist of her in Tucson during that period, and one of Ray's sons, Paul, indicated that Edith was in a promotional film from that time.

15 Across the United States, there were large-scale protests organized by students and other young people against the United States becoming involved if war broke out again in Europe.

16 Paul Brandes discussion with the editor, January 2016.

PART TWO

World War II

3

Edith's Red Cross Experiences

An Overview

On September 1, 1939, Germany invaded Poland. On June 22, 1941, Germany invaded the Soviet Union, and on December 7, 1941, Japan bombed the US fleet at Pearl Harbor in Hawaii. The US Congress declared war on Germany, Japan, and Italy. Like Eleanor and Franklin Roosevelt, I hated war. I had worked hard and long to prevent this one.[1] My brother Art had tried to stop the possibility of a renewed world war by going to Spain with the Abraham Lincoln Brigade and joining the fight against Franco's Fascist army, which was backed by Germany and Italy.[2] Now America had to join with our allies to fight and win. It would be the last, and then we would build a beautiful world of peace and humanity caring for one another. After Pearl Harbor, my brother Bert joined the army in March 1942 and was now a first lieutenant. But I was a woman and not a nurse.

Women were answering the call to support US war efforts in a number of ways. Nineteen million American women were part of the labor force, not

1 Prior to Germany's invasion of Russia (June 1941) and the Japanese attack on Pearl Harbor (December 1941), many Americans had protested against the United States becoming involved in the developing conflict in Europe. Isolationism drove some of the concerns. Socialists and those aligned with the Communist Party believed that as long as the non-aggression pact between Hitler and Stalin was viable the United States should not become entangled in another costly European war. After the events of 1941, most Americans supported the war effort. Robert Cohen, *When the Old Left Was Young: Student Radicals and America's First Mass Student Movement, 1929–1941* (New York: Oxford University Press, 1993).

2 Arthur Witt went to Spain in January 1937 to join the Abraham Lincoln Brigade, part of the international contingent of soldiers that joined Spanish government troops to fend off Franco's attempted coup. Arthur was killed in his first engagement, at the Battle of Jarama on February 27.

only as Rosie the Riveter in war factory jobs, from which they had largely been excluded until then, but also as office, agricultural, and transportation workers. Women also supported the war effort by planting victory gardens, canning produce, selling war bonds, donating blood, and sending care packages.[3] In addition, due to the shortage of men to fulfill non-combat roles, women's units were created in the US Army (Women's Army Corps—WAC), US Navy (Woman Accepted for Volunteer Emergency Service—WAVES), US Coast Guard (Semper Pratus "Always Ready—SPARS), and US Marine Corps (USMC Women's Reserve). Almost 350,000 women served in these units during the war.[4]

The American Red Cross (ARC) was another avenue for American women who wished to take part in the war effort. Edith appeared to be the type of woman sought by the ARC. She may have seen an ad for the ARC Club Service or heard through a friend that the ARC was recruiting women to be overseas club workers. Whatever the impetus, she applied to join the ARC as a member of the Club Department.

The ARC played an active role in supporting soldiers stateside and US and Allied troops overseas throughout World War II.[5] During World War I a number of organizations had provided such services, but there had been some overlap in services and management, and implementation problems had arisen with so many different organizations involved. Thus, in 1941 President Roosevelt ordered the merger of the war services efforts of the YMCA, YWCA, Salvation Army, National Catholic Community Service, Jewish Welfare Board, and National Travelers Aid Society into a single civilian United Services Organization (USO). In the United States, the USO was responsible for on-post entertainment and recreation and provided off-post information centers, railway station lounges and clubs, hostels, and information centers for on-leave military personnel. The USO was solely responsible for the coordination of overseas entertainment, and its camp shows would become its trademark.

The American Red Cross remained a separate organization, with responsibilities for in-country recreation services at military camps and hospitals, and was solely responsible for providing overseas recreation clubs, canteens,

3 Doris Weatherford, *American Women during World War II* (Edison, NJ: Castlebooks, 2008).

4 Michael E. Stevens and Ellen D. Goldlust, *Women Remember the War 1941–1945* (Madison State Historical Society of Wisconsin, 1993).

5 "Our History," American Red Cross, http://www.redcross.org/about-us/who-we-are/history.

and "clubmobiles" to serve the millions of American men and women abroad. The overseas ARC clubs and clubmobiles were intended to provide an escape, albeit temporary, from the harsh brutality of war, with clubmobiles serving soldiers in the field, often near the frontlines.

These converted buses, trucks, and jeeps were typically staffed by three Red Cross women. Each clubmobile had the ability to make doughnuts and coffee, with other services, such as the ability to play phonograph records, screen movies, and dispense candy, gum, cigarettes, and books, depending on the unit.[6]

An ARC "club" could be as simple as a tent near the front lines or located in more permanent facilities at a base or in a town near where troops were stationed. Coffee, doughnuts, and snacks were the staple of club offerings, but some also offered dancing, movies, and other entertainment, as well as cigarettes and supplies for writing letters. Some clubs provided overnight accommodations (with the claim made that the Red Cross ran the largest hotel chain in the world), a barbershop, and laundry facilities. Importantly, the clubs and clubmobiles provided an opportunity for servicemen to interact with American women.[7]

Women of the ARC Club Service and clubmobiles stood in for the sisters, wives, mothers, and female friends that soldiers had left behind. They were a reminder of home and the people the men believed they were fighting to protect. The ARC generally recruited women who were physically attractive, good conversationalists, and approachable. Thus, the women at least symbolically fueled the men's heterosexual desires and helped overcome the largely homosocial nature of military life of the day.[8] *As one observer stated: Red Cross "girls" represented "everything the boys admire in American Womanhood—vivacity, grace, charm, virtue, beauty, enthusiasm, intelligence and*

6 Foster Rhea Dulles, *The American Red Cross: A History* (New York: Harper & Brothers, 1950), 367–68.

7 In the terminology of the time, women serving in the Red Cross were often referred to as "girls." However, as noted by Julia Ramsey, "Make no mistake, they were not 'girls' in anything but name. Rather these were intelligent, tough, and educated women who were often fiercely independent and in most cases fit traditional female roles of the time much less closely than their 'on paper' qualifications would indicate." Julia A. Ramsey, "'Girls' in Name Only: A Study of American Red Cross Volunteers on the Frontlines of World War II" (master's thesis, Auburn University, 2011), 55–56.

8 Quoted in Kara Dixon Vuic, *The Girls Next Door: American Women and Military Entertainment.* (Cambridge, MA: Harvard University Press, forthcoming).

that wholesome friendliness and interest that reminds them of sister and wife, girlfriend and mother."[9]

The ARC clubs in urban areas were also important as a means to distract service members from frequenting bars and clubs and thus limit the possibility of their contracting disease through sexual contact with local women or prostitutes. Venereal disease was a significant health concern during World War II; penicillin did not come into widespread use until after the war.[10]*According to Red Cross historian Foster Rhea Dulles, "Wherever clubs were established, the rate of venereal disease declined."*[11] *At its peak of operations, the Red Cross operated 989 overseas clubs and 310 clubmobiles, with approximately six thousand women employed over the course of the war.*[12]

As alluded to above, the women recruited for overseas service by the Red Cross had to meet certain qualifications. They needed to be between twenty-five and thirty-five years of age (Edith was thirty-two years old when she applied), have at least a college education, have some work experience, preferably in the recreation field, and be healthy, physically hardy, sociable, and attractive. They were also expected to have a sense of humor, well-modulated voice, maturity of judgment, an appreciation of people from varied backgrounds, and be likeable.[13]

9 Vernon Pope, "GI Joe's Best Girl," *Los Angeles Times*, August 20, 1944.

10 Vuic, *The Girls Next Door*.

11 Foster Rhea Dulles. *The American Red Cross: A History* (New York: Harper & Brothers, 1950), 437.

12 Vuic, *The Girls Next Door;* American National Red Cross, *Red Cross Service Record: Accomplishments of Seven Years, July 1, 1939–June 30, 1946* (Washington, DC: American National Red Cross, 1946).

13 *American Red Cross, General Guide for Selecting Staff Assistants*, ARC 828 (Washington, DC: American National Red Cross, 1942). Allan Berube in his book *Coming Out under Fire: The History of Gay Men and Women in World War Two* (New York: Free Press, 1990) discusses efforts by the military to screen for gay men and women but also notes that in order to fill quotas, recruiters were often lax in the questions they asked or conclusions they reached, especially in the early stages of US World War II involvement. While the Red Cross had its own system for recruiting and interviewing potential staff, the same problem existed of garnering enough individuals to meet the demand. While "don't ask, don't tell" would not become a policy until the end of the century, it could be that recruiters were willing to ignore sexual orientation in order to fill quotas. In any case, it is likely that nothing about Edith's life to that point would have pointed to her being lesbian, and it is unlikely that she would have discussed her sexual orientation with recruiters. The major concerns seemed to be discouraging sexual interaction between Red Cross personnel and troops and maintaining an image of propriety and femininity among the women that served. See Leisa D. Meyer, *Creating GI Jane: Sexuality and Power in*

Together these requirements "produced applicants who were, by and large, white, middle to upper class and formally educated."[14] To serve, women had to be able to leave home, which generally meant that they did not have family responsibilities.

Red Cross workers received a $2,000 life insurance policy but were not eligible for GI benefits and had to sign a release that they would not sue in case of injury (and that their survivors would not sue in case of loss of life).[15] Pay for staff assistants was typically $150 per month. The women were considered officers, which would potentially lead to deferential treatment if they were captured by the Axis forces.

According to the 1942 "General Guide for Selecting Staff Assistants," these workers were tasked with providing for the club "an atmosphere of youthful hospitality and friendliness." They were to plan and conduct musical programs, parties, and dances; organize resources for quiet games; organize and direct skits, one-act plays, and concerts; organize resources for restful pursuits (e.g., reading, writing, conversation, and just sitting); and assist with outdoor activities, including nature outings and sports, among other duties.[16]

Prior to being assigned overseas, the recruits received training through a Red Cross–sponsored course on the American University campus in Washington, DC. At the time that Edith took the course, it lasted four weeks. The course included information about the history, organization, operation, purpose, and function of the Red Cross; policies and procedures for the administration of service clubs; the relationship of the Red Cross and the army (which coordinated, supervised, and governed Red Cross activities); and the type of entertainment that should be offered at clubs and clubmobiles.

During training, recruits also learned activities and techniques for breaking the ice when talking with servicemen. Being able to start a conversation was a prized skill given the variety of servicemen who would come through a club on any given day. Trainees also learned to play table tennis, chess, and

the Women's Army Air Corps during World War II (New York: Columbia University Press, 1996), 156–57.

14 Ramsey, "'Girls' in Name Only," 30.

15 Rosemary Norwalk, *Dearest Ones: A True World War II Love Story* (New York: John Wiley & Sons, 1999).

16 American Red Cross, *General Guide for Selecting Staff Assistants.*

board games (if they hadn't already learned) and how to talk about sports, deal with wolf whistles and sexist or sexual comments, and rebuff advances without being dismissive. The women were also advised to have plenty of perfume or cologne so they would "smell like someone at home."[17]

Not only was smelling good considered an asset and desirable quality, there also seemed to be considerable attention given to women looking good despite having to wear the Red Cross's required uniform. The only time wearing the uniforms was not required was when the women were at their living quarters. Uniforms were intended to convey a professional appearance yet present the women in an attractive and feminine manner.[18]

While Red Cross women were not expected to be beauty queens, physical appearance was emphasized by reporters covering the war. For example, in a 1942 New York Times *article headlined "Girls with Red Cross in Britain Learn One Duty Is Always to Look Their Best," Tania Long wrote:*

"The girls say the soldiers have taught them one lesson, and that is that it is their duty always to look their best. The first thing Americans long for is to talk to a girl from back home. But they want to see that girl looking just as pretty as she would appear if she were back in New York or Kansas City or a little village in Illinois. . . . Although they are all chosen partly for their looks, there are no glamour girls among them and they all have to be hard workers."[19]

In another Times *article, James MacDonald clarified that while physical attractiveness was important, qualities like intelligence and personality were equally or more important in order for the women to do their jobs:*

"A steadily increasing corps of American women acts as hostesses for the Red Cross. It isn't fair to call them mere glamour girls, as [they] were unhappily termed when the first contingent arrived in the British Isles. True, many of them are as beautiful to look upon as the doughboy or gob far from home could wish, but they were not selected for their beauty. They were picked for intelligence, character, personality and general ability, and they represent a cross-section of American women."[20]

17 Mary Thomas Sargent, *Runway towards Orion: The True Adventures of a Red Cross Girl on a B-29 Air Base in World War II India* (Grand Rapids, MI: Triumph Press, 1984), 23.

18 Vuic, *The Girls Next Door*.

19 Tania Long. "Girls with Red Cross in Britain Learn One Duty Is Always to Look Their Best," *New York Times*, October 5, 1942.

20 James MacDonald. "With the Red Cross in Action Overseas," *New York Times*, February 21, 1943.

As suggested, one of the valued qualities of women selected by the ARC was their ability to talk with the soldiers with whom they interacted. Edith recorded in the notes she kept about her experiences details about the content of a number of gripping and poignant conversations she had with GIs. Here are examples that show the range of concerns voiced by the soldiers:

> Lewis—got a letter from his wife, wrote it on their anniversary, how much she loves him, misses him—he went to pieces, cried, hard to see a man like that, took him out of the tent, went for a walk, try to help him from being alone, what can I do.
>
> "I gave up a drinking bout tonight. . . . so long since I've been able to be with someone I can talk to, who understands. I want to take care of you, I'll treat you so nice, I wish I were good-looking, imagine, a thousand GIs and me with the only girl, I dreamed about you last night, I never said good night to a girl before without kissing her all night—pardon me, I mean kissing her good night—I'm not a wolf, just a little coyote—when I leave I'm not going to remember you, that'll be the end of it, I don't want to get too fond of anybody over here—being up there, seeing the things you do, going through what you do, it does things to a fellow."
>
> "My wife writes that the little boy brings in a piece of wood from backyard wrapped around in an old piece of paper, wants to mail it to daddy, package—he's two." He's going nuts—his mother died, his father's 60, very ill, all alone, that's the hardest thing, to see the fellow next to you get it, to see the man in front of you disappear, to hear the man behind you cry out—why not you—I've seen men go out of their head when their buddy got it.

Based on her writings, Edith was deeply touched by her interactions with the soldiers. She knew that it was her job to listen to their concerns about what was happening at home and about the struggles of being in a situation where they did not know if the next bullet would be for them. We can only imagine the toll these conversations took on Edith and the other Red Cross women. For three years Edith listened to the troubles, concerns, and fears of the men who came to her clubs. What were the consequences?

As we will learn through Edith's writings and postwar advocacy, she deeply questioned the impact of the war on those who served and those at home. She believed in the necessity of answering aggression but always hoped that future generations would find other ways to deal with disputes and differences.

On January 28, 1943, having completed her ARC training, Staff Assistant Edith Witt received her orders:

"Proceed without delay to the New York Port of Embarkation, Brooklyn, New York, reporting upon arrival to the Commanding General for suitable assignment and transportation."

She departed on a troop ship along with other Red Cross workers on February 7, 1943, to an unknown destination, as great secrecy surrounded troop movements, and after two weeks at sea landed in Oran, Algeria, in North Africa on February 21.

Before shipping out, Edith received her orders regarding expected dress.

Troop Movement Officer L. G. Meyer directed that "American Red Cross Casual Groups Nos. 30, 31, 32, 33, and 34 will wear the following uniform and accoutrements:"

Females
Field helmet
Musette bag
Gas mask
Web pistol belt
First Aid Pouch & packet (front right)
Canteen filled—water (rear right)
Galoshes or rubber boots
Raincoat over overcoat
Winter uniform (grey in color)
Winter hat to be available for use on board ship
White T-shirt or blouse (jersey)
White muffler
Pocketbooks to be out of sight in hand bag

In her 1990 autobiography, Edith provided an overview of her war experiences and wondered about what the future would hold once the war was over.

I spent a year in Algeria and two years in Italy.[21] I helped open and worked in clubs in a large empty furniture store on the main intersection of Oran, an empty art gallery in Naples, a villa on the sea at Agropoli, the railroad station in Florence, and in tents in an alfalfa field north of Florence, and ran cookie bakeries in Livorno and Bologna.

The clubs had cookies and coffee, chairs and tables, stationery, paperback books, chess, Ping Pong, movies, music, and dances. The clubs had Red Cross women who soldiers could talk to. We worked long hard hours with sometimes a day off a week. I was always tired, high on excitement, adventure, joy and sorrow, and thousands of people, mostly men. I got to know more about my country and about Americans than I had ever known before, and I loved them dearly. I also loved the French I met, the Arabs, the Italians, the British.

Before the daily club opening in Oran, sometimes we'd stand around outside in the sun, and GIs would gather around. Many had come through England, and what they talked about was how the English girls dated American Negro soldiers, liked to date them, could we imagine that? What did we think of that? I thought it was funny that they were shocked.

A month after we landed, we were asked to meet a hospital train passing through the station, give out ditty bags with comb, mirror, deck of cards, et cetera, and talk with the soldiers. It brought us up short. At the station there was a long, long stretch of cars pulling out toward the front on a far track, soldiers crowding the windows, laughing, singing, calling to us. On the near track, inching into the station, came the quiet hospital train from the front. We felt awkward. We told one another, "Just be yourself." We went in twos, walking slowly down the aisle. The soldiers smiled and received our presence and our meager presents as

21 When Edith arrived in Algeria in February 1943, the Allied forces were in the final months of defeating the German forces in North Africa. The Allies then moved troops to Sicily and proceeded into Italy where they steadily moved north in a series of battles that contributed to the surrender of the German and Italian armies in 1945. Edith was transferred to Italy in early 1944 and moved north with the troops as they continued their efforts to defeat the Germans and Italians. After Germany and Italy surrendered, the Red Cross continued to operate in support of the Allied occupation forces.

if they were great treasures. Chit-chat. "What state are you from, soldier?" One soldier asked us to sign the cast on his thigh where his leg had been amputated. One soldier sat alone, and when I sat down beside him, I knew it was the wrong thing to do. He didn't want anyone to talk to him. He didn't smile. He didn't hear. He didn't talk. We waited for lunch to be brought up, hot dogs and two tablespoons of canned sauerkraut. We were given soup to feed to the most injured. I sat at the edge of the bunk of a soldier whose face had been burned. The pink flesh of his face had been burned black. His lips were a jagged hole. I fed him the soup, and he swallowed it spoonful by spoonful. There was another man in the bunk above him in the same shape. The face of war, I thought.

A cluster of men had gotten off the train. One of them, his open great coat flapping around his shins, came flying toward us, a great grin on his face. "I came over with you on the *Flossie*," he said. "And now I'm going home. They say I'm out of my mind. They say I talk too much. I'm going home."

I organized a caravan of horses and buggies that were for rent around town to take soldiers up to the top of the mountain for a picnic—Spam, bread, coffee, canned peaches. Some charming Arab boys were playing around. When we cleaned up, I remembered seeing local people using empty tin cans and I offered the boys the large peach can. One of them stepped forward. "You," he said, "You eat and eat. Your bellies are out to here. And you give us tin." We had no food left. We had shared our food with the drivers. We hadn't had much ourselves, we thought.

One night I walked home across town from the club with a navy friend. The blackout was darker than usual, and there was no one on the street. Suddenly there was a blasting sound, planes above, a ship in the harbor a sheet of flame. Terror. We walked on, trembling, and turned in to the naval hospital. No lights at all. Corpsmen talking quietly to patients to calm them. Now the terrible racket of anti-aircraft guns from our ships in the harbor. I thought my skull was going to burst. We decided to go up to the roof "to see the show," a stupid, ridiculous thing to do. We felt our way up the steps and out onto the roof. The air felt good. We stood against the parapet. The ship was burning like a waterfall of flame. We could see the Nazi planes. Terror.

How could human beings do this to one another? My heart was

leaping against my ribs. So was my friend's. We went inside and stood there, trembling. We began walking down. My friend didn't have his cap. We went back to the roof and got it. We stumbled down the stairs. Finally, finally, finally the "All clear!" sounded. On the seawall outside my billet [assigned housing] a few people were standing together just to be together. A phonograph was playing "Begin the Beguine," and two couples were dancing on the sidewalk. Someone told us that the admiral had gone on the burning ship to take it outside the harbor where it could not damage other ships if it exploded.

As the war went on, all I wanted was for it to end. "Well, it will be over by Christmas," we said. I began thinking it shouldn't take a war to produce this fellowship we felt for one another, the trust we had in one another, the help we were offering one another. It shouldn't take a war to produce this intensity of life, of love, of work, of appreciation of this world. It shouldn't take a war to inspire us to rise to the occasion, to be able to do things we never did before, to do whatever needs to be done by doing it oneself or turning to those around for help. But the war went on and on and on.

I was in Bologna when the fighting ended in Italy. I woke sleepily one morning to the cry of the woman news vendor, "In Italia la guerra e finita! In Italia la guerra e finita!" [The war is over!] We had thought we would celebrate wildly, but instead we walked the street aimlessly, talked in flat voices, asked ourselves, "How should we celebrate? What should we do?" There were too many dead, too many maimed and crippled and out of their heads. Too many homeless, hungry, far from home, families decimated, separated children; the earth and the sea too bloody; the wounded, stabbed, and gashed. We met two soldiers in the same mood. They invited us to have a drink. The bar was very nice, very quiet, almost empty. We had one almost silent drink, a Brandy Alexander.

How wonderful the world would be after the war was over. All that we had produced to destroy and to be destroyed, to kill and maim other people, we would now produce for peace—food, clothing, houses, books, schools, music, parks, art, dance, theater, gardens, health facilities, libraries, transportation. We would sit on the earth and watch the grass grow to cover the dead.

Then one day the Americans and Soviets shook hands on the Elbe River. All the Allies were in Berlin. The war in Europe was over! Oh, what a wonderful world we would build now! One world, one humanity.

All the men wanted was to go home. All I wanted was to go home. I began hearing disturbing statements from the men. "Well, there's no sense sending us home. We'll just have to come right back and fight the Russians." Our gallant allies, Eisenhower had said. I was in a miserable small town the day the *Stars and Stripes* had an article about the mysterious bomb that had destroyed the city and people of Hiroshima. An Italian woman had come in to our building, looking for insulin for her diabetes. She was out of it, and she needed it badly. I took her over to the medics. "No, no, we need it for our people," a medic said. "Suppose she were your mother," I said. "Just a little, until she can get to her own doctor." The medic got up, handed her a packet. Then I went back and continued reading about the bomb.

I tried to understand it. Why had we done that? I had been reading that Japan had been putting out feelers for surrender. I walked over to army headquarters and talked with some of the men about it. But they were glad. They had no doubts. They did not want to be sent to the Pacific. I did not want them to be sent to the Pacific either, but I did not think they would be. Japan was through before the bomb was dropped. "Better them than us," they said. Sweet boys, and I loved them. They didn't know what kind of bomb it was, and they didn't care.

What kind of world was it going to be? What a wonderful world it could have been!

4

The Adventure Begins

The Trip Overseas

After Edith returned from her World War II Red Cross service, she wrote a series of accounts about the first four months of her service in Oran, Algeria. The accounts were based on copious notes she had kept about her experiences and material from the many letters she had written home to her mother, other family, and friends. These accounts convey insights and observations of war and its impact on soldiers and those, such as the Red Cross workers, who supported their efforts.

The accounts begin with her trip from New York to North Africa on a troop transport ship. She then describes her involvement in setting up the first Red Cross officers' club in Oran, her interactions with soldiers who frequented the club, a Sunday picnic she organized for some of the soldiers, her trepidation about meeting a troop train carrying wounded soldiers back from the front, her fears when the harbor at Oran was under attack, and even the simple joy of a hot shower. Edith's accounts, including dialogue, allow us to feel like we are there with her. She provides us with a rich understanding of what it was like to be a Red Cross Club Service worker as the campaign in North Africa was ending.

The North African conflict between Axis and Allied troops had been going on since June 1940. By the time Edith arrived there in February 1943, the final push for Allied victory was well underway, with the Axis powers finally surrendering on May 13, 1943. While Oran was away from the front, it served as a major staging area for troops and supplies for the Allies' North Africa campaign, and after victory in May 1943 it served in the same capacity as troops pushed on to Sicily and the invasion of Italy during the summer of 1943.[1]

1 Rick Atkinson, *An Army at Dawn: The War in North Africa, 1942–1943* (New York: Henry Holt, 2002).

The Six

Every morning, on the trip going over, I woke rejoicing that I was still alive. There were twelve of us in the cabin, in four tiers of three-high bunks, our group of six Red Cross club girls, three nurses, and three other Red Cross girls attached to the army hospital unit aboard.[2] We had distributed ourselves pretty much according to choice, top, middle, or lower bunk, all except Janie [aka Tillie Jane], who had been the last one in and had therefore drawn the upper berth beneath a battery of steam and water pipes. I used to think of Janie and the pipes long after and be amazed at how immature we were at that point in social feeling, fresh from civilian life, to have let Janie suffer the pipes for fourteen nights, instead of taking turns.

If I was the first one up, the cabin would be pitch-dark. I would have the sense of morning, of the torpedo-twilight having passed. I would feel the motion of the ship and the whirring of the life-giving ventilator and the other human beings alive in the cabin with me and in the hold below, carried like cargo, shelf on shelf and tier on tier, the strong, tender, pulsing humanity of three thousand American boys.[3]

And out beyond us the sea-spread convoy, brave rolling transports, and the lumbering old battleship, and on the edges, like nerve-tight terriers, the destroyers and corvettes. But most of all I felt—*I am alive. Another day has come and we are still alive.* And I would reach my fingers out and touch the cool, moist, steel side of the ship. Six-tenths of an inch between us and the sea. Good old ship. Carrying us all safe and sound to war.

It was February 1943 and there were seventy-five of us Red Cross club workers in three groups in the convoy.[4] The other two groups were

2 As noted above (chap. 3, note 7), in the 1940s women in the Red Cross were commonly referred to as girls, even though they had to be at least twenty-five years old to serve. Edith was thirty-two when she went overseas, but in her writings she sometimes refers to herself and the other women who served as Red Cross girls. Likewise she sometimes refers to soldiers as boys, as was common then.

3 German submarines patrolled the Atlantic Ocean. American troop ships traveled in heavily protected convoys, but there was always the fear of being torpedoed, especially at night.

4 Sixteen Red Cross workers were with the troops during the Operation Torch landings in North Africa in November 1942. Thirty-five additional workers arrived in January 1943. It was difficult for the Red Cross to get workers and supplies to North Africa due to limited transport space. General Eisenhower had to intervene to get space authorized. Robert Bremner,

large, but our group, which we called The Six, had been separated off, alphabetically, so that we were R's and S's and W's, and we speculated greatly on the reason for this. Our most logical conclusion was that we were going to be dropped off at some island somewhere. We had visions of the convoy steaming off without us at the first likely island, and then our good ship steaming off without us so that we would never be reunited with the rest of our group again.

The bonds among The Six were close and indestructible. Although our reason for being was purely alphabetical, we were The Six. It was our primary identity of the war, and even though we would be quickly separated and did not keep in touch with one another, the bonds remained.

Beyond that, we were bound to the larger group of seventy-five Red Crossers with whom we had come up from training courses in Washington and with whom we had staged for an exciting week at the St. George Hotel in Brooklyn. This was our group, and, ever after, when two of us would meet we would know one another as part of "the group who had gone over together." Then, as the ship progressed, our fellow feeling grew with every other fellow on the ship, our ship, both navy crew and army troops, with a very special feeling toward the crew, who brought us through.[5]

The *Flossie*

She was the *Flossie,* most beautiful, beloved in her dull gray paint, her ropes and grease.[6] She was a thing alive as she rolled with the roll of the sea and swung with the stars by night. She was the strongest,

Minna Adams Hutcheson, and Lucille Stein Greenberg, *The History of the American National Red Cross*, vol. 13, *American Red Cross Services in the War against the European Axis, Pearl Harbor to 1947* (Washington, DC: American National Red Cross, 1950), 159–60.

5 The Red Cross reported that in April 1945, at the height of the deployment, 2,686 Red Cross Club Service personnel were deployed overseas to 787 club facilities. In addition 141,725 paid locals and volunteers helped staff the clubs. American Red Cross, *Red Cross Service Record: Accomplishments of Seven Years, 1939–1946* (Washington, DC: American Red Cross, Office of Program Research, 1946).

6 The actual name of the ship is not known. Edith refers to it as the *Flossie.* Records of troop transport ships used during World War II are poor, and I was unable to find records indicating the ship name beyond the nickname that Edith used. For information, see World War II Troop Ships, http://ww2troopships.com/.

staunchest as she trembled to the storm; she was the keenest, surest as she zagged and zigged in her outwitting dance among the German subs. She was a strange world of exciting exploration, with throbbing motors and her limitless horizons, full speed ahead to the venture, her strange messages ("Now hear this: the smoking lamp is lit"), deck and bulkhead and ladder, officer's country and scuttlebutt and head, and her strange gear of guns and rafts and life jackets, and her taut, restless cargo of men on their way to war.

The *Flossie* was an old eight-thousand-ton freighter that in civilian life had not ventured out of inland waters, but when we sailed on her she was already a veteran of the war. We rode in luxury—sheets, pillows and pillowcases, soft white navy blankets, springs and mattresses, bed lamps, hot and cold running water and showers down the hall, three meals a day of good navy food, eaten sitting down at a table, served by mess men, with china and silver, polite conversation. We were surprised at how comfortably twelve women lived in a space that might normally hold two, with our suitcases and musette bags, our helmets and gas masks and canteens, and the clotheslines strung among the bunks. We learned to edge our way about and keep our elbows to our ribs and be careful where we came down with our feet.

Below, the enlisted men and some of the officers slept on bare canvas stretched on steel frames five-high, strung with ropes, with all their gear around them and breathed away each other's air. They stood in line for chow and standing ate two meals a day on one tin plate and had their water and their time in the topside air rationed. We knew it wasn't fair that there should be such differences in our lot, that we who were not going to fight were privileged simply by being women and designated by the army as "assimilated second lieutenants," but that's the way it was, and we took the first awkward steps along the road of taking things the way they came.[7] We took our guilt and shoved it down or scattered it or hid it, and we licked our lips over our extra lunch and snuggled in our beds and stretched out in our extra deck space.

7 As noted in chapter 3, Red Cross personnel were named officers to protect them in case they were captured.

Planning an Onboard Recreation Program

The first day out we met with the Special Services officers aboard to plan a recreation program for the trip. We knew the answers and so did they because we'd all been in training or read a bulletin. There were Red Cross ditty bags aboard, made up by home-front women in towns across the country, that had things in them like a paperback book, comb, handkerchief, writing paper and pencil, razorblades, and mirror. There were cigarettes donated by the Amalgamated Clothing Workers union. There were reels of motion pictures and a projector but no space on board to show them. We went over and over the ship trying to find a space, but in the largest common area meals were dished out all day long in shifts, and every other space was taken up with bunks. Live shows were possible, though, topside, and guys could sing. There were records onboard, but the navy understandably did not want its loudspeaker system diverted from the business at hand. We thought we might be able to use their mimeograph, however, and get out a ship newspaper, and perhaps the navy would cooperate on a daily news broadcast.

At first there didn't seem much that we could do, but as we talked it over we realized that the men aboard had plenty to do and had their own initiative and talents for entertainment. With the newness and excitement of the trip they certainly didn't need any stimulation from planned recreation the first few days, and we decided that our job was to gauge the moment when the excitement ebbed away and come up with some diversion from the thick blue thoughts that would be gathering.

We Red Cross girls, restricted so far to officers' quarters, wanted to be able to go down to the enlisted men's deck and just spend time there, sit around with the fellows and shoot the breeze. There was some hesitation about this idea on the part of the officers, but they finally agreed that some of us could distribute cigarettes so the men would know we were on board, and maybe later on there might be other things that we might do that would take us among the men.

The next day the officers organized men in queues, and four of us went down into the cargo hold with Spike, the head Special Services officer, and found the cases of cigarettes and had some fellows lug them up and then stood by two hatches, fore and aft, and gave out the packs. It wasn't much, just a tentative reaching out toward men for whom we felt an overwhelming complex of emotions. On the surface it was this:

"Hi." "Hi-ya." "Where're you from?" "Brooklyn." Repeat, with different place name.

"Where're from?" "God's country. Never saw the ocean before, and only time I want to see it again is going the other way. What you doing tonight?"

"First pack of tailor-mades I ever smoked. Thank you, ma'am. You got another pack for my brother?"[8]

"You look just like a girl I knew back home."

"Say, nurse, I need someone to hold my hand. Say, nurse, I wish I was homesick."[9]

Actually, it was surprising how much conversation there could be with the passing of a pack of cigarettes from hand to hand.

The Measles

By nightfall the middle nurse with the red hair had her forebodings confirmed that what she had broken out with was the measles. There was a great to-do. We were in quarantine. Our supper was served to us on four aluminum trays and six bedpans were distributed beneath each tier of bunks. We were restricted to our cabin. The pharmacy sailors who had taken over were delighted. Our spirits sank. We moped about the cabin glumly. "My mother told me there'd be days like this," said Angel. "But she didn't tell me there'd be so many of them in a week." No matter how we figured it, the horrible fact was that it would be at least a week before we might be rescued from the black hole of isolation. "Three thousand men on board!" moaned Tex. "And me all set to go howling tonight," said Angel. "You mean after we rot down here for seven days," said Swallow, "if someone else breaks out we have to stay down here for another week?" We looked at one another. "Listen," said Swallow, "the first one gets a rash goes overboard." It wasn't comforting conversation to the poor nurse who had the measles. I felt sorry for her, but we weren't wasting sympathy on anyone but ourselves. "I'm sure

8 "Tailor-made": a mass-produced, factory-made cigarette.

9 The soldiers on the ship had no way at this point to distinguish a nurse from a Red Cross Club Service worker. All the Red Cross personnel would have been in uniform, without a designation as to their responsibilities.

glad," Tex said privately, "it wasn't a Red Cross girl who got sick." We went to sleep. It was a terrifying responsibility: "Suppose I wake up with a rash all over my face?"

That night the convoy headed into rough weather. The ship rocked, and all night the bedpans slid across the deck and clattered like a set of dodge 'em cars in a carnival. Next day the army and the navy set about trying to raise the morale of Red Cross girls whose job it was to raise morale. We didn't object at all to having breakfast served in bed. The bedpans were removed, and we were allowed to use the head. Everyone who could invent an excuse to come by our cabin dropped in to visit. Enlisted men weren't able to, but the pharmacy boys came every half hour to sweep the deck, fix the lights, see if the ventilator was working, sing us a song, or show us a dance. And in the afternoon they brought us their phonograph and more than a hundred records. The doctors came, of course, and the ship's officers, and brought us messages.

Then Spike came, grinning, and very formally announced that he was in charge of conducting us on a one-hour airing mornings and afternoons. That was great news, and we trooped up the ladders after Spike with as much glee as if we had been let out of a ten-year stretch of solitary confinement. We were assigned an isolated section of the officers' deck within hailing distance of the other officers and nurses and within whistling and waving distance of the men on the deck below. And again we could see the other ships of the convoy to know that all was well with us. Spike insisted on boosting our morale still further by giving us judo lessons, but it wasn't much fun because we had only one another to practice on, and the only thing I remembered was how to break the grip of someone coming head on trying to strangle you, but I would never have a chance to use the knowledge.

We settled down to the now delightful routine of being the Measles Kids. A penciled "Quarantine" sign was put on our door to keep visitors out, but Mike and Al, the pharmacy boys, could come in, and others slipped anonymous and mysterious notes under the door and sent us presents of books and games and candy.

On Valentine's Day Ardith got out her crayons and drew hearts and flowers and ships, and we made up verses for each of the units on board:

Oh, men of the Nine Hundred and Seventeenth Anti-aircraft
with love for you we are all daft
When we get out of quarantine
Will you be our valentine?

Where Are We Heading?

Next day booklets were distributed to everyone on board: *A Pocket Guide to North Africa.*[10] It had seemed our inevitable destination, but I was glad to have it confirmed. First of all, that's where I wanted to be sent, because I wanted a European and combat area assignment, and in the spring of 1943 North Africa was the only place in the European theater where American troops were in combat with the Nazis. I knew that many of the men on board had good reason to feel differently. For them combat meant different things besides being in the mainstream of things, adventure and excitement, and a keener sense of being of service. We knew, from the fact that our port of embarkation was New York, that we were not headed for the Pacific. We might, however, be headed for some place like Iceland or Bermuda or some spot we'd never heard of. But it seemed unlikely, with so many army troops aboard and that large of a convoy, that we would be destined for an inactive area.

On the other hand, it was possible that the convoy might keep dropping off parts of itself at various spots as it went along. But we were the first large group of Red Crossers going overseas together, and we knew there were only a handful already in North Africa, and it seemed to us that that's where we'd be needed. Of course it might be England, and if the invasion had been the second front instead of North Africa, I would have wanted it to be England. I wished there was a second front. I wished there was some sign of a second front soon, and then I would have wanted to be on the way to England. But in the spring of 1943 there seemed a better chance for an American to get to Europe fastest

10 Special Services Division, Army Service Forces, United States Army, *A Pocket Guide to North Africa* (Washington, DC: War and Navy Departments, 1943), www.ibiblio.org/pha/world/Pocket-Guide-to-North-Africa.pdf. The forty-four-page guide provided information about the people of North Africa, customs, dress, food, shops and markets, and social life, along with general rules about health, interaction with locals, and "List of Do's and Don'ts." Among the latter: "Don't refer to the people as heathen—they are very religious." "Don't drink liquor in the presence of Moslems." "When visiting, don't overstay your welcome. The third glass of tea or coffee is the signal to go, unless you are quartered there."

via North Africa, for that was where the Americans were currently fighting.

The day before we left Washington [where they had trained at American University] we were each issued two tropical-weight uniforms, and in my ignorance that was another sign of our destination. Now and then we speculated on our landing place, and most of us thought North Africa and were glad, but there was the lurking chance of someplace else, an island, say, where we six would be dropped off. Mostly I was sure it would be North Africa because I was a lucky person, and that's where I wanted to go, and I couldn't imagine going anywhere else. In a long white envelope stamped "SECRET," kept in my money belt or under the pillow of my bunk, were the orders of our group, not to be opened until we were again in sight of land.

During the day, our flat rubber life belts slung across our shoulders, we lay on deck in the sun. It was a beautiful wide world of sea and sky and ships, and we had nothing to worry about and nothing to do but lie in the sun and experience the cradle-rocking of the ship. We grew tan and healthy and lazily relaxed and watched the horizon dip and rise and the foam whiteness of our wake and the gleam of sun on water and the rainbows in the spray. Oh, this is the way we go to war, go to war, go to war, this is the way we go to war—

Sometimes there were porpoises and the sharp, quick maneuvers of the tiny destroyers far off, and always the rolling of the other ships to watch. And when we were allowed on deck at night I lay on my back on the lifeboat stanchion and was lost in the stars, wrapped in the sphere of sea and sky, and swinging with the stars. During the day we talked and read and looked at the French and Arabic in our North African guides and made up games to play. We started playing Battleship, a game on paper ruled in squares, where each player tries to sink the opponent's fleet. It helped the torpedo anxiety to play it, and everyone around us began ruling squares, and we mimeographed sheets and took them down on the enlisted men's deck, and for days and days people played Battleship as if we were on an idle pleasure cruise. The sailors played a kind of solitaire over and over again where you took off cards to make fourteen until all the cards were paired, and the reason they played it was that the whole pack was held in your hand—you didn't need to set cards down and so none would blow away. At night the tiny wardroom became grotesque in thick blue smoke, with grim and shadowy figures jam-packed and concentrating on a blackjack game.

During the trip there was nothing more lovely and heart-turning than the men singing out on deck. Sitting cross-legged on every inch of space, shoulder to shoulder or leaning back to back, lounging, hands beneath head or elbow bent and cheek on palm or chin on fists, knees high with arms wrapped round, squatting cowboy style, or perched on hatchway, rope, or gear, the whole mass swaying with the ship and sea, and the quiet slap of the waves and the taste of salt on lips and the voices of a hundred men. Oh, sing! O joy of life, with the sea and the wind and the sun. O world ahead for all of us who have just begun to live! O man, the sweet green earth is yours, alive or dead. So let me call you sweetheart, that married dear old Dad, America, America, with brotherhood, from sea to shining sea, oh, I've been working on the railroad, Dinah, blow your horn, down by the riverside, ain't gonna study war no more, the white cliffs of Dover, remember the Red River Valley, and the skies are not cloudy all day, it's a long way to Tipperary, it's a long way to go, when the lights come on again all over the world. Let the sea roll, and let the ship rock, and let us sing our way to war. This is the way we go to war, go to war, go to war, this is the way we go to war, all on a Thursday morning.

For three days the convoy ran through moderate storms. The sea grew higher, and the sky grew lower, and the wind ripped cold and wet across the decks. Rain splashed down and blew and slanted, whipped and flooded across the ship. The sailors grinned at us and said "you ain't seen nothing yet" and watched to see us take to our bunks, but we bore up and called to them in blithe and cheery voices and saw them turn with sickly grins on greenish-yellow faces as they climbed about their tasks. The second day of the storm the wardroom was considerably less crowded, and we clung to our seats while the dishes scooted across the table until they hit against the board that had been raised and came scooting back. Next day even the cooks acknowledged the storm and served sandwiches on deck. We ate because food and air were the rumored preventives for seasickness. But down below, where there was no air and the odors of the food were thick and stale, homesickness and fear and gloom rose in a thousand gullets and misery was epidemic.

We gave out Red Cross ditty bags that had no seasick pills, no little bit of Texas soil, no clod of red Georgia earth, no Minnesota sod, no New York City heat wave, no one-way tickets home hidden in the seams. We were on deck briefly, breathing deeply and storing air, pacing in circles and exercising to keep warm, and standing aslant in the wonderful feeling of leaning on the wind. At the changing of the watch we saw a sailor climb the long thin climb to the crow's nest and stand suspended in the storm. At night topside was a fantastic world of heavy gray clouds scudding lightly across the moon, of sudden moon glow and foreboding dark, of wet-whipped deck aslant and veering and cables trembling in the wind, of black cold sea below in turbulent surging and falling to hostile depths.

In my top, wall-less bunk, my insides followed the unfriendly churning of the sea. I rolled to starboard and my feet slid aft. My head slid forward and I dipped to port. Storms were bad for aiming torpedoes. I slept.

Boat drills were a part of ship routine. Sometimes they included passengers, and we lined up topside until the deck was a solid mass of human beings. Sometimes drills involved the crew only: fire drills, abandon ship, and various alerts. We didn't like those at all. Gongs would sound so urgently and sailors scamper about so fast. All we could do was to get down to our cabin and stay there. We never knew whether it was real or not, and even if it wasn't, it stirred up all sorts of possibilities. And then they closed us off. They pushed the big heavy bulkhead doors shut and clamped the bolts and sealed us off. Ah, we didn't like that at all, and one of us would call out, "Don't forget us!," and we would sit in nervous chatter and jittery jokes, wishing we could work off the anxiety in some more active assignment.

Dangers at Sea

There were always rumors that we were being chased by a pack of German subs, and whether any of it was ever true, we never knew. Occasionally there was gun practice, when we had to go below and feel the ship reverberate with the recoil of the guns; and sometimes, when we went aloft, the covers of the guns were off and their crews stood by. Practice, they would tell us. Just a drill. Always, throughout the trip, the convoy zigzagged its way up and down and across the ocean. Even after we had gotten the North Africa guides we thought sometimes that they must be blind—it seemed that we were going in every direction but east. We'd feel a sudden lurch, and our ship would point around, and we'd feel her swing over and settle down again into another tack. Mostly we seemed to be going north. By day the sun was always in the wrong place, and at night the North Star was never where it was supposed to be. One evening our whole sphere of sea and sky boomed and shook as if from monstrous underwater drums. Our destroyers were dropping depth bombs. Ba-ha-h-ooooom-m-m-m. Ba-ha-ha-oooooommmmm. Practice, the sailors said. By that time we were skeptical that the navy would toss those tin cans overboard for fun. The German subs must be practicing too, we said.

After the storm the sea was bright and calm. Again we lay on deck in the sun under the soft blue sky. We were cradled and felt the gentle motion of the ship and the caresses of a mild, sweet breeze. How could there be war in a world like this? What had happened to man that he should be intent upon blasting his life and ripping the earth, the lovely earth, and man created in the image of God. In the beginning, God created—

At night the moon shone silver on a peaceful sea, and on the top deck men and women sat in close comfort to one another and dreamed of a life full of living and of love, and on the lower deck men sat alone or close to other men and remembered their women and their loves. But what we had to think, beneath our thoughts, was this: moonlight and calm water are best for torpedoes. Ah, it shouldn't take a war. It shouldn't take a war for us to be sailing to new lands. It shouldn't take a war for us to be meeting one another, to be learning of America from one another. It shouldn't take a war for us to be crossing the ocean to see the wide, wide world. It shouldn't take a war for us to be able to lie in the sun on the deck of a ship and feel more alive than we'd ever felt before. It shouldn't take a war.

Mutual Attractions

It wasn't long before most of the girls had felt specially drawn to some particular male aboard. We had slight opportunity to get to know any of the enlisted men, but we mingled freely with all the men in our allotted territory. They happened to be officers, but to us civilians they were men. From the moment that the soldiers on the dock had grabbed our suitcases as we got off the army bus and the sailors had grabbed the suitcases from the soldiers and had led us up the gangplank and down the ladders to our cabin, we had reveled in our new delightful status of being scarce women among a multitude of men.

I had thought beforehand that I would surely think some ponderous thought as I climbed the gangplank of the icy ship that would take me from homeland to participate in the history-making of a war. But all that I had in mind as I watched the lovely sailor up ahead with my suitcase in his hand was a laughing thought about the person at headquarters who had warned us sternly: "Don't take any luggage that you can't carry at least a mile yourself. Remember that from now on you're on your own." And another laughing thought at how good it was to be a woman with the army and the navy on your side. Never before had we had such an opportunity for selection: tall ones and short ones and medium ones, slender and broad-beamed, redheads and light-heads and dark-heads, baby faces and boy faces and man faces, indoor and outdoor faces, inward and outward faces, blue eyes and brown eyes and gray eyes, deep eyes and bright eyes, piercing and faraway eyes, young boys and older ones, country boys and city boys, prairie boys and mountain boys and woods boys, doctors, engineers, salesmen, soda jerks, auto mechanics, teachers, bank tellers, farmers, fighter pilots, air corps intelligence specialists, medics, signalmen, tank men, and sailors.

We talked and sang and ate and joked together and studied one another. There were magnetic fields at work and chemical reactions and gravitational pulls, and out of the mass, for each woman, stepped forth a man declaring "I am the one," and for some it was flirtation, and for some it was love, and for some it was a special bond of fellowship. For some it was forever and for always, and for some it was here and now today, and for all it was as if there would be forever, as if today would continue.

As for me, I loved them all and shied away from letting my affection gather in one spot that might be shot away or scattered at any moment. But one day the middle Red Cross hospital girl and I were alone down in the cabin. "There's a fellow," she said, "who says he'd like to know you." "Which one?" "One of the tank men." And I knew. I waited for her to go on, but I knew. That very quiet one from Illinois.

And it was him. The tank men were all boyish-faced and shy, with close-cropped hair and quiet eyes. They stayed pretty much each one alone and hardly spoke except what could be said with eyes and quiet gestures. The Air Corps boys were gay and jittery, their nerves sharp-honed, garbed in restless glamour, with their yellow loin-slung life belts and their devil-may-care squashed caps. They were charged with nervous energy. They spilled over with the joy of living. They grinned and laughed uproariously and egged one another on, told tall and taller tales and sang, wise-cracked, shot the breeze, cut up, snapped their fingers, shrugged, and grinned. "Rolling home, rolling home, rolling home, rolling home, by the light of the silvery mooOOOON. Happy is the day."

The intelligence men were older and mature. They were a close-knit fraternal group of individualists. They had been around. They all spoke several languages. They had complex personalities, with minds both sharp and deep and both a cynicism and warm humanity that comes of mingling with all sorts of people. They were a moody lot, gay and gloomy and full of fun—and sunk into despair.

The signalmen were all sorts of men and not a unit yet, from Spike, the Special Services officer, just out of Brooklyn College, short and stocky and muscular, tough and fighting his way through Brooklyn and through life, to the regular army colonel, slender and shy and homesick for his wife and not knowing what to do with women under his command as senior army officer. The medics were just doctors and nurses in uniform disguise, talking shop and using their own jargon, an ingrown group already with their private jokes and common memories.

The navy. Ah, the navy. A special breed of men was stamped "navy," but all were individuals underneath, their individuality tailored and trimmed to the navy uniform. And these were extra-special men, the men who took us overseas and cared for us through measles, storms, and packs of German submarines, and who sailed our ship and got us there. I loved them all most dearly, as I did the anonymous men below whose names were All Those Who Came Over on the Same Ship with Me.

I was filled with love for all of them. I cared what happened to the ugliest, most obnoxious, worthless of the lot. I felt a common bond with everyone, no matter the distance between us in background, outlook, thoughts, and interests. I loved them all, and how could I narrow down my love to one disparate part of them. Yet if I would let myself be drawn to anyone it would be the armored man from Illinois, I thought.

"Why doesn't he speak to me, then?" I asked.

"I guess he's shy," she said.

That day at lunch, by chance, I sat across the table from him. He had pale marble-blue eyes and small pointed ears. His cheekbones were high, and his skin was tight on the bone of his jaw. His light-brown hair was soft and short and frayed down over his forehead. He was of medium height and slender, and he sat quietly, a perpetual question in his eyes, and now and then he ran the tip of his tongue along his full lower lip.

"What's your name?" I said.

He swallowed and wet his lip and brushed the hair back off his forehead. "John Adams—like in 'apple.'"

"Where are you from?"

"Peoria, Illinois."

I told him my name and where I was from, and we ate our lunch. After that we said hi to one another, and once he came and stood beside me as I lay on the lifeboat cradle, and we watched the swinging stars. Johnny became a symbol then of all of them, a touchstone for us all. What Johnny would do, we all would do, and what happened to Johnny would happen to us all.

Nearing Our Destination

As we neared the land masses of Europe and Africa, with the weather relatively calm, the feeling gathered that we were almost there, that we had crossed the ocean safe and sound, eluded flaming oil and splintered steel and hostile waves. Our torpedo anxiety relaxed, and we were gay with our victory over German subs until one night when we were brought up short. We were out on deck, and it was a dark, clouded, moonless night with a gentle sea. It was so dark we could not make out even a dim form of the ship nearest to us in the convoy. We were lulled by the dark, by the soothing motion of our ship and the quiet, now-customary sounds of sea and ship, and our growing feeling of being almost there. Suddenly something strange, something unaccountable was happening. A brilliant glow of light was on the sea ahead.

We rushed to the rail, staring into the darkness, trying to comprehend the weird phenomenon. A large white ship, all lights ablaze, was slowing coming up the middle of the convoy, throwing into bold relief against the sky the blacked-out hulk of every vessel of ours. It was an eerie, spine-chilling thing to see a ship alight, a phantom ship, it seemed, in ghostly silence, moving like a white-draped death among us, pointing a finger of translucent bone to mark us for the enemy.

A Spanish ship, the sailors said, and they cursed it, spitting bitter strings of epithets about all "neutral" Spanish ships and Franco Spain. "They always send one out," they said, "whenever we go by, and make us sitting ducks for subs." "The Straits are worst of all," they said, "because Spain is where the German subs hang out and wait."

Shock and anger gathered in us as the evil ship sailed on. Spain—Republican Spain, which should have been on our side now, tortured and trampled and bleeding, the knife plunged by the hands of fascists and twisted in the wound by democratic friends. Spain, whose Madrid might have been the tomb of fascism, as this might have been a pleasure cruise in a brave new world of peace. From now on, the sailors said, there was danger also of German planes, but mostly subs. Tenseness gathered on the ship, in anticipation of our landing in a yet-unknown port and what came after that—and in nervous alertness for what might come before.

In the morning we watched half our convoy take off for Casablanca. It was a sad, heart-wrenching sight, like losing part of ourselves, to see the ships veer off and steam away, the destroyers with them, until they were a file of silhouettes on the horizon. We watched them go out of sight along the sky until they dipped beneath the curve of sea. We wished them well now on their own and felt torn of half our strength, abandoned and forlorn. Little British corvettes came to take the place of our destroyers, darting like hungry watchdogs sniffing the scent of danger. And for the first time we learned firsthand reliance on an ally, of different nationality, for our lives.

We strained ahead for our first sight of land. Twelve days of sea behind us, and we felt as if we had never known a thing like solid earth. It was Africa that loomed up first, dark rugged mountains in the dusk, the Pillar of Hercules [the mountains that signal the entrance to the Strait of Gibraltar], the sailors told us, majestic rock and furrowed earth, solid and peaceful in the quiet night. We were hushed on our blacked-out deck, as we beheld the land of Africa, as the ship moved slowly, secretly, as if the earth had been created as we watched, created for us to live on and enjoy. We stayed on deck long into the night to see Gibraltar, to see if the rock looked like it did in pictures. Most of us, from our schoolbooks, had expected that our first sight of Africa would be a narrow strip of steaming sand. And now we were determined to see if this was so.

Our ship moved almost silently in the night, and we kept watch for Gibraltar. There were sudden blazes of dancing light on shore, a whole city reveling up the hillside in a carnival of light, mocking our world of darkness and the world of rubble and holes dug in the ground. Tangiers. We waited for Gibraltar on our left. We saw land continuously now, the continent of Europe, rock and earth rising proudly from the sea, free this peaceful earth—ripped and torn and shredded, this proud rock and fertile soil strangled and choked with blood and shattered bone and flesh. We gazed at the wondrous earth, watching for Gibraltar, and now and then a massive rock would loom up darker than the night and we would whisper to one another, wondering if it were Gibraltar.

And, bit by bit, more people went below to go to sleep, satisfied that one of those dark brooding rocks had been Gibraltar even though they didn't know exactly which one. And some of us stayed on till two and three and some all night, waiting for the picture of Gibraltar to appear and knowing we had passed it, too uneasy to go down to bed with nothing in the world the way we thought it was, the way we'd learned it was, the way it ought to be, the way, the beautiful, wondrous way, the world might be.

The blue, blue Mediterranean we'd expected was wide and gray under a clouded sky. From day to day we had been waiting for tropical weather so we could change to our tropical uniforms, but we were still wearing winter-weights. Finally word went round the ship that we would come in to our unknown port the following morning. That last night we carried white gloves to dinner, and Tex and Swallow draped theirs through their shoulder tabs. The air was electric with excitement. We ate with a hectic gaiety. The next day the human components of this ship, which were its life, and through which each one of us had lived as only one small, intense, blood-beating, deep-breathing, nerve-tight part, would scatter out to re-form into new multi-being groups. The scattering would come hard, as if the ship itself was torn apart and each of us had become an anonymous rivet or an isolated link of chain, a scrap without identity. And at the same time we still felt part of a larger group, the war, and were impatient to attach ourselves again to the new entity we would be.

For the men, the end of the trip was the start of things very different from what they would be for us. For them the anticipation was mingled with dread and fear and foreboding, yet their anticipation was one of impatience and urgency, for some just to get their feet on solid ground again, but, for many, to get down to the business at hand, to get going, to get the job done, and to win the war and go home.

Arriving at Oran

Next morning we were up early, waiting for the signal—"Smoking lamp is lit"—so we could go out on deck. We rushed up, and there it was, our port, Africa, the war. It was a drizzly, misty, gray day. Gulls wheeled through the air, and the sea around us was filled with little boats. And there was land, green hills crouching to the sea and a host of gleaming white houses climbing up the hills. Brown earth and roads and palms. A beautiful city clinging to the cliffs, washed by the sea. Oran, the sailors said. Oran. A name that we had heard for the first time only some months before. Oran. That was one of the places they came during the invasion. Oran. Wasn't there some fighting here?[11] And that's all we knew. Oran. And high above the city, on the highest steepest hill, a white rounded building and a tall standing female figure. It looked like a chapel and a shrine.

We stood on the deck in a circle, we six, and together held the envelope stamped "SECRET." We opened it and withdrew the papers, unfolded them, and waved them with ceremonial flourish. I read the

11 Operation Torch was a joint British-American invasion of North Africa beginning on November 8, 1942. Troops landed in and around Casablanca (Morocco), Oran (Algeria) and Algiers (Algeria). Troops of the French Vichy government defended Oran, but after heavy bombardment from British naval vessels and landing of US troops, the French surrendered on November 9. Williamson Murray, "Operation Torch: Allied Invasion of North Africa," *World War II*, November 2002, http://www.historynet.com/operation-torch-allied-invasion-of-north-africa.htm.

words as if they were a proclamation: "And proceed to Algiers." Algiers is where we wanted to go because Algiers had Pepe Le Moko, Hedy Lamar, and Humphrey Bogart. Algiers had glamour: and the Casbah. And Algiers was nearer to the fighting front.

"We're on the wrong boat!" exclaimed Swallow.

"Ship," corrected Tex.

"We better tell the captain," said Marge.

A fine way to start out! Getting to the wrong place to begin with.

We decided that the captain probably knew and that the ship wasn't going any farther and that there was undoubtedly some form of land transportation between Oran and Algiers and that we might be a little late but that we'd finally make it. We were supposed to be given an order of disembarkation so we'd know when to get off, but it hadn't been sent around yet. We didn't know what had happened to the rest of our group of seventy-five, whether they had already landed or were farther out waiting to come in or had actually gone on to Algiers. We were the only ship around.

Suddenly Tex said, "Let's stick together, us six, no matter where we go." "Okay," we said, "us six."

We were in the harbor then, close enough to see the busy little boats around us, motorized fishing vessels mainly, and rowboats, and a couple of small navy craft. And then we could see the people in them. People!

Tillie called from the port side, and there was a tug maneuvering near us. A tug, just like a tug in New York Harbor, snub-nosed and shaggy and determined. And on the tug there was a man, a man in blue jeans and striped T-shirt, a big white walrus mustache and a blue beret. Suddenly he called to another fellow on the tug who was trying to throw us a rope. "He's speaking French!" cried Marge. He was speaking French. He stood, gesticulating angrily to the fellow who was trying to get the rope over, and he was yelling at him in French.

The disembarkation list came around with the order in which troops and passengers would get off the ship. First on the list was a category called civilians. Last on the list were the hospital unit and Red Cross personnel. "Last," the major told us. "Take it easy, plenty of time." We were downcast. How could we ever wait? And who were the civilians? There were no civilians aboard unless they meant us, we thought. The "Red Cross personnel" might mean the three girls attached to the hospital unit since they were listed together. Maybe we were supposed to go off first. No, said the major, who had brought the orders around. We had been first on the ship, wouldn't it be logical that we should be the first off? "Logic?" said the major.

It seemed a shame that a group of six should have to wait for hundreds and hundreds and hundreds to go by. It would only take us a minute. We were all ready. Let us get off now. No one will even notice, and we'll be gone. "No," said the major. "What's your hurry?" The war would wait. The war would not end that day. But we were here, and how could they get along without us another minute? We had come three thousand miles to do a job, and how could we serve the troops if they went off and left us? We waited.

The men began going off the ship, walking down the long, long length of the white concrete mole, where some were met by trucks but some continued walking on, up the curving road that led to the town, and on and on. It was our first sight of troops walking, and, as they did, we wondered *where* they were walking. *On* was where they went: on and on. We sat moodily on deck and waited. It was intolerable. A whole new world within our grasp if we could stretch our arms so far. Our muscles were tense for action and our nerves taut for seeing, hearing, smelling. Besides, we had to get to Algiers.

We went below and brooded on our stripped bunks. The cabin was bare, our things all packed away, as if we had already gone. The ship meant nothing to us any more except something to get off of. Home was so far away, and how long would it be before we would see it again? Would we ever see it again? They had told us back in Washington to pack enough to last a year, but that, I thought, was cautious prudence. Six months. The war would be over in six months, surely. Six months! How long they stretched ahead—like the solid ranks of men in olive drab, shoulders burdened with their barracks bags that moved along the mole, in the cold damp gray. At one o'clock they decided to serve us lunch, and we ate, annoyed that we were hungry.

In the middle of the afternoon, we were moping, as if doped, some of us on deck and some below, when a land-based colonel came aboard. Come on, he said. Where have you been? We've been waiting for you all day. You were supposed to have been the first ones off. What are you doing here? Come on!

We didn't know who he was, and it seemed like a gag, but he spoke with curt authority, bawling us out with impatient gestures. We came to life. We babbled with hysterical joy and stumbled, fumbled gleefully, and tumbled down below. We wore our raincoats over our overcoats over our winter uniforms over our sweaters. We strapped our weapons belts around us with their dangling first aid kits and canteens. We slung our gas masks and our musette bags across our shoulders and stuffed our pockets with our books, our Kleenex, shoes, or whatever had not fit elsewhere. We set our uniform caps askew and tied our helmets to our backs like turtle shells, or to our belts like redwood burls, or held them in our hands like flower baskets, and grabbed our suitcases and staggered up topside and latched on to the colonel. We floated off two feet above the gangplank with never a backward glance, our pulses pounding and our eyes shining, open to adventure.

5
Getting Started

First Impressions

"I have a jeep," the colonel said. "Just set your luggage here." And abandoning the cardinal principle laid down by our Washington headquarters, "Never be separated from your baggage," we flung our suitcases onto the pier and leaped into the jeep. It was a glorious ride, careening down the long white pier at what seemed like a hundred miles an hour, the wet wind in our faces and our hair blowing: an exciting entrance. This is the way we would go on, speeding to victory.

Up a red earth road a Red Cross man stood by an army truck awaiting us. We fell out of the jeep, and the colonel, whose very name we did not know, like a knight errant who had rescued us damsels in distress, disappeared, never to be seen by us again. We surrounded the Red Cross man in respectful admiration, eager shyness. He was a veteran. He was already here, and we had only just come. He was of medium height, dressed in army olive drabs, and had orange hair and mustache and a furrowed face with that special sort of farseeing blue eyes that one associates with people of wide spaces of either sea or land. We thought that he was wonderful to know now that we were in Oran, even though we were supposed to be in Algiers. He told us that the rest of our group of seventy-five had already come in, having landed a few miles down, at a place whose name we couldn't pronounce and then couldn't remember, even after we had chanted it over and over, enjoying the feel of its lovely strangeness in our mouths: Mers el Kebir. They were all waiting for us so they could get started with a meeting and get everybody settled so we could go to work.

We stood chatting beside the truck, and suddenly we became aware of the crowd of children who had collected, having sprung up from nowhere. We were enchanted. They were so dirty and so ragged, their feet mud-caked and their hair all tousled, and their dark Arab skin and their dark liquid eyes were so lovely and their faces so wondering and sad.

At first they stood silently, off a bit, but then one or two stepped out in front, and the whole group drew toward us, cupping their hands. "Bonbons, chingum [chewing gum],'" they murmured. It was like a muted choral chant, beseeching. We had been about to climb aboard the truck, but now we paused, a pull between us, the kids solemn-eyed and wary, and we bubbling over with excitement. How cute they were, we thought. We dug into our pockets for chocolate bars and fruit drops and chewing gum, and the tension broke. The children crowded in and pushed and shoved and stretched their arms in front of one another's faces. How magnanimous we felt! Americans! Bestowing our bounty on the world!

"Allez!"[Go!], shouted the Red Cross man at the children. He looked up from unchaining the tailboard of the truck. And to us he said, "You'll never get rid of them if you start giving them stuff. They'll strip you if you give them a chance." "Allez!" he growled again, as the tailgate of the truck banged down. "You'd better get on or we'll be mobbed," he said.

The children seemed poised for flight, yet they held their ground. The Red Cross man gave each of us a helmet, gas mask, canteen, musette bag, and bundled clothing. Then we scrambled into the truck as the children inched closer. As we reached down with our last bonbon or stick of gum, they were silent and unsmiling.

The truck had two board seats along its length and giant naked ribs from which the canvas had been rolled. The Red Cross man got into the cab, and we felt the live throbbing of the motor, and we pulled up the hill, and it seemed as if the group of children backed away from us and kept backing off until they disappeared. We were all eyes and nerves. We bounced with the truck and twisted and turned and craned our necks, tingling with new sights and sounds, tangled in a jumble of impressions: giant paddle cacti, a Jantzen bathing suit billboard, a saddle-packed burro and an Arab out of the Bible, apartment houses (which I had thought were only in the United States), soldiers (American, British, French and Arab), parks, palm trees, and a sidewalk cafe with well-dressed North African French customers and a sign, "Brasserie," that looked to us like misspelled "brassiere." And a shroud with feet, it seemed—an Arab woman. I felt a knot of terror at this. She was a woman, I was a woman, and how very lucky was I. We moved through the hustle and bustle of traffic: army trucks and jeeps, horse-drawn wagons, burro carts, bicycles, and people walking, everyone carrying something on her head or his shoulder or her back or in his hand: bundles and jugs and wood and baskets. It began to rain, a soft gray drizzle, then pelting drops, and then drizzle again, and the Red Cross man called back to us: did we want him to put the canvas on? "Oh, no!" we cried. "We want to see!" The rain was fresh and good, caressing, part of the inevitability of everything we saw, of the way things were.

Suddenly we were there. The truck jolted to a stop in the middle of town, and the Red Cross man came around to the back.

"Okay. This is it. All out."

We didn't give him time to get the tailgate down. One by one we crouched and jumped. Then we stood for a moment, steadying ourselves and gazing around with swivel necks. We were too excited to know what we were seeing except that we were right on some main intersection in the pulsing heart of town. And in that moment a crowd of people gathered, half-circling the truck, this time adults as well as children, French and Arabs both, and studied us with as much curiosity as we felt looking back at them.

We made our way into a wide doorway on the corner, entering a cold, dim, barnlike place, a shabby, high-ceilinged room of about twenty by thirty feet. Its walls were cream-colored or covered by faded brown wallpaper, and it contained no furniture or furnishings except for some folding chairs set up at one end. It had four big windows that stretched almost from floor to ceiling and overlooked the street, and its floors were rough, worn boards. It was hard to figure out what the place was or had been. It didn't look to me like North Africa. It didn't look like anything but a bare, dismal space enclosed by walls. It had no character, nothing but emptiness and cold.

There were a few Red Cross people standing around, however, and we greeted one another with the warmth of long and intimate friendship, of strong ties, as people who recognized each other as fellow workers in a common cause. We did not know them—they were some of the few who had come from England or over from the States before us, but with the first hand clasp it was as if we had always known them, human beings who needed us and with whom we needed to achieve a mutual goal. We looked them over, eyeing them covertly, wondering what would happen to us when we were veterans, what changes we could expect in ourselves. They were tanned and healthy-looking, with deep-lined faces and bright, feverishly eager eyes and something tough about them that we knew we didn't have, as if their faces had been carved from granite and ours molded so far only in clay.

They told us that others had gone out exploring and that there would be a meeting at four o'clock, so we had an hour or so to look around. We rushed outside. In order to disguise our sightseeing and be less conspicuous we decided to split up into two groups of three. Tillie, Tex, and I wandered about the streets downtown. It amazed me that there should be such a good-sized bustling town, with so many human beings living in it, that I had never known existed.

We stood on the main street, and across the intersection of the two angled streets that came into it was a gray, stone, rounded facade of a building that looked like a bank except that it had a little stone balcony above its front steps. The streets were lined with little shops, many of them with apartment houses over them, with stone or metal balconies. We went window-shopping, and the most notable thing was the bareness of the windows and (as we saw by peeking into the stores), the bareness of the shelves. There were handmade Arab products of wool and leather, blankets, tea wallets, hassocks, slippers, and some metal jewelry. Some seemed to have nothing but a picture of President Roosevelt, a vase of flowers in the window, and little else inside, or a few items in the window but not another thing in stock. We saw no dresses, no men's suits, no children's clothing, no toys, no hardware, no meat or eggs, no bread, no dishes, no pots and pans, no stationery. There were no five-and-dimes, no soda fountain drugstores, and no supermarkets. There was one store that had a window full of men's cheap work shoes, with little red-white-and-blue tags on them inscribed "Fabriqué aux Etats-Unis" [made in the United States]. The only other American product we saw must have just come over by the shipload. In one shop window, large blue boxes of this product were displayed, circling President Roosevelt's portrait: sanitary napkins. Up and down the streets went men and women carrying the same blue boxes. Here and there were postcards, some paperback books, a half-bolt or so of cloth, and some urns of colored water in the chemists' shops. I thought of what we had considered shortages at home and got a first glimmering of what it means to be a country caught in war. I remembered reading that a German commission had come requisitioning in North Africa, and I thought of this now not as a small item in a newspaper but as a real locust plague.

The people on the streets were a fascinating parade of strange faces. We saw the high wooden platform shoes of bare-legged French women, the caps of French officers (like the Foreign Legion hats we had seen in movies), the baggy pants of Arab men, and the Arab burnoose [hooded cloak] and fez. We saw scurrying Arab women trying to be invisible in their draped sheets, ragged shoeshine boys calling "American poleesh, Joe!" That first day we saw them all as tourists. We were Americans in a foreign land, and it was colorful, picturesque, and strange.

We wanted to go into some of the shops or stop some people on the street and speak with them, but whatever French we had ever learned was tongue-tied in our English-only-speaking mouths. Even the few words we had practiced on the ship were lost, and the speech that went on around us was a babble that added to the charming strangeness of it all.

Suddenly we came upon a store that had "English Spoken" painted on the window, and we gathered up our courage and went in. It was dim and cold inside and very neat, larger than most of the shops, with what looked like polished mahogany woodwork. There were shining showcases, empty, and rows and rows of shelves, empty but for a few partial bolts of cloth. One of the two sisters running the shop indeed spoke English perfectly and was eager in her friendliness. She told us how many months there had been no cloth, no thread, no needles, no buttons, and no hooks, but she thought that now that the Allies had come things would be better, and as we were leaving she impulsively reached down beneath the counter and brought out three thumb-sized sewing kits that she presented to us gratis as souvenirs. *How do they get along?* we wondered on our way back.

Checking out the Clubs

The meeting was a reunion of long-lost sisters and brothers, the rest of our group of seventy-five, with whom we compared notes on our journey over, although by now the trip seemed vague and in the distant past. Beside a greeting and a welcome, we all got a briefing on what work the Red Cross was already doing and something of what it planned now that we were there, as well as a few remarks about living conditions (in a nutshell: don't drink any tap water). We were asked to fill out forms indicating preferences in assignment—whether we wished to change from the Club Department to Clubmobile Service, whether we preferred working in a small or a large club, and whether we had a preference regarding where we wished to serve, among Casablanca, Oran, and Algiers. The six of us got together and conferred. No one had seemed a bit perturbed about our landing in Oran instead of Algiers, but we were still sure we were destined for Algiers because the secret paper had said so. We all wanted to stay with the Club Department, and although some of us preferred small ones and some preferred large ones, the only thing that seemed to matter was that we all stay together, so that's what we indicated. The Red Cross was operating the Quantin restaurant in Oran then, and that was where we would have dinner, but we needed to get washed up and settled first. Bill, the man running the meeting, ended it by announcing that the men would be taken to their hotel and the women to the maternity hospital.

"Fast work," we joked.

"Wait till I write that home to Mother!"

Nothing had been heard of our suitcases, and Marge had been especially concerned about them all afternoon. At dinner there was a report that a barge of luggage being towed to shore had capsized, with the total loss of its cargo.

"Our suitcases!" cried Marge. She then became annoyed with the rest of us, who had apparently lost interest in our possessions, thought the story to be a rumor, or didn't much care if it was true, or that the suitcases would show up by themselves or that some colonel would suddenly appear with them. After dinner she attached herself to a corporal with a jeep and eventually returned triumphantly with all bags intact and dry.

"They were just exactly where we left them!" she exclaimed. "And that ought to teach you that you have to do things for yourself from here on out."

After dinner Walt [another Red Cross worker], Swallow, Tex, and I roamed through the town some more. We went to see the two Red Cross clubs that were already in operation. The main one was the Empire Club, a block and a half from where we had had our meeting.[1] It was a tremendous stone building set back by a courtyard from the street, U-shaped, with a wing of apartments on each side. With the soldiers of our convoy out in bivouac areas, there were not many troops in town, but the Empire Club was going full tilt, as if all the men who *were* in town were there. One climbed a flight of steps and entered the maze of the lobby, crisscrossed with men in ODs [olive drab uniforms] coming from and going to the honeycomb of rooms beyond and below and above, all clustered about the French girl at the information desk. We scattered, and I stood for a moment in the lobby, watching the grave faces, the sharp-creased and rumpled clothing, the funny droop of pants looped into boots, the angle of the caps, the swing of arms and jutting shoulders, the pert uniform of an occasional sailor, our American boys.

A soldier approached me, swiping his cap from his head.

"Say," he said. "Where can I get some wrapping paper to mail a package home?"

Four thousand miles I had come, and I couldn't even answer the first question that was put to me. I thought through all my luggage, even the footlocker and bedroll at the bottom of the *Flossie's* hold, for any scrap of wrapping paper. Of all the things that we had brought along, including shoe tacks and rubber bands and a Boy Scout knife. I stammered. I thought maybe the club might have some somewhere. Maybe the girl at the information desk would know.

"I just got here," I confessed. "Today."

"Saaaaaay," the soldier said. "You an American girl?"

"Sure."

"From the States?"

"Sure thing."

The soldier stepped back, wide-eyed with astonishment. He laid a

1 The Empire Club was located in a building that had formerly been the Empire Theatre.

finger lightly on my arm. “Do you mind if I touch you?” he said. “She’s real,” he whispered. “A real American girl. It’s eight months since I talked to an American girl.”

His buddy came along, and the soldier explained that I had just come over.

“What for?” his buddy exclaimed. “They’re not drafting women are they?”

“Red Cross,” I said, “pointing to the insignia on my sleeve.”

“That’s voluntary, ain’t it?”

“Yes.”

“You mean you didn’t have to come? You mean you volunteered?”

“I wanted to come.”

He ran his finger in circles by his temple. “She’s crazy,” he told his buddy.

“It’s different for me,” I said.

After a bit I found my way over to the Allied Club a few blocks away. This was a former automobile showroom and was open not only to Americans but also to French and Arab soldiers. There was a long information counter at one end of the back wall, a Ping-Pong table, piano, tables and chairs, and a snack bar on the other side. It was crowded with a motley assortment of soldiers, swarthy and pale-skinned, in uniforms that included bright red or blue pantaloons and cummerbunds. Arab and American soldiers ate thick peanut butter and jelly sandwiches, a Frenchman and an American played a fierce game of table tennis (spectators’ fez-topped heads turning from side to side as the ball clicked from court to court), and others read, played chess and checkers, chatted, and wrote letters.

There was a pleasurable sense of excitement in both clubs, the excitement of many people coming and going, of men seeking something, a cup of coffee, a shower, a sheet of writing paper, a place to sit, news of the front, a movie. Of the possibility of running into an acquaintance from home. Of getting away from the war, the army. Of the mingling of strangers and meeting of new people and conversations that ensued. There was also excitement in sensing the pride of the Red Cross people in their club and in doing their very best, their restless, driving energy and their outpouring of human warmth. My muscles tensed, ready to get to work. My heart swelled, and my lungs expanded in the beautiful thought that tomorrow I would have a club. I would belong. I would not be clueless about how to help a soldier wrap a package to mail home.

Finding Our Billet

By the time we were ready to get back to the billet, Walt, Tex, Swallow, and I had gathered together, and Walt offered to see us there. It was pitch dark outside in a blacked-out town under a clouded sky. We had no idea in what direction to go. We started walking, and in a few minutes we had no idea where we were. With glad cries of relief we came on one of the horse-drawn hacks we had seen earlier near the Hotel Continental, and we piled in gaily.

"Avance!" we cried in our approximate French, urging him to proceed.

From the shadowy bulk on the coachman's box came a throaty voice asking something that we took to be "Where to?"

"We can't tell him we want to go to the maternity hospital," said Tex, flatly. "The news would be all over town tomorrow about the American women."

We all agreed.

"Do you know the address?" asked Walt.

The horses were jangling the harness and stomping on the pavement.

"Square de Souvenir," I said, but the driver was not impressed. "Square de Sou-veh-neerrr." I tried again.

"You go down the street that the Red Cross Club is on," said Walt in a loud, firm voice.

"The street the Red Cross Club is on," Walt repeated louder still. "To the sea!"

"Au mer," I said.

"Past zee Raid Cruss Cloob," drawled Tex in what she thought was a French inflection. "To zee sea." Now Swallow joined Walt to augment the volume of their voices, and there we were, three schools of thought to bridge the gap of language—pidgin English loud enough for even a foreigner to understand, meager French, and English with a French accent, like in the movies and on the radio. All accompanied by gestures that no one could make out in the dark.

"The guy must be deaf," said Walt, and he and Swallow started up again in a frustrated shouting.

I chanted my few words, with dim memory of three years of French in school. Only Tex was having fun with her French accent from deep in the heart of Texas. The driver growled and grunted, the horses jolted off and then picked up speed, the carriage rocked and threw us back into our seat, and we sprawled, relaxed, and laughed in the blacked-out night. As if we were in Central Park. It was a wonderful ride, a fitting first night overseas, with the clop-clop of the horses' hooves on and on, the dark, wet wind in our faces, the creak and sway of the careening carriage through unknown streets and past blacked-out houses, downhill and uphill, the lurch around corners, and the short, sharp cries of the driver to the horses. We were sure we had gone too far. We were sure we were going in circles. We were sure he was taking us Americans for a ride.

Suddenly we were almost catapulted from our seats, the horses almost backed into our laps. The carriage shuddered, the wheels screeched, and we were stopped. The driver sat, placid and immobile. We peered about with eyes that had become accustomed to the dark. It was lighter here, with the sky less dark above the sea and from the reflection of the bright floodlights of the army supply depot down on the beach. We were on the boulevard above the sea, all right. We could make out the palm trees and the little square with the monument in the center and finally, on the corner, the gray, balconied, three-story maternity hospital. We abandoned Walt, and he abandoned the driver to make his way back to the men's billet on foot. We found our way up the steps to the rooms we had chosen earlier and undressed in the icy dark.

"Do you believe it?" we whispered to one another. "Are we really here?" "Is this really me?" "Am I awake or dreaming?" "Is this real?" "Is this me, and am I in North Africa?" And we thought we were too excited to fall asleep.

I crawled, shivering, into an envelope of army blankets. *How close,* I thought. *Only six hundred miles away from the war. If I were in New York, that would be as if the Germans were a little west of Cleveland!* Astonished, I fell immediately to sleep.

Next day, with those in charge apologizing for unavoidably breaking up The Six, Angel, Marge, and Tillie Janie were assigned to the Casablanca area, and Swallow and Tex were assigned to the Empire Club. I was assigned to a new officers' club to be opened in Oran. It would be a long time before any of us saw Algiers.

The Officers' Club

I was really pleased with my assignment. I liked Oran. I liked the way it climbed up from the sea, that it was a port town, and I liked the sea itself. I liked the coming and going and the ever-changing motion of it. I liked our billet, and I liked my room, and I liked the towering fortress and the shrine.[2]

Of course, it was a disgrace to be assigned to an officers' club, and it made me feel that something must be wrong with me to have been so chosen. I tried to rationalize it by pointing out to myself and others that I had requested a small club, and an officers' club was bound to be smaller than an enlisted men's club. Also, I was older than some of the other girls, and on the whole the officers were somewhat older than the enlisted men, and the powers that be might have felt I would get along more easily with an older group. But both of these reasons were weak and failed to comfort me or convince anyone else, and I just had to learn how to take the hurtful looks of disgust when I told someone where I worked. I learned not to divulge the information whenever I could avoid it. Some fellow would say, "I've never seen you at the club." And I would swallow and cough and murmur, "I've never seen you there either." But when the chips were really down and I would have to confess that I worked at the officers' club, then I would grit my teeth and stand my ground while the others shrank back as if I had admitted to some crime.[3]

2 Fort Santa Cruz and the whitewashed Santa Cruz Church sit on Mount Murdjadjo overlooking Oran, which is about thirteen hundred feet below. The fort was rebuilt by the Spanish on a site captured from the Ottomans in the sixteenth century and served as the seat of city government. The chapel was built by orders of the bishop of Oran in 1847. A large statue of the Virgin Mary is a visible landmark at the site of the church. "Fort Santa Cruz, Oran," *Wikipedia.*

3 Edith's concerns about working at an officers' club were not without basis. A Gallup survey conducted in 1946 indicated concerns enlisted men had with the Red Cross. Chief among these was the feeling that Red Cross personnel showed favoritism to officers. Red Cross

I didn't really care. Since the first time I had come across that army phrase "So many officers and so many men," I had discovered that there were men among the officers too. I was a civilian, and it didn't matter to me how many stars or stripes a man was wearing, except I had to learn what each one stood for so I would know what to call him in some unforeseen official moment. And anyway, I thought, there are as many second lieutenants as there are enlisted men. And besides, the reason we're opening this club is so that the officers will have some place to go so they won't be getting into the hair of the enlisted men at the Empire Club, so actually I'm working for the enlisted men by taking the officers off their hands.

I was glad it was a small club where the staff did not have to be departmentalized. Even more, I relished the prospect of starting with a new club right from scratch, of being able to start to make something out of nothing. The officers' club was to be in the very place we had used for meetings, and I liked the idea of making a club out of the first spot I had landed overseas. The nearly empty barn-like space had been a furniture store we learned. How could we make it warm and cheerful? How would we ever fill it? I smiled. We had no problem. It would be filled with people.

There were three of us on the staff—George, as club director, and Liz and I. Gil was food man for the area and made his headquarters in our club and was responsible for our snack bar. George and Gil were both hotelmen at home, George in a small town in Alabama and Gil in upstate New York. Liz was a schoolteacher, from, she always said, eastern Kentucky and western Alabama. In two weeks people listened to me talk and asked if I was from Alabama. George, Liz, and I got together and made our plans. The most important aim, we all agreed, was to get the place open as soon as possible. It would be geared to second lieutenants, and if the higher brass wanted to come in, the door would be open, but no one was going to crowd out the shavetails [newly commissioned officers, especially second lieutenants] by pulling rank or scare them off

personnel could not date enlisted men but could go out with officers. They could dine at the officers' mess, and officers were financially better able to entertain Red Cross women. Robert Keith Murray, *A Study of American Public Opinion on the American Red Cross from Newspapers and Periodicals, 1881–1948*, Monograph 30 (Washington, DC: Privately printed, 1950); Gwendolyn C. Shealy, *A Critical History of the American Red Cross, 1882–1945* (Lewiston, NY: Edwin Mellen Press, 2003).

with any fancy stuff. As for what the club would offer, we would have to find out from the men what they wanted and then figure out how we could get it for them.

George got to work on the basic engineering problems. Plumbing needed to be installed (toilets, washbasins, and showers), and so did lights. The snack bar needed gas, the floor had to be tested to make sure it would hold the weight of dancers, and carpentry and masonry work was required. George also needed to hire civilian staff. Liz and I worked on indoor decorations, blackout curtains, and a powder room for nurses, and Liz was the inside person and I the outside person when it came to procuring supplies. There were five sources of supplies for us to draw on: Red Cross supplies shipped from home, Red Cross purchases made locally, army supplies through official channels, army supplies not through official channels, and whatever we might find to buy ourselves.

I was elected to do the local shopping because I knew three more words of French than George or Liz. For days I wandered through the streets, the main boulevards and little alleys, from the center to the far reaches of town, scouting the shops. All I could find to buy were Arab woven rugs, and I bought them wherever I could find them, two here and three here, and "maybe we will have some in next week." Their soft, soft wool was so lovely to the touch and evoked for me images of Arabs on the wide desert with their flocks of sheep. I would make my selection, ones with bands of harmonious shades of green and rose and blue, and then peel off thousand-franc notes while the shopkeeper piled the rugs on the shoulders of a tall sandaled Arab. Then we would make our way to the club through the teeming streets, and I would think, *They never told us in Washington that this is how you start a Red Cross club.* Our headquarters had unpainted wooden furniture made locally, square tables and straight chairs for the snack bar, for writing, and for games, as well as low, cushioned lounge chairs, broad end tables, and bright canvas beach chairs.

I hung most of the rugs on the great expanse of empty walls with a hammer and nails. And as the furniture came in, we set a rug down on the floor and made a conversation space. The information counter was built, mostly for leaning on, to the left of the doorway as you came in, and Liz and I began boning up on information: where to get clothes cleaned and pressed, where to get shoes fixed, what movie houses showed American films and what was playing, where the bars were located and what hours they were open, where one might find a French-English dictionary, where US money could be changed to francs, and where the PX, barbershops, Red Cross restaurants, and army messes were located.

Around the corner from the information desk, in two partitioned cubicles, were Gil's office and the club office. In a long and narrow ell were the beginnings of the snack bar and rows of tables and chairs. The far end opened broadly to a lounge, with an informal scattering of more tables and chairs and a platform along one wall that could easily take the part of a stage. The basement, smoothed and whitewashed, would have the Ping-Pong table, badminton court, darts, restrooms, and showers.

Liz and I concocted the powder room in what had been the one toilet facility in the place, what Americans called a Turkish model. This was a small, cement-floored cubicle with a small hole in the middle of the floor and two raised footprints in front of it. A fragile chain hung from the ceiling, which, when pulled, caused a spurting and gushing of water across the floor, so that one had to pull and jump to safety at the same time. This intrigued Americans so much that mimeographed diagrams of the contraption passed from hand to hand and were sent back in letters to the States. Where George found more modern plumbing apparatus he did not say, but this was a basic problem for every club—and our Washington headquarters had never mentioned it.

From the Red Cross warehouse came checkers and chess sets, cribbage boards, decks of cards, Red Cross stationery, penholders and nibs, pencils, soap, toilet paper, paper towels, a beat-up typewriter, blackout cloth, sewing kits, cigarettes, razor blades, pocket combs, an old upright piano, a spindly secondhand French radio, last year's magazines, Ping-Pong balls, badminton birdies, and darts. In the local shops I found scrub buckets, vases, ashtrays, and ink that was labeled with American names but was not the same grade as found in the United States. Early one morning as we came in, a crew of women, their skirts tucked up, pushed rags about the lounge floor with their bare feet, being human mops, as they sang some local version of "South of the Border."

Bit by bit the empty furniture store began to look like an American club. Every day more men found our unmarked door and pushed it open. "Is this the Red Cross club?" they'd ask. How did they know about it? "Oh, word gets around." When were we going to open? Why didn't we open now? And they would stay a while to chat. In the first week or so most of these men were those who were stationed in town and worked in offices, ate at their assigned army mess, and were billeted in dismal apartments around town. You're ready, they'd say, looking around at the cold, half-furnished place. All we want is a place to come to. All we want is a chair to sit in. All we want is someone different to look at. All we want is a decent light to write by.

So one afternoon, with the snack bar gas line still under construction and the plaster still wet downstairs and no sign yet out front, George said, "Let's open."

"Sure," we said. "Let's open." We looked around. It had been eleven days since we had landed.

"Wait," I said. "We have to get some flowers." Liz and I went down the street to where we had passed a flower vendor each morning on our way to the club. He had baskets at his feet, baskets of mimosa, narcissus, and violets bursting with spring in the cold gray street. At that time of day there were not many left—the people there bought flowers along with their daily groceries, and in those days there were more flowers to be had than food—and those remaining were drooping. But we wanted all there were.

The children began collecting around us first and then the women and gradually a few men, closing in and watching the transaction. We were beginning to see beyond our tourist eyes, and I saw the flower vendor now, thin and undernourished, with drawn face and pale eyes and thinning hair, hunched in his worn jacket. Finally he understood that we were not trying to choose which bunch to take but wanted them all. We asked him the price, and he told us fifty francs, and we handed over the outsized Algerian notes.

At this the people behind us, especially the women, began calling out to the vendor, with hostile gestures and angry voices in words too fast and shrill and no doubt too colloquial for me to understand. Liz and I conferred, trying to sense what was taking place, wondering if we had done something to offend these people, perhaps fostering resentment by coming along with our American riches and buying the last of their flowers. We looked about at the people, the women with their bare legs, some of them scarred or covered with sores, and their odd, mismatched clothing and their strong, work-reddened hands and their hair oiled to bring some life into it or otherwise dull and listless. Now children were joining in the clamor, and a crowd was closing in, but their anger seemed not at us but at the vendor, who backed off, worried and blinking and pulling his head down between his shoulders, nonplussed, until they closed around him. He remained silent, with the franc notes crumpled in one fist and the flowers still held tightly in his arms.

Then suddenly his resistance seemed to snap, and with a limp arm he handed us back the fifty francs. And now the women spoke again, their anger softened. Still wary, they were talking to us as well as to the vendor, and as their tone softened and their words slowed, I began to understand, with wonderment, what it was all about. The vendor had overcharged us, and they were protesting. The flowers should cost twelve francs, not fifty. And they did not think we should be overcharged just because we were foreigners. For we were not only foreigners, we were Allies, Americans, come to help drive out the Germans, and it was a shame and a disgrace that one of them should overcharge us. This they told us over and over again, in bits and snatches, piece by piece, as thread is spun.

I was quite tangled up with emotion. I wanted to embrace them all, the righteous people and the flower vendor as well. And failing to be able to do that or to think of some symbolic way to show it, I would have liked not to have been there then at all. I could not even muster the beginnings of the words I needed to tell them the first part of the things I felt. But now all they wanted was for me to give the vendor twelve francs so they could witness the completion of the transaction, and they were puzzled at my hesitation, as if they might be thinking that now I was hesitating to give him anything at all. And I hammered at my brain to find some more gracious thing to do than just to hand over the required francs as if the whole thing were only a matter of business, money. And at that moment a French soldier stepped forward from the crowd with a little bow and gesture of salute.

"Permettez-moi" [Permit me], he said. I should be very grateful if you would allow me to present you with the flowers. And he took a few crumpled bills from his pocket, and, straightening them in his hands held before him so that all might see they totaled twelve francs, he handed them to the vendor. A murmur of satisfaction went through the crowd. The women smiled and nodded. The vendor laid the flowers in our arms with care. We bowed and smiled. The soldier bowed. The women turned to one another, talking it all over as they went their ways. The children followed us a bit, not asking for chewing gum or candy, and then ran off. The deep rich fragrance of mimosa and the delicate fragrance of narcissus mingled with the odor that was Oran.

A few minutes after we had the first vase of mimosa on the information desk and while Liz was scattering smaller vases on the tables, the front door opened slowly, and a young crew-cut head appeared.

"Are you open?"

"You bet," said George. "Come on in."

6
Settling In

The Stork Club

Someone called the former maternity hospital the Stork Club, and that's what our billet was known as from then on. As a billet it grew with us, with all the people who slept there from the time we came and all the things that happened. The place had been emptied and washed clean. Its previous occupants had left no traces: no ghostly footprints on the tiled floors, no evident fingerprints on the bare tiled walls, no pictures or old greeting cards, no safety pins or broken combs. It did not smell like a hospital, but we knew its history. It had been a private hospital directed by a doctor who was now in the French army. His wife and children continued to live in their apartment on the top floor, and now and then we glimpsed the small, dark woman or one or another of the dark-haired children moving like wraiths up or down the broad stone stairways, shrinking to be as invisible as possible, clinging to the curving balustrade as if to blend in to its stone uprights. The children must have been instructed not to speak to us, and even the woman never gave any smile or sign that we were visible to her. Not having been overseas long and not yet having learned much of war, we accepted the situation, and none of us ever knocked on that door as we went by it on our way to the roof, and none of us did more than perhaps occasional vague wondering about what they were eating and how it was with them with the man of the family gone and hordes of strangers in their house.

The rooms were of good size and those on the second floor all bright and cheerful, with French windows opening onto a narrow balcony, overlooking either the inner courtyard, with its flash of purple bougainvillea, or the palm trees of the boulevard, the Square de Souvenir, the seawall, and the sea. In the center of the grassy square rose a clean-cut pedestal, with the carved inscription "Mort pour la France," on which were mounted three figures of French soldiers. It was a monument in honor of those fallen in the prior war, not this one, and it stood before us day after day and loomed in the darkness of the blacked-out nights. The soldiers stood, solid and unmoving, forever and ever, with their sad, determined eyes that spoke in silence. Stop. There is no more room. We shall not move over. We are the last war—the last—the last.

When we came into the place that first day it seemed an incongruous mixture of Arab artistry, monastic asceticism, severity, remoteness, retreat, and army barracks utilitarianism. In each room was an iron hospital bedstead, narrow and shorter than average, with army blankets and a washbasin with running water, which we learned later had been the guest bed for each patient in the hospital. And that was all. Yet we knew these were luxurious accommodations: a lovely, graceful, spacious, light, airy, clean building in a wonderful location, rooms to ourselves or shared by no more than one roommate, a curving staircase, and lovely tiled designs. But tile and stone give no warmth, and that first night we were shivering cold. It was, people told us, the tail end of the rainy season, but the rain and clouds and damp and cold went on and on. Very unusual weather, people said. We laughed to learn they used the same expression way over in North Africa that we used at home. That first night we thought we were as cold as we could be, but in the morning we were even colder. As we would do each morning until we discovered that one can live for quite some time without a bath, we shivered as we took sponge baths with the cold saltwater that came from the tap. There was no heat anywhere—no hot water, no sun—and the damp cold ate its way into us layer by layer, gnawed through bone, and settled in our marrow.

The men, meanwhile, had problems of their own in their billet. One night, after we were through at the club, George took me over there to let me see the raw nightlife of Oran. The men's billet was a fourteenth-rate hotel on the other side of town that was still partly used by civilians. They seemed eerie to us as we passed them climbing the long, long flights of steps barely illuminated by tiny bulbs. The rooms were small and airless, with an odor of squashed bugs, and seemed ready for a hanging, each with one bare bulb suspended from the ceiling. The filthy peeling wallpaper seemed to crawl before my eyes. George had been sleeping on the rough, unswept floor rather than come in contact with the bed, and he had his gear piled in the center of the room.

There was one narrow window with ragged curtains, and George motioned to it and said, "Look." The window opened onto a narrow, cobbled alley, garish in the glare of headlights from an army truck. Singly and in pairs, soldiers moved slowly, doorway to doorway, white-helmeted MPs handing out slips of paper, directing men to pro-stations.[1] On one rough stone stoop sat a little boy who appeared to be six or seven, counting the wad of franc notes in his hand, elbows on his skewed knees, occasionally wetting his thumb with his tongue. Other little boys and girls, haggard-faced, in patched clothing, ran up and down the alley, scouting for their older sisters.

As soon the population of the Stork Club thinned due to girls' assignment to other areas, most of the Red Cross men moved in, while a few found rooms or apartments on their own in town. Then Walt and Gil got busy on an improvement program, and before long a kitchen was put into operation, and then there was breakfast every morning while the gas was on—until about eight o'clock. At first the men took whatever rooms were vacant, but gradually, in a series of checkerboard moves, a male and female wing were established in the interests of propriety, morality, and greater freedom in visiting among the girls in pajamas. Three sisters who had worked at the hospital came to cook our breakfast and clean and do our laundry, and their presence was like warmth and sunshine, with sparkling liquid speech and laughter.

Every morning two of them, Rosette and Juliette, were there before we woke to make use of the gas as it came on, having walked clear across the town. Rosette was perhaps in her early thirties, and her arms and shoulders were broad and strong. She lit up the place: her bosom large with love, her expressive face and dark eyes alive and gleaming, laughing at the world, her shoulders shrugging, her tongue swift and sharp.

Juliette was younger, dominated by Rosette, thinner, more given to moods but able to match Rosette's sallies when she cared to, and it

1 "Pro-stations" (prophylactic stations) provided preventive measures and treatment for venereal disease. The military went to great lengths to distribute information to troops about the dangers of sexually transmitted disease, but it was an ongoing problem. "Venereal Disease and Treatment during WW2," WW2 US Medical Research Centre, https://www.med-dept.com/articles/venereal-disease-and-treatment-during-ww2.

was our delight to have them go at one another, like the catlike play of light and shade. Annette was the oldest, more subdued, placid, and came only now and then to help with cleaning. None of them knew English, so it was a great help to us to have to speak to them in French, but they learned more quickly from us than we did from them. They could understand a look, a gesture, while we struggled with our French.

We ate our breakfast at a large rectangular table in the kitchen, a table covered by a checkered oilcloth. Nearby was our larder, unrefrigerated. It was up to Gil, who drew our rations from the army, to maintain the supply. We had canned grapefruit or tomato juice, well-salted bread for toast, butter, powdered eggs, oatmeal, sometimes canned bacon, tons of peanut butter, corned beef, marmalade, Spam if we could face it, cocoa, coffee, sugar, and evaporated milk. Until we got a Lister bag with regular deliveries of purified water, Rosette sometimes would resort to using tap water for making coffee.[2] She was always astonished by our screwed-up faces at first taste. Having used that water all her life, she could never realize how we could tell the difference.

Don't be afraid of it, she would protest. It is boiled. It won't hurt you. "But salt, Rosette!" we would exclaim. And she would shrug. These strange Americans with their strange tongues that had such a hard time pronouncing French and complained of salty water!

The kitchen was the only common room we had, and it became our hearth, and from there each morning Rosette sent us out with smile and cheer, and at night it became a last stopping place before we turned in for bed. After work, some of us would stop by the kitchen with whomever had brought us home—to see who else was there and what was doing and what there might be in the way of a snack. Hot chocolate mostly, after we acquired an electric hot plate, and maybe toast or a sandwich to go with it. We'd sit around the table, talking, joking, telling stories, singing, unwinding the tangled skein of the long day we carried home with us.

"That's why you run out of food for breakfast," said Gil. "If you want to feed the army and the navy every night, go ahead, but we only get a certain amount for rations."

"Oh, Gil," we said. "You can do anything."

2 "Lister bag": a canvas bag used especially for supplying troops with chemically purified drinking water.

"I get the food from the army, and then you give it back to them at night. Let them scrounge their own snacks."

And he put a lock on the larder. But it was a poor lock, and soldiers and sailors made informal contributions, and it was seldom that we had to skimp on breakfast. There was no other place like the kitchen of the Stork Club, where one could count on finding warmth and listening ears, where one might sit silently, where army and navy mingled and rank was checked outside, where there was no rivalry among the women for the men because of such a vast supply, where you could leave before the others and know you would not be talked about behind your back, where one's escort was accepted as a fact and not a subject of discussion (no matter whether he was the same one every night or not), and where newcomers were welcomed and those departing for new assignments given sendoffs. Allen's birthday was celebrated with anchovy paste and duck produced miraculously by Gil. Jo and Betty came down in evening dress and helmeted, because they had no other place to wear the things, bearing gifts of flowers and lice powder, and Allen held a slice of duck aloft upon a carving knife, proclaiming, "Next year, in Tenafly, New Jersey!"

Next year—of course, next year—back in the States. The war was going well now. The retreat had been stopped, and we were pushing back. Americans would not retreat again. Americans did not retreat. And Kasserine was just—Well, it was history.[3] We were going strong now, and we would push the Germans out of Africa and cross over into Europe and then, March, April, May, June, July, August. They had told us to pack our luggage for a year. A year! Just to be sure. Better to have too much along than too little. Six months, I had thought, surely six months is enough to win a war. Surely, I thought, we will be home by Christmas.

Ah, what did we know of the war? We read the news in the *Stars and Stripes* and studied maps and learned new names.[4] We read first of our

3 The Battle of Kasserine Pass, February 1943, in Tunisia, was said to be the first and one of the worst US battle defeats of the war.

4 *Stars and Stripes* is a newspaper that reports on matters related to the US armed forces. It has been continuously published since 1861. During World War II, a number of editions were printed, covering the news in the different operating theaters of US engagement. *Stars and Stripes* (newspaper), *Wikipedia.*

war in North Africa and then of what the Russians were doing and then of Europe and then whatever there was of the Pacific and then the home front. It was all remote. We were here and now, and the problem was to get our phonograph fixed, or to find a band for the first club dance on Wednesday night, or to run a club without having a vehicle of our own.

Old Friends, Race Relations, and English Girls

After the first few days of settling in, the men who had come over in the convoy with us were finding their way into town along with sailors from others ships that had not yet departed. Some units had set up here and there in the mud outside of town, but most of the men, the casuals, were out at Canastel, the big replacement depot about ten or fifteen miles west of Oran on a bluff above the sea. Meetings with these men were joyful dramas of reunion. We might have seen them on the ship so casually that we hardly knew their names, but we knew them—we had shared the close warm bond of the voyage and the ship.

Now and then the sun would come out during the middle of the day, and one or two of us would stand outside the club for a bit to catch the warmth. We would stand and watch the passing pageant, and all of a sudden we would realize that a crowd had collected, staring at us. Mostly kids, they would stand there, silent and immobile, ragged, barefoot, and dirty, their grave faces lifted toward us, looking us over, inch by inch.

"American?" one of them would say. And when we nodded, the word would murmur through the group—"Americain, Americain, Americain." And we would smile to show that we were friendly, that we liked them, that we wanted to be liked by them, and we would feel the awful weight of the responsibility of being an American in a foreign land, of being a foreigner in a native land, of being a representative in their eyes of the vast nation that was America. Soldiers would stop and stand beside us too, and sometimes they would act protectively when they thought the kids were closing in.

"Allez!" [Go!], they would say roughly, with a threatening motion of their arm and one step forward. The kids would back off, but it would take some more *allez*-ing before they actually would go. *Merci* had been the first French word we had learned to use, and now the second was *allez.* Thank you, go away. It was strange to ponder such an ironical relationship.

It was there too, chatting outside the club and catching the sun's warming rays, that we heard about the English girls from American men who had come from England. The men were incredulous. "Why, those girls went out with Negro soldiers. They didn't think anything of it." "Why, some of those English girls said the Negroes were nicer, more polite than the whites. And I don't mean only going out." "Why, some of those English girls liked the Negroes better than the whites. Some of them wouldn't have anything to do with a white guy if there was a black boy around." "Why, do you know there was a hospital in England full of English girls having black babies?" "Why, some of those English girls even married those Negro bastards."

Day after day such talk would begin. Different soldiers would repeat versions of the same: repeating and exaggerating, waiting for the reaction they expected, the shocked disbelief, the clicking tongue and wagging head.

It struck me as odd and stirred up feelings and thoughts. Americans were fighting a war for equality and dignity of the human individual against the racist brutality and dark ages of Hitler. Yet here were Allied soldiers saying these things. It wasn't so much their ignorance of the history of slavery in the United States that bothered me. It wasn't their ignorance of systematic and legislated segregation and discrimination, enforced by legal and extralegal means, the exclusion of Negroes from mainstream American life. No, it was that these fellows still believed what they had been taught, that it was some innate, inborn antagonism that kept Negroes and whites apart. That white females came bawling into life with a physical revulsion toward males of certain degrees of darkness of skin. I wondered if any of these men would die before learning firsthand that they had been wrong. I wondered if any of them would survive the war and eventually begin to understand the full meaning of what they had fought for, that all are created equal and that it takes a never-ending hammering and pounding, a chaining and straitjacketing, a blinding and a poisoning, and lynch ropes, bombs, and bullets to keep one part of humankind down and make the other part believe it is superior.[5]

5 Red Cross practices were impacted by attitudes at home about mixing of the races.

Sometimes, standing there outside the club, walking along a street, or in the club itself, we would catch sight of some familiar face, a long-lost buddy from our ship. And we would rush into one another's arms with a glow and tingling of delight as if we were the only two who spoke the same language in a throng of foreigners. Apart from all the new close contacts that we made each day, we two had a common past together. We had a private language of our own.

"Come have a drink," one would say, "and talk about old times."

And we would take off, usually to the Hotel Continental down the street on the corner of Clemenceau and Gallieni, where there was a long sidewalk cafe, where we could sit and talk over the three weeks that had passed and watch the passersby and maybe spot some other people we both knew and then find out how Bill was and where Eddie had gone and what had happened to Booth. And remember the time the major was—? And remember that night? And do you really think there was anyone in the smokestack when the colonel got so worried? And we would slap our hands down on the table and laugh and laugh and feel so fine and close with friendship, and lean back in our chairs, and maybe the sun was out, and we were in North Africa.

"Why, we must do this more often," we all agreed. Then those acquaintances were gone, and perhaps we never saw them after that.

Officially clubs were open to all soldiers, regardless of race, but at the same time certain clubs were designated mainly for African American soldiers. The result was that African American soldiers mainly attended segregated clubs, and, if possible, these clubs were staffed by African American personnel. Besides concerns about mixing of white and black soldiers, there was a fear among some white men of white women intermingling with black soldiers. Kara Dixon Vuic, *The Girls Next Door: American Women and Military Entertainment* (Cambridge, MA: Harvard University Press, forthcoming).

7

Dance Club

George and Liz and I stood nervously at the information desk the evening of the first dance at our club. We wanted so much for it to be a success, and we couldn't think up anything more that we could do. The Griffins, an army band of high repute, had agreed to play, and a truck was already on its way to bring them in from their area. The furniture was all pushed back against the walls, and here and there, almost lost in the wide stretches of empty space, were plants and flowers I had been able to scout up all over town. Gil was furnishing cake and lemonade and paper plates and cups. We had decided that the only admission ticket a girl would need was accompaniment by an officer. And so we stood inside the door, after our C-ration supper, and wondered and waited.

The French girls began coming in about seven o'clock. They came in twos and threes, in fours and fives and sixes, and if they didn't know an officer, they stood outside the club, like youngsters at a movie house back home waiting for an adult to take them in. The officers were delightedly gallant and would even escort them just inside the door and turn and leave again to catch the last hour at the bars. And with the girls came papas, mamas, brothers, brothers-in-law, cousins, and uncles—all chaperones. Liz and I attempted to play the role of hostess, one at the door and one in circulation, smiling in what we hoped was French when we could think of nothing better than to ask someone to sit down who was already seated. There were few nurses since most of them, stationed outside of town, were not able to get passes to come in. The band arrived shortly before eight and started setting up on the platform in the lounge.

The French sat along the walls, chatting among themselves, vivacious, in a party spirit, and the officers stood about, second lieutenants mainly, on one foot and the other, deadpan, corner-eyeing the girls, and afraid that they might have forgotten how to dance. Liz and I urgently conferred. How were we ever going to get the Americans and French together? We circulated among the men, urging them to mingle with the girls. "Wait till the music starts," they said. "Don't worry."

At eight o'clock the officers came streaming from the bars and brought more girls, more families came with eligible daughters, the music started with the sweet, spine-piercing notes of a trumpet, and suddenly the center of the floor was filled with dancing couples. They pushed the chaperones flat against the walls and spilled out down the snack bar corridor and eddied into every little pool of space between the furniture. "That Old Black Magic," "I've Heard That Song Before," "In the Mood," "Jersey Bounce," "When the Lights Go on Again," "Stardust," "Begin the Beguine." The club had come alive. Forget the war. Forget the long, cold, lonely nights. Forget that you are five thousand miles from home. Forget tomorrow. Dance, boy, dance, and wrap that music round you, and draw it deep inside you, and you inside the music, and feel the rhythm in your blood and beating in your brain, and hold a woman in your arms, and move together with a woman, man and woman as one, and nothing else. And nothing else.

As more people came into the club, as more couples wedged their way between the elbows of the dancers and became dancers themselves, and as they in turn were pressed by new dancers, the room became a frenzied human mass of motion. Looking out over the lounge one saw human heads tossing, bobbing, and swaying, cheek to cheek, wide-grinned, laughing, hair thrown back, eyes glittering or closed. A tossing sea of sweaty, shining, breathless, feverish bodies. The musicians caught the fever of the dancers, and the music grew louder and wilder, and the dancers threw themselves into the madness of the music, and the floor shook, the walls trembled, the whole room seemed to rock and spin, and the drums beat fast and faster, matching the pulses of the dancers, and the trumpet tore the breath out of their throats.

When the band took breaks after each three pieces, the room shuddered to a stop with a gasping sigh, and faces lit up with wide delight. The men beamed at their partners, mopped their faces and the backs of their necks, each threading his way to deliver a girl to her chaperones, to gulp down lemonade, to crowd to the front of the club for air, to eye the band expectantly for the next round, poised and ready, the dance already in their toes and up the muscles of their legs. Do not let the intermissions be too long, let not the letdown come, let us not give way to thought, this is a good old war, we will dance our way through this goddamn war, this is the best war I have ever been to, so dance, okay, *bebe*, let's dance, *voulez-vous promenade avec moi apres?* [will you go for a walk with me after?], and those poor guys out there fighting this war, maybe they'll dance again before they die, and they won't all have their legs shot off, and I'll be out there, let's go, *bebe*, you want to come to America after the war?

The stags pushed up the snack bar wing and clustered at the band pit and edged out all around the floor and closed in on the dancers and dove into the jumping mass and tapped a shoulder moving in rhythm already, and the girl changed partners without missing a beat, and the old one, now a stag, stood rooted, jam-packed, for a moment, and turned and tapped a shoulder and moved together with the mass, a new girl in his arms until in turn he felt the touch of fate upon his shoulder once again. There was the heaving mass of dancers, among which milled the aggressive stags, and then the ring of hesitant onlookers and those for whom there just wasn't any foot space, all closing in upon the dancers, and back of them, with craning necks and forward-pushing shoulders, the chaperones.

How strange a world. These girls, with husbands and boyfriends far off, somewhere in distant lands in the French army, in prison camps or Germany, and our men, far from home and wives and girlfriends, dancing with them in Algeria.

George surveyed the bulging walls. "Sure good doing business like this," he said. "No publicity, no advance ticket sales, and you got an overflow house."

It was a good dance. It was all the dances back home on a Wednesday night all thrown together. From then on the club was a live thing, with music in the walls and the air between them vibrant with the yearning breath for life and peace.

The All-Uniform Dance

On Saturday we tried what we called an all-uniform dance to cut out having space used up by chaperones. It was a day of rain, with sudden drenching downpours and walls of rain advancing along the streets.

All day the men came in with dripping clothes and water-trailing boots, and we wondered if many would come into town that night. Already men were coming in to say good-bye day after day, our fast friends of an hour, an afternoon, an evening, of being in and out of the club for the last three days, in the week it had been open. We were the only ones they knew to say good-bye to. What could I say to men like that? "So long, take it easy, good luck, see you." And press into their hands the words I did not have to say.

A few days earlier one had said that he would fix our phonograph and talked about the records he was collecting at home, still following the catalogs he had sent to him and ordering records, which he had sent to his folks. "I'll have a mighty fine collection when I get back home." And now he comes in, in his wet leather air corps jacket, with his hair wet-plastered down. "I'm sorry I won't be able to fix the phonograph," he says. "I came to say good-bye."

And this one, with his baby face as fresh as dew and wet with rain, who beat me at Ping- Pong just the other day.

And this one, grinning, tough, and swaggering, who asked me at the information desk how he could get in touch with some local person in Oran. And all the others in and out and gone and off to war and what.

The rain let up about the time the All-American Name Band came in, but it had been raining on their way, and they were sore and grumbling because we'd sent the only truck we could lay our hands on, which was an open one, concerned not for themselves but for their instruments.

The men came in all right. Rain meant nothing to them and to the few nurses who were able to get in. A number of Red Cross girls showed up, those who worked at headquarters and did not have club hours, and what really helped was a group of about ten French Red Cross girls. They were, unlike us, ambulance drivers, waiting for assignment. Fortunately for us, our club was the only place in town they were permitted to appear off-duty except for an occasional chaperoned movie, and they gladly came to many of our dances.

Uniform dances gave more room for dancing, but fewer women were available as dance partners. That meant great hordes of stags, for after the bars closed there was no other place to go in town except the movies, and there were always as many men as the club could possibly hold on a dance night, men who wanted to hear the music and watch even if they didn't get to dance all evening. And there were always a certain number of men who came into the club even on a dance night to take a shower, play Ping-Pong, and later on have a snack, or snag a corner or a table, despite the din and clamor, or maybe enjoying it all around them, to play a game of chess or read or write a letter. The success of uniform dances depended on how many nurses were in the area and how many could get into town, and Liz and I were all for letting French girls in to every dance, even though it was a greater strain on us. George was all for uniform dances only, so we compromised on one of each kind each week. George also got the bright idea of roping off the dance area, leaving just a narrow aisle around along one wall and space around the bandstand for stags so that they couldn't crowd the dancers out.

Controlling Who Could Come to the Dances

We tried all sorts of things to establish some control over the local girls who came into our dances. We learned early in our career that one of the main functions of a Red Cross club was to help keep the VD rate down, and it would never do to have us come all the way overseas to provide an easy place of contact for local girls who were most likely to send the VD rate up. For another thing, like money, "bad girls drive good girls out," it was pointed out to us by civilians. But how were we to tell?

Liz and I stood at the door as the girls came in and looked them over. We were to give each other signals, but the only signs we ever made were shrugs and raised eyebrows. There were too many girls and all at once and not the same ones each time for us to get to know more than a few. We might have developed a stable corps of hostesses as the enlisted men's club did, but the officers wanted to bring their own girls to the dances, and the enlisted men's club didn't want us to create hostesses for fear we'd wean their regular girls away with the glitter of shoulder straps and insignia, and we were all for letting any girl in who could dance. We limited the chaperones to one per girl, and very soon the girls came on their own without any chaperones at all, which pleased us not only because it gave more room for dancing but because we were touched by the trust their families placed in us after that first looking over. We could get help from civilians in identifying the local girls and the chaperones, but even their knowledge was limited. Jeanne was working at the club now, but her acquaintances were limited, and she had no more idea of how to tell than we did.

Finally we compromised again. We had cards printed entitling the bearer, whose signature was on the card, to admission to any of our civilian dances on Wednesday nights. We issued them first to friends of girls who worked in army installations and those requested by an officer and then to their friends and their friends and their friends. It was not long before about eight hundred cards were out. And soon the rumor rumored back to us that this card was one of the most prized possessions in town, despite the ease with which we knew they could be gotten. Possession of a card was a mark of prestige, and to be without one was to be in danger of bottomless embarrassment should an American officer invite you to a Red Cross dance. George had laid down the ruthless rule that an officer who wanted a card for a girl had to ask for it by the Saturday night before the Wednesday dance. This wasn't too hard on the town boys, but fellows who just had the night of the dance in town, maybe having come a hundred miles or more, raised a justified and angry howl. George gave way grudgingly and moved the deadline up to four o'clock on Tuesday afternoon, but that still left out fellows who had only Wednesday in town, who were most likely those who most needed whatever breaks in life that they could get. So, swearing underneath his breath, George gave in another inch and authorized us to issue cards to any officer, even if it was in the middle of a dance. But such cards were marked with the date or as temporary, and at that point there didn't seem to be any sense to having cards at all, except that they meant a great deal to the girls.

And then the rumor rumored back to us that girls with cards were lending them to other girls for favors or under threats. And so we started a guest book at the door, a roadblock of a little table set up in the center of the entranceway, for each girl to sign as she came in so we could compare the signatures. It was a bluff, a blind, a gesture since Liz and I agreed that neither of us were handwriting experts. Liz and I stood at the little table barrier, and the crowd came surging through the door, flooding over us and swirling around the sides and rolling up on one another like pounding surf until we had to stand our ground by digging our feet into the floor. And in that sea we were to stop each female wavelet and have her dig into her purse and find her card, and sign her name, to give us time to look her over with a graph of the VD rate in mind.

How could we tell? We couldn't. What could one woman tell about another, looking at her? Nothing. The girls came streaming in, and there were all kinds of girls. Mostly average height, mostly thin with bony arms and shoulders and hollows in their cheeks, mostly young, with hair mostly shoulder-length and dark and waved and oiled, mostly good-looking because they were young, wearing the best clothes or the only clothes they had—short, tight skirts and simple blouses, sewn to fit and freshly washed and ironed, and maybe a thin jacket, with the collar held close with two cold hands around the neck, and open shoes with high wooden wedges. We smiled at all of them and tried to get to know their faces and gave up trying to learn any of their names and let them in. So long as they had a card we let them in. Ah, what the heck. Most of them were okay. They were like girls in any soldier town back home except that French families were much stricter with their daughters than our own, and we were glad they came so that our men could dance, and we were glad they were our friends and looked on us as friends and could have a bit of fun.

And then one night an MP came into the club. "You know," he said, "your dance cards are selling for three hundred francs up the street. Your club is going to become another prostitute hangout if you're not careful."

"But what can we do?" we said.

"Keep 'em out."

"But how can we tell?"

"Oh," he scoffed. "You can tell just by looking at them."

"How?"

"You can tell," he said.

And the sureness in his voice convinced us that a man could tell, although a woman couldn't. Next dance, at our request, he came and stood beside us at the table, looking out above the crowd as it flowed through the door, to spot the prostitutes. "Coming up in the brown coat," he said. "Hangs out at the Chantilly." "Green jacket—hangs out at the Coq d'Or." "White coat, Chantilly."

We took their cards away. It was a smooth and simple thing to do.

When they presented them we took them in our hands and did not hand them back, and the girl was borne forward and beyond us in the press and excitement of the crowd before she had a chance to realize what had happened. Then, after a long and fruitless search for more to reject, the MP left. And now we were no longer sure that he was right. He seemed to have grown as confused as we were in the crowd, uncertain, standing on one foot and then the other, wetting his lips and wrinkling his forehead, indecisive. He may have pointed out three girls at random simply because he knew he was under an obligation to produce something to satisfy us. And even if he were right, if there were only three, that was nothing to worry about. The men would have met these three or others just walking down the street. And these officers were big boys now and could take care of themselves. The girls themselves would tell us if things ever got out of hand. So long as the "respectable" girls kept coming by the hundreds, it was all right.

We relaxed. Months later, the club had to be closed down for almost a week for repairs and rehabilitation. An officer at the Repple Depple [supply depot] told us some time afterward that the VD rate had risen sharply among his men right after that week and had dropped again after the club reopened. We felt it was one of the finest compliments we had had.

Setting Up the Nurses' Billet

The day of our first dance we set up an emergency overnight billet for nurses in a large vacant loft across the boulevard from the club. I had the job of setting up the cots, which Red Cross Supply had borrowed from the army. The truck pulled up with four Arab laborers to do the work, and they began carrying the cots up the long narrow stairway to the loft. They were all tall, slender men, dressed in tattered shirts and trousers and worn sandals. They moved inch by inch, it seemed, like a motion picture being run so slowly that one could see the stills, in a series of tableaus. Between each almost imperceptible move they paused for rest, so that I never felt sure that each step was not their last. And while they moved their bodies seemed to waver, with a sort of inward staggering, so that I was afraid each moment that any one of them would fall flat on his face.

The cots were of light metal, with flat springs, and folded in half, the legs jackknifed. There were about thirty of them, and after the men carried them up, two to each bed, they turned with timeless slowness and looked at me, and I pointed to the spot where they should set the cot. They came up the stairs not out of breath, as I would have expected, but hardly breathing, as if they had no breath to start with. There was one, younger than the rest and somewhat shorter, more lithe than thin, with jet black hair in ringlets, whose dark eyes flickered with a spark of life, but the faces of the others were unchanging, as if made from a hardened wax of listless pain. They bent down with the cot, lowering it quarter-inch by quarter-inch, while I wondered if they would ever make it and then if they would ever be able to straighten up again. They did, in the same agonizing manner, and tottered back and forth a bit as they stood up straight and worked to get themselves turned around and moved themselves with a tremendous summoning of energy toward the stairs as if each step would be their last.

Dates, I thought. *Arabs live on dates.* I could see the sentence in a geography book. *Americans,* I thought, *live on steak, roast beef, hamburgers, hot dogs, pork chops, ham, bacon, pot roast, stew, meatballs, lamb chops, potatoes, bread, spaghetti, rice, grapes, plums, corn, beans, peas, tomatoes, milk, coffee, cocoa, lettuce, cucumbers, oranges, apples, pears, prunes, peaches, cherries, watermelon, nuts, raisins, figs, dates, cabbage, carrots, eggs, cereal, milkshakes, and more. Arabs,* I thought, *live on dates.* Dates, period. I tried to realize just what it meant in terms of calories, in terms of energy, in terms of minerals, vitamins, proteins, carbohydrates, and fats. The great American energy was simply a matter of food.

Even the Algerian French, at whom Americans scoffed because of their unhurried pace, their siestas, and their putting off until tomorrow, moved slowly because they had less food than we. And the Arabs had less to eat than the French. Less energy to move with, to work with, to think with, to enjoy life with. *Colonialism,* I thought, and I saw it again as a chapter title in a book at school, a heading in a notebook. What did we know about colonialism until we saw it in action with our own eyes? And even then what did we know of it compared to the human beings who actually lived it themselves?

Two of the laborers came through the door again, and I pointed to the next spot for them to set the bed. Of course, these were city Arabs, and their diet, I thought, must vary somewhat from just dates. But not much, not much. Working for the army, they were fed one meal a day of measured calories to keep them on their feet. I had seen them down at the docks, long lines of men in rags, passing flour sacks, perhaps, from one to another, unloaded from a ship, or carrying them on their backs, with the same last-ounce-of-energy pace and motions as these men. And we had seen them walking through the town as if fighting their way through air, the way one walks through chest-high water, and we had seen them lie down on the curb or along the walls beside the road that led down to the sea, heaps of breathing rags, replenishing, conserving the bit of human strength that lurked beneath. We had caught a glimpse of the hovels in which they lived, the filth and unsanitary conditions. And we had seen the women and the children. And the contrast with the French, who lived, for the most part, in decent houses and had much more, although not anywhere near as much as we, to eat.

The men had now brought all the cots up. But there were no mattresses. Mattresses? I described the word in gestures. The men moved their heads from side to side, although I wasn't sure they knew what I meant. I ran downstairs, but the truck had gone. I went across to the club and made some phone calls. There were supposed to be mattresses. Weren't the mattresses with the cots? Hadn't the truck brought mattresses?

Nobody knew where the mattresses were. Didn't we have the mattresses? They'd check. They'd try to find out. Was I sure the mattresses hadn't come with the cots?

I went back to the loft. The men were sitting on the floor, leaning against the wall, each one alone, not talking. Laboriously they raised their heads, and I pantomimed the task of getting the cots opened up. They investigated them without apparent curiosity or interest and fumbled and fought them apart. Suddenly, as I resisted the impulse to show them how the cots worked, I wondered how it seemed to them to be directed by a woman, to see a woman in such a different role than that to which they were accustomed and must think the only proper one, unveiled. And then I noticed the young fellow grow curious about the working of the cot and stop his random ineffectual efforts and look more closely and study the hinges and learn that with a couple of deft movements he could get the thing to respond to his hands and spring into place. But the others did not even glance at him and continued on in their own fumbling way.

Two GIs stuck their heads in the door suddenly. "Well, hello," they said.

I explained what we were doing. They were looking for a photographer. There was supposed to be a photographer some place around there. No, I hadn't heard of any photographer, but if they found one I'd be glad if they came back and told me because it would be a good thing for me to know. But they stayed instead to talk. Al was the spokesman of the two, a short, dark, thin boy, quick with nervous energy.

"Where you from?" he said.

"New York."

"New York? No kidding. What part?"

"Oh, Brooklyn, the Bronx, Manhattan. Where are you from?"

"I'm from Brooklyn." And he told me the street. The street, just a little street in Brooklyn, with rows of brownstone houses, high-stooped and bay-windowed. Mentally I was going down the street from the elevated train, and turned the corner. I was a kid and I felt my steps get faster and faster, and about the middle of the block I ran up the steps, with a tingling of anticipation, into my grandmother's house. The minute you got inside the door there was a special odor to the house, a warm and comforting smell, of living and cooking, like the scent of a trail that I could follow way back to my family roots. In the dining room in the corner against one wall was a built-in floor-to-ceiling cabinet of dark brown wood. Beginning at just about the height I could reach, the lower half was made up of drawers. It was the highest of these drawers that was the special territory of us kids, a deep heavy drawer about four feet long with two brass pulls to tug at and the drawer apt to stick, heavy with what we learned was "miscellaneous" and through which we were free to rummage, to our great delight.

"What number?" I asked Al. And when he told me, I said, "Hmm, that's just the next block over from where my grandmother used to live."

We stood for a bit and marveled at the fact. Here we were standing in some loft in Algeria, a loft converted into a nurses' billet, and he had been looking for a photographer that wasn't there, and he lived just a block away from where my grandmother had lived.

We started on a do-you-know routine. Al knew the families on his block, and I knew some of the people on my grandmother's block, but neither of us knew anyone a block away.

"It's sure good to talk to an American girl," said Al. He was a telephone operator on the night shift. "Could I call you some time?" he said. "I get so lonely sometimes I think I'll go nuts. It would be wonderful if I could just call you some time and hear a woman's voice."

8

Interactions with the Locals

A Sunday Picnic on the Santa Cruz Mountain

That first Sunday the club was open I had planned a picnic up the Santa Cruz mountain [Mount Murdjadjo] that is the landmark of Oran. The club had no vehicles, and neither the Red Cross nor the army had any they would or could spare. All week I had been wondering how I could get up there, and the idea of making it an official trip by having a club picnic seemed that it would bring me closer to getting there. But without transportation, it seemed a hopeless undertaking. Until I passed the hack [horse-drawn carriage] stand again outside the Hotel Continental. I had envisioned a fleet of jeeps rolling up the mountain, but the idea readily transformed itself into horse-drawn carriages, and the thought was even more appealing than motorized vehicles.

After talking it over with George, Gil, and Liz, who sort of smiled and told me to go ahead, I asked Bob, a young Austrian refugee who was working at the club as an interpreter, to make the necessary arrangements with the hack drivers. Negotiations went on for several days, not so much about price but about our doubts as to whether the horses could make it and the drivers' doubts as to whether they cared to be part of such a crazy American venture.

Sunday was a beautiful, clear, sunny day, the most beautiful day since we'd been there. After Saturday's rain, the sky seemed freshly washed, the sea most blue of any day, a true Mediterranean blue. The sun was warm, and the air was cool and fresh and clean. The whole world we saw stretched tranquilly, calm and beautiful, to be embraced, beloved, and enjoyed. A day to breathe deeply in, to draw into one's lungs and feel the heart expand, the nerves and muscles ease.

Even at three o'clock, the appointed time, I was not sure our chariots would appear, and, as usual, as the time approached, my great enthusiasm spent itself and flattened itself into a deflated balloon of apprehensiveness that the whole idea was ridiculously unsound. Bob had made the round of sworn coachmen around noon and returned with the intelligence report that we had lost two waverers but that there were still six who were holding firm. That was fine if the six were men of honor and goodwill, for twelve officers had signed up for the picnic, and we reckoned that meant perhaps eighteen to twenty-four would actually want to go. From two-thirty on, I stood watch at five-minute intervals on the corner, my ears pricked, and at five to three I tried to persuade Bob to make the rounds again, but he explained that that would undo the sensitive relationship he had built up.

"They come," he said. "They come."

And at five minutes after three by my watch, which I am sure must have been five minutes fast, Bob came in to tell me that the caravan was assembling outside. And there they were, lining up along the Rue de la Paix, six men of honor and six magic carpet coaches and six horses—sturdy, reliable, trusty steeds.

Gil had prepared us a box of special treat food, and Bob was going along to help me serve. There were twenty officers in the picnic group, and we climbed aboard and sank back against the well-upholstered, springy, roomy, black leather seats. The lead carriage started off, and the second carriage started off and stopped. The rubber rim of one of its wheels had slid off. Three of the drivers conferred and then got to work and pushed and tugged it on again. Then—with whip-flicking, a mighty pull and heaving of the horses, a creaking and straining of the carriages, and grunting of the drivers—we were off.

We clopped along, following the winding of the empty streetcar tracks to the other side of town and the bottom of a hill marked by a giant sycamore. It was good paved road, up past an Arab village of clay huts, mud caves, and shacks patched together from tins, packing case boards, cardboard, and rags. There we saw a roofed-over, open-air, swimming-pool-sized community laundry, with stagnant, scummy water and women kneeling and beating clothes against the stone, and we heard them talking, laughing, calling to one another as scrawny chickens and barely clothed children ran about and solemn goats stood perpendicularly on the hillsides and terraced gardens scratched out of the clay, green and yellow green, beneath tall palms. And on up we went, winding, the horses now wet and straining, and the third horse stopped, and we all stopped, and the third horse shook the harness and turned sharp left to head for home downhill and swung his carriage across the road.

The driver leaped down and held the reins close to the bridle and stroked his horse's neck and spoke with him, and after a while he gently slipped blinders on the horse and pulled him back in line, and we went on, slowly and more slowly, and I began to feel for the horses and think that I would just as soon walk the rest of the way. And the coachman came back to explain to me, "Is good horse. Just crazy." But we do not think he is so crazy. And now we are beyond the palms and into pine and fir, with yellow flowers sprinkled bright along the road edge and now and then a comfortable, middle-class French villa and neatly dressed small children running out to see the carriages and shout "Americains!"

Then there were no more houses, and the road went winding up through sunlight woods, and men and women and children in family groups were climbing up the paths with picnic baskets and flowers in their hands as on any peaceful Sunday afternoon. The carriages pulled off in line along the shoulder of the road just where there was a path that led up to a piney level camping space with a great flat rock to set our food upon. We walked on out beyond the rock to a point that dropped down a sheer cliff, and there it was, the world before us, the lovely curve of hills around the sea and the sea so clear and calm and blue with the breeze and sunlight on it, and the graceful ships at rest in the harbor like toys and the barge balloons silver and gleaming in the sun above them, and the city all spread out.

All was quiet. Below: an open hand of crisscrossed streets and sweeping roads, clean white buildings in clean air. Above, built into the top of the now gently sloping hill: the silent brooding fortress and—higher still, on the topmost pinnacle of earth—the smooth, domed shrine and the towering figure of Santa Cruz that we had first seen from the sea. The navy men stood way out on the cliff and sighted their own ships, and all of us could pick out the garish dome of the cathedral just off the main part of town and, far across the curve of shore, high on a bluff, the pink casino of Canastel.

A Feast to Share?

We laid out our food on the picnic bench at the edge of the cliff with the world spread out before us like a dream. Ah, what a lovely spot to be. Almost unbelievable that I am here and that there is such a thing as war. We had bread, Spam, cheese, California sardines, and grapefruit juice in paper cups—a feast, and the sardines were something we hadn't had before. The men got out their Boy Scout knives, and we opened cans and sliced the meat and cheese and cut thick slabs of bread to pile them on. As we gathered around our fare, feeling at the top of the world, being very witty and gay, appreciating one another, and declaring we would stay up there forever, through the trees and bushes came the civilian picnickers, gathering around us, edging closer, closing in. The kids came right up and ringed around us, both French and Arab children, and stood rooted, staring. The men stood off entirely, appearing unconcerned, and the women took the middle ground, some hanging back yet not able to turn their heads from our picnic table, and others striding up to where they could see the details, commenting to one another, and a few, scornful and aggressive, marching right up to the table, bending over, poking fingers at the food, and commenting.

"Hmm, meat. Enough for a whole city." "Hmm, white bread." "Hmm, fish." "Hmm, cheese. See how thick they slice it." "Meat and cheese and fish all at the same time, all three at once. They will eat all of that now at once, do you think?" "Hmm, in cans, from America. They bring it over by the shipload, but it is only for Americans."

Our food stuck in our throats. Our jaws stopped working. A moment ago we had been joking about how much food Gil had sent with us, but suddenly it seemed to dwindle into crumbs and fragments. For if we could steel our nerves and stop the trembling of our backbone long enough to raise our eyes and meet these people face to face, their numbers seemed legion, infinite, limitless, and alarming. First the children, some of the French well-scrubbed and neatly dressed yet with the same solemnity of hunger in their eyes, little girls with beltless, unstarched dresses hanging loose and limply to their scabby legs, and little boys in too-big or too-little clothes, patched and holey and ragged, barefoot or shod in ill-sized shoes that barely hung together. Our food was not one good slice for all the kids. Yet beyond them were the adults and more youngsters held back by a restraining parent's hand, and back of the adults we could see were shadowy figures among the trees as if each tree would come alive.

It would have been good to have been able then to talk it over with the people surrounding us, to be able to put into words the feelings churning up inside of me, to take their hand at least, but what are gestures to satisfy years of constant, gnawing hunger, and what words are there to explain why some have more and others never, never enough, their whole lives through. And so we stood there, we and they, avoiding one another's eyes, and bit by bit the grownups drifted off, with reluctant dragging steps, and the kids moved back, and those who had come with parents rejoined their family groups to nibble at whatever it was they carried in their picnic baskets, a cut of tough, dark bread perhaps or what. And the urchins on their own backed off an inch or two and sat or crouched and waited.

Just then one of our drivers plodded up the hill from where he had stayed down with the carriages and proffered us a gift, a paper-stoppered bottle of red wine. How moved can one be and go to pieces all inside and keep the tears from showing and bow, all on a level of politeness, saying thanks, thanks very much, thanks, thanks. And then one of our group, a decent soul, said, "Let's send them down some sandwiches in exchange. We have enough. Don't we have enough?"

And I shriveled with shock and burning shame and felt bereft of all humanity, like a shell from which all life has crawled, to acknowledge that I had not thought of sharing our food with the drivers, had not thought whether they had anything to eat with them or not. What manner of human being was I? Even when all the people closed in on us I had not thought of our own drivers at least. And now a dozen of us sprang to make sandwiches for the drivers, full of activity and purpose and consultation, all our pent-up feelings of a few minutes before unloosed. And then when two of the men went down to help carry the food to them, we awaited their return impatiently.

"What did they say?" we asked. "Were they glad to get them? Did they seem pleased?"

"Oh, yeah," they said offhandedly. "They thanked us."

And we tried to be satisfied with that and finished quickly the food we had been eating without remarking on its taste. We lounged around a bit, bathed in sun, quiet and drifting off, each one to his or her own thoughts or thoughtless in a dream world of beauty and peace without war and want. We began cleaning up, wrapping the leftovers to take back with us and collecting the paper cups. We wondered where we could throw the empty grapefruit juice cans, and someone said, "Let's give them to the kids. They'd probably like to have them." We agreed enthusiastically, feeling thoughtful and magnanimous, for we had all noticed the many uses to which the Arabs put old American tin cans. We called the kids. There were only half a dozen or a dozen left, and one boy came forward to represent the rest. He looked about nine or ten years old, which meant he was probably twelve or fourteen. He was a handsome boy, full of charm and grace, full of life and spirit. His lively liquid eyes, quick and dark, darted from one to another in our group, trying to surmise our purpose, ready to react instantly. One of the fellows held out the two tin cans.

"You want?" he said.

The boy shrank back, his thin shoulders tightened in horror and disgust.

We stared, bewildered, fascinated by the mobility of the boy's lovely face. Dramatically, he held the moment of our amazement, drawing himself up with the aloof, scornful pride not only of a little boy, a human being, but of a whole people. There was dignity in the wry angle of his little wool skullcap. There was dignity in the tangle of black ringlets beneath it. There was dignity in his threadbare jacket and his tattered pants, frayed short above the knee. He stood with dignity, his bare feet planted on the earth.

"Ah," he said, waving the tin cans off with the back of his hand. "You eat like this," he said, spreading his legs and arching his back to push his stomach forward, putting his hand way out in front of him to make a fat and well-filled belly. And then drawing himself up again, "And you tell me to take these?"

We didn't laugh. The navy fellow put the empty tin cans out of sight in our carton. Finally I found my voice.

"You want a sandwich?"

"Sure. I like eat too."

Already I was slicing meat and bread. I looked up, smiling. But the boy did not smile and did not take the sandwich yet. He turned his head to the other children, watching from a distance, then back to me. Bob helped me make the other sandwiches.

Mohamed Ben Ali, shoeshine boy. From you we learn. And now you smile with us and seeing we can learn, you become our friend and have your picture taken with us and tell us your name and use such English words as "plentiful" and "difficult" and explain that you have learned English since the Americans have come. Mohamed Ben Ali, Arab boy, bright and beautiful, barefoot shoeshine boy, will you grow up to be president, and how will it be between you and Americans when you grow up? Will we remember what we learned?

Before we left some of us climbed up the lovely grassy, meadowy hill, higher and higher above the world to the thick-walled fort, with the shrine still farther up above us. "So beautiful," I said.

"On this hill," said a soldier, "350 Americans were killed in the invasion." They'd had no cover, and the enemy had looked right down upon them from the fort and mowed them down.

We walked down to the others, with the grass golden in the sun, glowing, waving.

When we got back to town, people asked us, "How was the picnic?" "Oh, wonderful, we said. It's beautiful up there away from everything."

Interactions on the Street

In the morning I woke to the sound of big guns booming out at sea. Practice, perhaps. From my balcony I saw the water calm and blue to the horizon and arched above it the soft blue sky. On the boulevard below, the tops of the tall palms swayed gently, and in the Square de Souvenir the sunlight lightly touched the monument to the dead of the last war. After breakfast I walked the mile or so between the Stork Club and our club, along the street to the Rue de la Paix and down the Rue de la Paix to the Boulevard Clemenceau, and my feet took the path they had worn on previous mornings. It was still quiet and unhurried on the streets, the town waking slowly. There was a group of washed and polished French children playing on a stoop, and on a dare, perhaps, one of them called after me: "Bon jour!" I turned and smiled and waved and said "Bon jour!" They were delightedly amazed and flung their arms about, jumping up and down and shouting to one another and to their mothers who were chatting at the door, "Elle parle français! Elle parle français!" [She speaks French!]

On the Street of the Peace, a soldier was suddenly beside me.

"Hi, Red Cross," he said, grinning that warm, expansive, open-hearted grin that is only American.

"Hi," I replied, and we walked along.

"Where you from?"

"New York."

"New York! Don't you wish you were back there right now?"

"Someday," I say. "Where you from?"

"Kansas. And I wish I was there right now. God's country."

"Ever been in New York?"

"Yeah," he laughs. "Going through, from the train to the boat. At night. I never did see nothing. I'd like to see it. When I get back. When. You notice I said 'when,' not 'if.'"

We smile to one another.

"Say, where'd you get your freckles?"[1]

"Brooklyn."

"Brooklyn? The sun shine in Brooklyn?"

"Yeah, you know the subway in New York gets to be an elevated train in Brooklyn and the sun shines through the spaces of the elevated tracks in spots."

"They look awfully pretty with the sun on them now. Makes me think of a wheat field, all yellow in the sun. You ever been in Kansas?"

"No, I haven't."

He shook his head, expressing his sympathy for my misfortune, pity. And then he brightened.

"Tell you what. After this war is over, you come out to Kansas and I'll show you some real country."

"Okay."

"Well, I got to turn up here. Say, what's your name?"

"Edith. What's yours?"

"Bill."

"Okay, Bill."

1. On March 23, 1944, about a month after she arrived in Oran, Edith wrote home to her mother: "Finally, finally I have discovered the raison d'etre of my freckles. Here I am, the living symbol of all the freckled-face gals that ever saw the sun from coast to coast back home—and last night, even England. I am sure I have met every man on this planet who somehow or other has come to have a special fondness for freckles. And the Red Cross did a noble job to ship one freckle-face to North Africa to help men think back to the sun over Lake Michigan and on the wheat fields of Kansas and in the mountains in California."

"Thanks for letting me walk with you. You don't know what it means to talk to an American girl."

"Thanks for walking me down."

"Well, I'll be seeing you." He half-turned and then turned back. "You know, my sister has freckles too," he said.

I smiled. "See you, Bill." And for a moment I watched his lonely back go down the street.

From across the street two GIs called. "Hey, nurse, I'm feeling sick. Hey, nurse. Please take my temperature. Hey, nurse. Please count my pulse so you can hold my hand." Clowning, staggering, going limp, letting their heads roll.

I smiled and waved, and they straightened up, embarrassed, and walked on quickly.

There were still men who hadn't quite got us figured out, why we had come, and thought we must be nurses.

Now Arab shoeshine boys and street urchins were trailing in my wake, with their chant of "Chocolate! Cigarette! Chewing gum! Shoeshine, Joe!" And suddenly from one shop entranceway one lad charging, with finger pointing and thumb cocked, in perfect Hollywood greeting: "Stick 'em up, *bebe.*" And then he leaped on his imaginary horse with a battle cry, "Hi-ho, Silvairrre!"

Day Off in the Country

Sometimes we have a chance on a day off to get a ride out into the country, perhaps along the sea, the blue Mediterranean, and the young, curling vineyards, the tender green wheat, yellow bright fields, flashes of poppies, and people working in the fields, women and children squatting, backs bent, and men plowing, with their horses one behind the other, not side by side like ours, down to the sea.

And here and there a man straightens up and waves from the midst of a red earth field, and we have come four thousand, five thousand miles, and we will never speak to one another or meet again, and we wave back, and we are brothers and sisters of one world, part of a fight for humanity, a fight for life to be lived, a fight for the life that is in us and the earth. We roll above the sea, where the white surf breaks against the sand and rock below, and fields turn to cliffs, and cliffs to bare earth hills, and hills to dunes. And there are fishermen below, in little coves where cabins stand on stilts, and fishing nets are spread, and the wind comes in gusts and chops the sea to whitecaps and slaps against the battered boats.

The road turns somewhat inland and races through the villages with their little squares and monuments to the dead of the last war, and storks stand one-legged by their great nests on rooftops, and little children run out to the road wearing only shirts and stretch their skinny arms up in the V-salute. We pull up in a little town, where the fellow who has let me come along goes into a stone house that has been requisitioned as headquarters for the outfit he has business with.

As I wait in the jeep, two Arab women across the road eye me furtively from the folds of their white shrouds. A little French boy in tattered shirt and shorts studies me from the side of the building, but is more interested in the jeep than me. The two women have their heads close together, whispering, and suddenly one nudges the other, encouraging, and they cross the road to stand beside me at the jeep, looking me over with simple curiosity. With no man in sight, they have let the folds of their capes fall loosely to their shoulders so that their faces are uncovered entirely, and I look into their dark eyes as if across a barrier of centuries, wishing for some means of communication with them.

In the city the Arab women stay away from us, and now I do not move or speak for fear of startling them away. They are speaking to one another, however, in low tones in Arabic, and then one, gathering firmly her wrap with one hand, reaches out her other hand and pinches the cloth of my uniform between her fingers, feeling it. Then the other one steps closer and lays a finger on my sleeve, sliding it up and down a bit. They smile at me, and one of them calls to the little boy, Gabriel, and speaks to him in Arabic. He translates into French for me. The women want to know, are my clothes from America? I nod to the women and we smile to one another shyly. They study my face and my hands for a moment and speak again to Gabriel, and he interprets.

The women want to know, am I married? I shake my head, and we look into one another's faces, but this time they do not smile. They talk again to one another and then to Gabriel, and this time he too is interested. He lifts his face, hanging on the answer. Do I know how to drive the car? I nod, watching their faces, but I cannot tell what they are thinking, and their boldness has lasted long enough: they gather their cloaks around them and cross the road and disappear. Gabriel leans against the jeep. He is ten years old. He speaks four languages—Arab, French, Spanish, and "American."

"What can you say in American?"

"Yes. No," says Gabriel. "Give me cigarette. Chewing gum. Chocolate."

9

Interactions with the Troops

At the club workmen labored on the snack bar's gas pipes, and Liz and I beheld a wondrous thing that had come over from the States for us, a crate of books. We ripped it open with fingers trembling between hope and dread, and hope won out because they were new and wanting to be read: 150 books, including novels, biographies, and books on music, mathematics, travel, history, geology, and philosophy. We drew each one from the box excitedly and held it in our hands reverently. A book. The feel of it in one's hand and the smell of the ink and paper and binding. And then we dared to open it, and there were words, communication, the world we knew before and worlds we hoped to know.

The club opened at ten o'clock, and when men came drifting in we took each by the arm. "Come look at the books," we said. And soon a carpenter had built a counter in a corner of the lounge and shelves behind it, and we had a circulating library whose only rule became "If you can't bring it back, please pass it on to someone else."

During the day men dropped in to sit, doze, thumb through the latest three-month-old magazines, write letters, get a drink of water, wash their hands, find out where to get something to eat (the Red Cross Quantin restaurant), where to get a watch crystal (almost impossible to find), and ask how they can have a radio sent over from the States (they couldn't). I remember the Red Cross people back in Washington who told us that if a man comes into a club and leans against a post, that's recreation. Don't make him do anything else. The men who came to the club were good people, and they gave us a decent perspective, a solid slant. And talk. And talk. And talk.

I remembered Washington and our training group, and what worried us was how we would break the ice, how we would start conversations, get over the first stiff, stilted moments and put a man at ease.

I thought of all the card tricks, coin tricks, riddles, match and toothpick tricks we learned as conversation pieces. Cards? And where would one find a coin amid all this wallpaper that passes for money here, and who has a toothpick or a match? The fellow chatting beside me, batting the breeze, said nothing much but was warm and close as if we'd known each other all our lives. The economy of words, the sentences understood before they're halfway spoken, the thoughts and feelings of long hours alone ticked off in single words and pauses, a look, a gesture, a breath, a snort, a smile, a shrug, and then long pauses of understanding.

What would a fellow have thought if I were to have suddenly broken in and said, "Now you put the two nickels here and you put the penny there." A nickel, what's that? A telephone call, a subway ride, a Hershey bar, a ferry ride, a Coke, a cup of coffee in the middle of the afternoon, and long pauses in between.

"You want to play a game of Ping-Pong?"

Our first mail came. How strange that a simple piece of paper can set the fingers trembling and the heart to pounding. A pressed jasmine blossom in one letter and the locomotive rushes, its whistle hooting, through the great sweep of America to Arizona where the jasmine grew. Andy got a letter, his first letter overseas, from the St. George Hotel in Brooklyn, and it said that they want him to know that his credit had been established and that they would be very happy to serve him.

"The honeymoon suite," he said. "Day after tomorrow."

After french-fried Spam for lunch I come back to the club, and a fellow in an armchair by the office looked up and smiled and said, "Someday soon a short story will be told about a nice freckle-faced girl."

"Tell me now," I say.

"Soon—soon but not now."

And his buddy came up from downstairs, and he hoisted himself up out of his chair, and I never saw him after that.

At two minutes after five, Minn was in the office. Short and thin, wiry, with a young but shrunken face and two large, dark, mournful eyes peering out on either side of a bone-ridged nose. Every day at five he scooted over from the office in which he worked and sat astride one of the hard old brown office chairs and put his chin on the backrest. George would lean back in the swivel chair at his desk and put his feet on top of the desk, and the two would talk in monosyllables, hardly moving their lips for three-minute intervals, keeping company, close companionship, comforting, easing one another's loneliness, softening, smoothing. When I came in, Minn reached deep inside his field jacket, stretched, and put something into my hand. A box of thumb tacks.

"Oh, Minn. You're wonderful. A whole box! Thanks so much."

Liz collected men from eastern Kentucky and western Alabama. They clustered around her, and she adjusted her dialect accordingly. "Now where did you say you were from?" She wrote down their names and hometowns on her private list. "Why, there was a fellow from Butler in just the other day." And they would go through the do-you-know routine and discover that they were practically kin. It amazed me how many people she knew and had in common with others, from one town to another, maybe a hundred miles apart away. We New Yorkers spend our lives bumping into one another, elbowing our way, breathing down each other's necks and into one another's faces but do not know the fellow who used to live next door.

Art came rushing in, his calm and easy office manner a thin, tight skin over his constant inner excitement, and beckoned me over. He had a mysterious air of secrecy. "Brace yourself," he said. And then from a pocket he whipped out a folded paper, flipped it through the air to open it, and carefully, tenderly smoothed it out on the information desk counter. It is a subway map of New York City. We huddled over it, the breath knocked out of me, and people flowed behind our backs as they entered the club, and we traced imaginary journeys with our fingertips, express and local, Forty-Second Street, the shuttle.

"Ah, let's go up to Central Park. You want to go to Central Park?"

"Okay. Where shall we start from?"

"Let's start some place way out in Queens."

Suddenly Art pricked up his ears and lifted his head and stood rigidly, listening, and then I heard it too. Jeanne was playing her violin in the lounge. "Violin?" Art breathed. I nodded, and he grabbed the map and leaped across the club, and by the time I had made my way through the crowd, answering questions, chatting, retrieving a Ping-Pong ball, and procuring a deck of cards, and a checkerboard along the way, Art was up on the stage sawing the fiddle, sweat glistening on his face, while just below him a group of air corps nurses in leather jackets and slacks were dancing away with the air corps and RAF [Royal Air Force] men with whom they had come in, with throaty exclamations and gasps, while the rest of the lounge went on reading, talking, playing, sleeping, hearing or not hearing, and seeing or not seeing. Suddenly, without warning and without pause, Art shifted into a Tchaikovsky concerto, and the fiddle became a violin, sweet, heart-piercing, and the dancers kept going for a moment in incongruous, feverish motion, then they faltered, looked up bewildered, laughed, caught their breath, and relaxed, standing with arms limp at their sides. Then Art swung back into a jump, and the dancers readied themselves for more action, but he cut it short, handed Jeanne her violin, leaped off the platform—"Gotta get back to the office!"—and was gone.

The CO [commanding officer] of Canastel looked in for a game of Ping-Pong. He seemed to be a nice guy, but I didn't like to play table tennis with him. We were fairly evenly matched, and I knew he should have won but being a gentleman by act of Congress and by nature he couldn't get himself not to ease off—because I was a woman. And because he was a colonel and a commanding officer and I only a second lieutenant assimilated in case of capture, I knew that *he* should win, by virtue of rank. I couldn't keep myself from playing hard, as hard as I could play and better than I played with anybody else, but even when the score got to be 20–20 I didn't want to win. I didn't want to win, and I ground my teeth and felt every nerve on edge, and then I took two points and won. He was a sweet guy, and we got along fine, but I hated to play Ping-Pong with him.

And so there was constant coming and going. There were grins and handclasps, winks and nods, and wisecracks. "Hi, Edith." "Where you from?" "It's so good to talk to an American girl." "How you doing?" There was warmth and comradeship, the feeling that I had known these people all my life, people about whom I knew almost nothing. There was a strong, sure bond that made us all a part of one another, our lives all intertwined, part of something bigger than ourselves, making a decent world to live in. Suddenly, as if the lights had been dimmed and a spotlight focused on one individual in the crowd, Johnny was there, his hair cut short again and his pale eyes shy and questioning, and wetting his lips before the words would come. He was all right. He was staying out at Canastel waiting for assignment and wanted to know if I would go dancing with him that night at the Coq d'Or. The only time I had was my half-hour supper, and that was easy to give him because the only way one could achieve a change in menu was to skip a meal.

The Coq d'Or was only a few blocks from the club, on Boulevard Galieni. The Chantilly was a nicer place but about a mile away and with a smaller dance floor, and those were the only two civilian places open to Americans. The Coq d'Or was just a dive, furnished in dark, gloomy wood, but the dance floor still had some polish here and there and the musicians played loud and desperately in a jerky, two-beat rhythm—"Madelon," "Roll Out the Barrel," "Stardust," "Lili Marlene," "South of the Border"—and the cognac tasted only slightly of kerosene. Johnny danced stiffly, with the music in his ears instead of in his feet, face deadpan, humming a snatch of tune, and on the way back to the club he sang Cole Porter verses close to my ear so I could hear beneath the noise of traffic. He was an office clerk back in Peoria, but he wanted to write songs.

"You know that bench in Central Park?" he said. "You go in the Columbus Circle entrance—it's a green bench, and there's a squirrel there and some grass and a water fountain."

"Oh, yes," I said. "I know the one."

"That's where I spent two years of the Depression. Being a songwriter."

He left me at the door, and I rushed downstairs to start the Ping-Pong tournament. The town boys, who were in and out each day, stood back and let the boys on leave play. Red Percy from New Jersey had a side bet with his bearded, somber buddy, and Red poured twenty-one years of life into each stroke. His carrot hair flopped about, his tongue seemed to follow the ball from side to side, and he danced like a boxer, his eyes gleaming. On the back of his shirt a wet patch grew ever larger, and all his energy flowed down his arm into the paddle. "Three things I like," he said: "I like to jitterbug. I like to play Ping-Pong. I like to fly as if the war was to be won or lost that night."

An Evening Show

One evening a variety show called "Strictly GI" came in from La Sénia airbase [in Oran], with singers and tap dancers, a harmonica player, a magician, and a mental telepathist. The chairs and couches were lined all across the lounge, and down in front those in an overflow section sat cross-legged or hugging legs, while others leaned against the walls and perched on windowsills. The magician made eggs appear and disappear, suddenly roared and plucked coins out of the air, and flipped a deck of cards from one hand to another and found cards in his hair and behind his ears, but nothing up his sleeves. "Is there anybody here from Boise, Idaho?" That got a few laughs and catcalls, as if it was part of the act. The American, British, and French faces all around the room were rapt with solemn wonder, big-eyed like little boys.

The mind reader gave a demonstration of his phenomenal memory. He had the big club blackboard at hand, and he asked the audience to call out words or phrases, and as they yelled them out he had someone write them on the board while he faced the audience so that he couldn't see the list. Finally, when the board was full, he rattled off the list in order: hot dog, watermelon, featherbed, soldier, bad condition, Budweiser, Coca-Cola, double chocolate soda, Statue of Liberty, dirty Gertie from Bizerte, Forty-Second Street, Billy Minsky's, Brooklyn bums, I'm forgotten at Fort Totten, Chewing Gum Johnny, and on and on.

The mind reader, we learned, was from Youngstown, the second helper in a mill, a tamper of open-hearth furnaces. "You work," he said, "until your pants are smoking. I got six months deferment, and when the second one came around I turned it down. So what's a pair of smoking pants if you're wearing them in Ohio? If I only would have known."

The magician, he told us, was from Boise, Idaho, and he was no youngster. "I enlisted," he said. "I had a nightclub. Used to do magic, palmistry, got into the nightclub business. And one by one the boys went off. And then we had a farewell party for sixteen kids, and their ship was sunk in the Java Sea, and there were stools they used to sit on at the bar. I couldn't stand it any longer. Gave up my business, sold my car, told the girlfriend I didn't have time to get married, and I haven't met anyone from Boise since."

The club empties quickly after the show, the fellows spilling out to catch their trucks, to find their drivers, to thumb a ride. A few town boys and stragglers lingered, a fellow racing his pen to finish a letter, two diehards at a chess board, and some just not wanting to go, never to have to go wherever it is they must, and others edging in to see if they could walk home with Liz or me, helping to close windows, turn out lights, and put things away. Ralph, who was working as a porter at the club, recently released from a French-run concentration camp for Spanish Republicans, came up from downstairs.

"One more in the shower," he said. "Almost finished." We waited, and all but a couple of escorts drifted off, and finally we locked the door behind us and gave Ralph the key and stood for a moment at the entranceway to let our eyes adjust to the darkness. It was quiet and black, and in the night we heard the rolling of a lion's roar.

"Ah, Africa!" we sighed. We knew that it was the moth-eaten, anemic lion in the one-tent circus that had set up down the street.

Getting Walked Home

At night there were scarcely any civilians on the streets, and the soldiers were shadowy figures in the dark. The bars and shops long since closed, apartments shuttered for the blackout, in the soft, thick, purple dust of the parking area behind the Hotel Continental enlisted men and officers stumbled, muttering profanities, searching for their jeeps and trucks. Motors ground, and wheels spun in the dust, and vehicles lumbered up the steep grade to the street. Men called to one another, moving and cursing, and flung themselves onto the backs of trucks. In front of the Empire Club shadows stood or sat along the curb, waiting for trucks that might be late or might have gone already. Along the Rue d'Arzew, the street of silent streetcar tracks, misty figures lined the road like trees, with arms out and thumbs pointed in sudden bold relief with every flash of headlights and the anxious, plaintive chant, like wind through leaves: "Canastel? Canastel? Canastel?"

Each night almost, a different fellow walked me home, with tired steps that echoed slowly in the night and sparse and quiet conversation. One night it was Ridge, tall, clean-cut, American junior executive type and one of the few men I had met who was a few years older than me yet unmarried. Ridge was a petroleum engineer, a civilian in army clothes, doing the same job he had done at home and for whom the war was only something that kept him from the States and from his mother and five sisters who took care of him. We went across the street from the Stork Club, but Ridge was not one with whom one sat upon the seawall, dangling one's legs, and so we sat properly, at severe straight angles on a bench, and Ridge produced two oranges from a pocket and peeled them precisely with a pocket knife, and we sat savoring the delicious segments, the first for me since I had been overseas, and looking out across the dark and quiet sea to where red flares were bursting silently in the sky.

He held the oranges in his hand and let me hold them too, to feel the cool, smooth skin and let the scent drift upward to my watering mouth. He also let me know that before we Americans had come to Algeria the people had had no oranges. Although oranges grew everywhere there, they had been shipped to Germany, but now we could enjoy these two, he said, and know that there were plenty for the people in whose land they grew because Americans were there.

At lunch one day we learned that finally the Hitler laws against Algerian Jews had been abrogated, that once more Jewish children could go to school, and that Jews could again practice their professions and join the French army.[1] And as we exited the Quantin restaurant with the news the sun seemed even brighter and warmer and the air more clean and fresh than usual. I walked along with Andy, director of the Red Cross Allied Club, and we could not bear to go back indoors right away, and so we went on past his club down Boulevard Galieni to the little park that overlooked the sea, a lawn of grass, and, down a ways, a little country-fair merry-go-round playing "Penny Serenade," a toylike carousel with bright, bright colors made even brighter in the sun, round and round and nobody riding. Around us Arab shoeshine boys had gathered, and among them was beautiful Mohamed Ben Ali, jet black ringlets and jet black eyes, very shy and very dirty. And alone on a bench sat an American soldier. And in a moment all of us were on the merry-go-round, Andy and I and all the kids, and the soldier and I got to sit on the flame-yellow rooster with his proud red comb and tail, and around and around we went in the sun and round and round went "Penny Serenade" in the

1 The Vichy French had stripped the Jews in Algeria of their rights to French citizenship, required them to wear an identifying mark, implemented admission quotas for Jews in the schools, prohibited Jews from working for the government, and severely limited the occupations available to Jews. The Special Department for the Control of the Jewish Problem was created in Algeria to enforce the regulations. Sheryl Orchayon, "The Jews of Algeria, Morocco and Tunisia," *Teaching the Legacy* (Yad Vashem e-newsletter) 25 (October 2011), http://www.yadvashem.org/yv/en/education/newsletter/25/algeria_marocco.asp.

music box high above the Mediterranean shining in the sun, in celebration of the repeal of the fascist laws against the Jews.

And then we procured an American radio on which sometimes we could get the BBC from London, and we listened with close-held breath to the clipped British voice and thought that perhaps someday we might perchance, oh wondrous thought, pick up the States. We listened to the news, and suddenly the man said we had taken Gafsa![2] It was true then. We were one step nearer to home. We were on our way to the Promised Land through Gafsa.

At breakfast I looked curiously at a can of evaporated milk and took it in my hand and pondered the stories of fascism and democracy it held. I had learned that under Nazi occupation a woman had to have been six months pregnant before she could get any milk, but by this time the milk stations now distributed canned evaporated milk that had come over from America for children and pregnant women.

Welcoming the Newcomers

One morning when I looked out my balcony, the sea was full of ships.

It had been almost a month since we had come, and this was the first convoy from the States since ours. Not quite a month yet it seemed like years, ages, a timeless time that we had been here, since we had been back home. These ships, lying serenely in blue sea and sun seemed visitors from some far-off land dimly heard of in our youth and dimly remembered as if a country in a fabulous tale, a land of peace and plenty, whose inhabitants spoke a language much like ours in sound but whose words had unbridgeable differences of meaning for us both. George and I walked to the club together and detoured around by the port road and stood above the harbor elbows on the seawall and gazed at the ships, a few already docked but most outlying in the harbor. We wondered if it might be possible that our own ships were among them, and we stared and stared but could not be sure one way or another. And we wondered who and what they brought, and the wondering churned up the feelings we had had on the trip over and during our landing and since. We felt stirred by these feelings yet did not quite remember.

2 The capital of Tunisia fell to Patton's army on March 18, 1943.

By night the town was full of navy and a few army officers who had managed to get in, stamped as new by their new field jackets and gaiters, their lost, bewildered looks, and their strange, pathetic questions. Where's the nearest drugstore? Where can I get a chocolate soda? Where can I get a bottle of Scotch? What's the best restaurant in town—with real French cooking? And everyone was looking for someone he thought might be in the vicinity: a brother, a sister, a buddy, a cousin. There was the great joy for us sometimes to be able to cut through all the obstacles and, mostly by chance, bring two people together.

After work there was a welcoming party in the kitchen of the Stork Club, with tongue and wine and cocoa, for the new Red Cross group that had come over. I was worn out with the emotions of the day and the great influx of newcomers in the club with their myriad questions. So many of them, beneath the surface, were on a quest for an answer to their fears and uncertainties and loneliness. I lingered in the excitement of the kitchen, not being able to think of sleep, wanting to be near these people with the freshness of America, their gentle and eager faces, their clear, clean, sweet-smelling skin, their well-groomed hair and nails, and their new uniforms. But I did not know what to say to them.

"How is it in the States?"

"Fine," they said. "Fine."

There was not much communication between us at first, but it wouldn't take long to grow very close, living and working together, and next to our own group we would be closest to this one, the first that came over after us! That night I leaned against the wall and eyed them sitting at our table, eating their tongue sandwiches as if tongue were no special thing at all. The room seemed filled with fresh, invigorating air that apparently lingered on their clothes and skin. We were the veterans, and I remembered how we looked upon the veteran Red Crossers when we arrived. But I did not feel wise or hardened. It seemed I had been here a long, long time, yet I'd had only a glimpse of war, of poverty and hunger, of colonial degradation and fascism, of loneliness and homesickness. There was a great gulf between me and these girls fresh from another world, but there was a greater gulf between me and the men to whom we had to say good-bye each day and the people who had lived there under colonialism and fascism and war.

Being There for Johnny

One afternoon Johnny came in to say that he would be back to beat me at a game of Ping-Pong, and then he went out in search of a watch crystal. A few minutes after he had gone, his buddy Wayne was in looking for him anxiously.

"If he comes back before I find him," said Wayne, "tell him to get the hell right back to camp. He's leaving, and the trucks were about ready to go. He isn't supposed to be in town, you know. He'd better make it back, or he'll really be in trouble."

I played Ping-Pong hard. I ran up and down stairs between the lounge and game room, chatting, kidding around, and fetching records, more stationery, new Ping-Pong balls, decks of cards, cigarettes, matches, and razor blades. I played Ping-Pong some more; talked about Connecticut, Minnesota, Oklahoma, Arizona, Chicago, St. Louis, Yakima, and Three Forks; drew maps with Xs marking the Quantin restaurant, the bars, and movie houses; gave advice on what to pay for Arab slippers, wallets, and jewelry; sewed a shoulder patch on; wrapped some packages in some crumbly paper I had bought in a local store; told people there were no cameras, no film, no whiskey, no milkshakes, no shoe repair stores; and played more Ping-Pong. Wayne came back, his brow knit with worry, went out in search again, and then came back to tell me that he had to make it back to the depot himself.

More than an hour later Johnny appeared, and his eyes lit up when he saw that I saw him. He scraped one shoe and then the other on the floor, licked his lips, and swallowed.

"You ready to be beat?" His face gleamed mischievously like a kid's.

"Johnny," I said. "Wayne was looking for you. You have to get back to camp. Right away."

"Yes," he said. His hands went up to the tank insignia on his lapel, fingers fumbling with the catches on the back, fingernail digging in to flip them off. He laid the little metal tank in the palm of my hand and turned and hurried out the door.

A fellow I didn't know came up. "How about a game of Ping-Pong, Red Cross?" he said.

"Sure. Bet I beat you too."

"Yeah. I'll play with my left hand."

"You left-handed?"

"Only at Ping-Pong and marbles." We hurried down the steps. "You going to dance with me tonight if I stay for the dance?"

"Sure. I'm going to win this war, playing Ping-Pong and dancing. Rally for serve?"

"Okay. Did I ever tell you I liked your freckles? Where you from?"

Getting to Know the Men at the Club

In the club things went smoothly enough. George had battled through to get showers installed for men and even emergency towels for men who didn't have their own. There were some records for the phonograph and needles kept in the safe in the office. The radio was working and picking up the early evening BBC news, for which the whole club stopped to listen. The piano was out of tune, and nobody seemed to mind, and the magazines were two or six months old, and we didn't know the latest songs. We got more books for the library and found a local store that still had Ping Pong balls and got a Lister bag for which the army delivered water every day. There were dances, variety shows, Ping-Pong tournaments, a chamber music concert, a Negro quartet called the BonBon Boys, who made up songs out of their own experiences (one about Oran and one about how it was to work down at the docks), and local entertainers, community sings, and picnics.

The men came and went. There was Tucker, who had run away to sea at sixteen and was now in the navy, who liked to sit alone under the stars and think. He was thinking that a lot more depended on environment than on heredity. He was thinking that if you wanted to raise a garden, you wouldn't cut the weeds off only on the surface, you wouldn't plant your seeds until you had turned over the earth and fertilized it. He was thinking that if you had the most beautiful rose seed in the world it wouldn't grow if you planted it in gunpowder, for instance or in blood. He was thinking human beings were like that too.

There was Roy, air corps from Mississippi, who stood over the vase of roses on the office desk with tears rolling down his cheeks. "You don't know what it means to be able to see the roses. I couldn't see for two weeks, and I didn't know if I would ever see again. My eyes were full of splintered glass, and they had to keep poking after them to get them out. I was afraid I would die and afraid I wouldn't. Those are beautiful roses."

There was Don, who had come over on the same ship and was in the medics, who sat by as we listened to a swing quartet play "Blues in the Night" and "Hawaiian War Chant." He'd been in the army eight years—Hawaii, Egypt, and Libya—and been a reporter before that. His father had been killed in the First World War. "You can't understand what it's like in the army unless you've lived it. You have no roots. You live hour by hour. You're detached from everything, from the fierce competition other people must live in to make a living. Ah, five months from now, we'll be back in the States. You've got a duplex apartment in the Village, and I come up for Sunday breakfast. 'Marcella!' you call to your maid. 'Put on the eggs!' We have six eggs apiece. And we laugh, and we say to each other, 'Remember those powdered eggs?'"

There was young Captain Levin, infantryman, who sat against the wall through a dance, with people taking turns to sit beside him the moment the chair next to him was empty, to ask him questions, to learn, to try to understand. His arm was in a cast as a result, he explained, of a booby trap that had gone off after the ostensible wire of a landmine had been removed. And he explained the diabolical three-fused landmines of the Germans. "Sure, I want to get back," he said. "I want to get back to my comrades. I want to finish the job. Not that I like it. But it's not so bad up there. At least you laugh up there," he said. "We're learning. The British Eighth is really an army. They know what they're fighting for. Our boys are just beginning to hate, just beginning to know what it is to hate fascism. The German prisoners are still cocky. But wait till Tunis. Watch the Russian front. The Germans do not like to fight the Russians. They say the Russians do not fight like gentlemen. That's what we have to learn, to make them dislike fighting us as much as the Russians. It's no pushover. There's plenty of tough fighting ahead."

There was Lee in again, reckless and tight, not letting anyone cut in on a dance. He came to say good-bye. "I can't wait to get back up there. I don't care. I got nothing back home. They got me once; maybe they'll get me again. I want to get back. I wonder who's left in the outfit." And when the music reached its wild crescendo: "I found out my brother was killed. I met a fellow who told me. His jeep hit a mine. Three out of four of them were killed."

Another convoy came in, but the *Flossie* was not in it, and we went down to meet another hospital train. New people came into the club, asking where they could buy some Scotch, get a fountain pen and an ice cream soda, where they could send a cable home, where they could get some film, a watch crystal. A merchant marine engineer came into the club office to ask if merchant marine officers were welcome in the club. All day we had seen his crippled freighter being towed into port. It had been torpedoed just two hours from shore. "It's the third time I've lost a ship under me," he said. "Makes me a little nervous," he apologized. "Can't seem to do anything." We had heard the rumor that the crew was Senegalese and that all of them had drowned. "You know," he said, "they were colored boys. They weren't even Americans. But we've got feelings. They were human beings just like us. We did all we could. To see them go down—" And you knew he was seeing it, still seeing it, and you saw it in his eyes. "I thought maybe if I could come into the club—"

In the evening I fled from the club to steal time out and walk along the Promenade de Letang with Dave, at sunset. The promenade wound up above the port road on the other side of town from the Stork Club, above the sea on many levels, through cultivated garden borders of trees and vines and flowers and shrubs. Not many local people seemed to use it, and few Americans seemed to have discovered it, and it was always quiet and peaceful, with hardly ever anyone else about, like a secret garden. It was always lovely and almost unbearably so at sunset, when the clouds leaped in flame through the trees and set the whole world aglow, a soft glow, as if with an inner life of joy. Across the soft blue water lay sweeps and patches of lavender and pink and darker blue. Molten sun poured over the cliffs and lay in pools in the hollows and licked into the crevices and ran down again to the sea, and the ships at anchor became graceful shapes and shadows and not instruments of war. Dave and I walked slowly together along the path with scarcely a word, each in turmoil of our own.

Dave was four years younger than I but matured suddenly, violently by war. His whole life before the navy had been shattered by the war: the things he had been taught, the values he took for granted, his parents' lives, the Grosse Pointe [Michigan] world in which he had been encompassed, the future he had taken for granted and accepted, the pattern charted and inevitable. He was picking up the pieces and examining them, trying to fit them together again, discovering that he could use them only in an altogether different pattern, in which there were still many gaps. Dave was stationed at the naval base in Oran. He knew how his particular job fit into the whole scheme of things, knew it was a necessary link, and he applied himself to it as if winning the war depended on him alone, even though it dealt with paper and not bullets. But he hated it. He was bored to death with it and the whole routine of the land-based navy, and he was tired unto death with the long, long days and nights of work and the endless months. He was worn by the constant gnawing of shame at the safety of it, and he lived in hope of being transferred to a ship.

There were great gnarled and gray-barked trees whose lower branches curved and twisted down into the earth. There were truncated pines that slanted from the wind and squat and tousled palms. The colors of the sunset grew gentler and gentler, and earth and sea softened and quieted in twilight mist, violet and tremulous. It was more beautiful than one could stand. But, oh, this same sun rose and set above a blood-soaked, bone-splintered earth, a corpse-tortured sea that lay so serenely there.

"Let's go back to the club."

"Okay," said Dave.

Ahead of us clumsily tramped four ragged Arab boys, their arms around each other's shoulders, in huge GI shoes and singing out lustily, in English, "Oh, Susannah, oh don't you cry for me—"

Doing Our Part

A few people still carried around with them remnants of a past dog-eat-dog life, but most of this sort of thing had been shredded off by circumstances. Brass polishing or playing the angles or finding a soft berth or getting ahead were sorry pastimes looked on with contempt. Money didn't mean anything, possessions didn't mean anything, family background didn't mean anything, formal education didn't mean anything, clothes didn't mean anything, and good looks didn't mean anything. What counted was you, the work you did, the capabilities, adaptability, inventiveness, skills, decisiveness, judgment, determination, originality, energy, spirit, humor, dependability, and sympathy you dredged up from the depths of yourself and poured into your work and the people around you.

Each day you spent yourself, again and again and again. If you were a Red Cross volunteer, your way to win the war was to make your club the best, to search out the hottest, sweetest music, the most varied and entertaining entertainment and hidden talents, and to discover, borrow, or cajole transportation, and to keep up with the endless and repetitive requests for supplies: paper in the restrooms, pen points in the holders, magazines with pages still together. To help a man find what he wanted: his brother, a present for his wife, the music for "I'm Dreaming of a White Christmas," baby clothes for an Algerian infant adopted by his hospital, some ice, anybody from his hometown.

The thing was to have the club work so smoothly that it didn't seem as if you were doing any work at all. And then just to be yourself, a person, a woman to whom a man could smile, with whom a man could talk and have a cup of coffee, with whom a man could play a game of Ping-Pong or dance, to whom a man could say good-bye, for whom a man became himself, in whom a man might lay the burden of his thoughts for a moment, to whom one might not only be a soldier but also a man, a human. You lived a hundred lives a day. Sleep restored energy and calm temporarily, but it was the men who drained the wells of emotion or kept them filled to overflowing, brimming with their moving gratitude, their solicitude, that let us know that we were needed and belonged.

I was more than tired. I was exhausted. There had been a week or more of grayness and rain. In Tunisia the Allies were driving toward the conclusion of the war in Africa, but it was not over yet. Each day it was not over yet. Each day more men were killed, butchered. Each day more men were hurled into an inferno of life more horrible than I could even guess at.

A letter came through from Johnny saying that he was all right, but it had been written weeks before. I wore his tank insignia beneath my pocket flap and rubbed it with my finger now and then, for Johnny and for all armored men and for the infantry and for the air corps and the navy and the merchant seaman, for the engineers and signalmen, artillery and anti-aircraft, ordnance and paratroopers and quartermasters and medics, for all of us. I wondered how a man could pray for his life to be spared or how a family back home in the States could pray for their one man of all the men to live and not die.

On another gray morning, George and I stopped, on our way down to the club, to watch another convoy coming in. The ships were strung in single file, diagonally, across the sea, the last ones lost in fog at the horizon and then emerging, dark smudges suspended slightly above their white-churned foam, and moving slowly, gray on gray, becoming ships, and sailing close below us, with landing barges on their decks. We waited until the first one turned, with its tug guide, and slid into the dock.

10

Attack in the Harbor

Downstairs there were three sailors sitting on the steps and another astride a sea bag. For a minute or two we stood near their dim forms, and then we sat down at the foot of the stairs close by them. The noise kept on at the same terrific volume and tempo, every minute, every moment, every second, every instant, a million hammerings pounding on every nerve, on every bone, breath, pulse, on every inch of flesh, with never a respite. For a while nobody spoke but just sat there, cringing, recoiling, waiting for it to stop, to stop, to stop, each feeling one's own tension in the others, consoled, at least, that one was not alone. But it went on and on, and the tension couldn't continue without snapping. Someone lit a cigarette and others took out cigarettes. We moved around, stretching legs, leaning elbows on the step above or resting arms on knees, trying to get comfortable.

"We sure got to get us a new screen door," said one of the sailors. "You should have seen Lou come through there when it started. About took the door right with him."

I remembered that the screen door opened outward, and I tried to figure out how anyone could take the door with him in rushing in. But I felt a warm little spreading spot of gratefulness, as if somewhere way deep in a hidden center a part of me had thawed to humanness, for the plump shadow on the steps that had started us back to normalcy.

"I wouldn't mind," another sailor said, "if the guns didn't make so much darn noise."

We all chuckled, and the noise slapped the walls together, beat the ceiling down against the floor, clapped the steps on one another, and tossed the whole dispensary down a sliding cliff of prehistoric boulders. The sailors did not talk to us directly, but they were conscious of us in the group, and I was touched by the sailor's saying "darn" at a moment like that instead of whatever it was he would have rather said. They were our own guns, and we hadn't heard any other bombs after the first one or any other planes, and it was ridiculous to let the noise of your own guns disturb you.

"But what the heck are they shooting at?" the man on the sea bag asked indignantly.

We all laughed quietly. There were long pauses between one remark and another, and, when they did speak, the men spoke slowly in low voices, beneath the thump and rattle of the guns. No matter what was said we all chuckled, and the good feeling of shared laughter and the warm, soft sound of a human voice and the words said lingered on in the pauses deep inside of us beneath the battering of the noise until another man thought up something that he could put into words.

The sailors concluded that the guns were just being fired for the heck of it. Those guys had been manning those guns for so long with nothing to shoot at that now that they'd started they just couldn't get themselves to stop, and they were just having a heck of a good time. Just trigger-happy. It was impossible that enemy planes were still around for that length of time. And all we heard were our own guns, nothing else. With the harbor clogged with ships, and guns on every ship, every gun on every ship was just blazing away, and they'd probably keep it up until they ran out of ammunition, and nothing was going to stop them, not even orders, but they sure made one big heck of a lot of noise.

"I don't begrudge them a little fun," said the sailor on the lowest step. "But right in the middle of a good poker game!"

It seemed like ages. And it was. Every so often someone would say what time it was. Ten minutes, fourteen minutes, seventeen minutes, twenty-two minutes, half an hour. We didn't get used to the noise. We wanted it to stop. Stop! We didn't know if the planes had come back or whether other planes had come. We didn't know how many other planes there were beside the one that we had heard. We didn't know what might be happening in other parts of town, and we didn't know what might happen at any moment right where we were.

"Anybody got any bicarbonate of soda on them?" said the plump fellow on the upper step. "My stomach feels awfully peculiar." That drew some laughs. "Wonder what I et could have upset it like that?" More laughter. "If I only had some bicarbonate of soda."

It was easy to imagine oneself lying wounded or dead at the foot of the steps. It was easy to picture flying daggers of glass showering the area. It was easy to see the whole staircase caving in on top of us. These possibilities flashed like tracer bullets in and out.

Time went more slowly and then didn't go at all. Thirty-two minutes.

"Your watch stopped? It was half an hour an hour ago."

"Tell those guns to hush a minute so I can see if this thing's still going."

"Thirty-two minutes and a half."

Finally, finally, the solid mass of noise became disjointed. One gun and then another sputtered and then went quiet. We begin to breathe again, tentatively. We felt our flattened cells expand, our spirits rise. After a piercing all-clear sounded, the world went silent for a bit. Then some gunner somewhere took a few last shots.

"Oh, shut up!" one of the sailors said.

Even before the lights could be turned on the telephone rang, and men grabbed gear and jackets and rushed outside, started up jeeps, and took off. There were casualties out at the navy's tent city. The momentary joy one felt at its being over, at being alive, like clear water bubbling to the surface of a spring, hit bottom like a stone. The shadowy figures with whom we had spent the air raid had gone off to emergency duties. How strange that I had never seen the men with whom I had shared the most shocking experience of my life so far. I wondered if I would recognize them by their voices and thought I would only if I heard them again in darkness and amid noise and danger.

Now the building was quiet. There was no sound but the lowered voices now and then of the remaining men and their brief, hushed laughter. I thought of the patients in the wards and what it must be like to be pinned down to a bed by illness or wounds under the avalanche of noise and peril. I thought of what it must be like for one who had gone through much worse than this, for hours and hours, for days, for nights, whose nerves had already been bruised and tangled, who now lay upstairs. Forty-five minutes.

Dave asked if there was anything that we could do to help, but the doc said no, and with formal naval courtesy Dave thanked him for his hospitality.

"Any time," he said. "Nothing at all."

In the misty moonlight the whole town moved in silence to the seawall. The dull glow of a burning ship was like a magnet, and people gazed upon it with wide eyes and vacant faces. Now and then new flames would leap up, in bright intensity, accompanied by dull explosive thuds. Dave and I stood together with the rest. We felt a physical ache in all our muscles hoping that the men on the ship would be able to bring the fire under control before the whole ship burst into smithereens. We walked along the seawall to the Stork Club. We watched the ship. We turned and crossed the street and sat down on the Stork Club steps. We were both trembling inside, and we both felt drained to weariness. We had the feeling that the Germans would come back at any moment. We went into the Stork Club to see who was around. People greeted one another dully. "Hi." "Hi." Then after a few moments, "Where were you?"

There was apparently no damage except to the ship and to the tent city. People spoke in flat tones as if they were too tired to speak. We went out and walked farther along the seawall to the navy base apartments, where Dave found his roommates among the people congregated on the street and gave them the apartment key. A French naval officer and his wife who lived in the same apartment house smiled and waved to Dave. The man's smile seemed a leer. He and his wife both looked very pleased. Their eyes were shining. I wanted to give that man the back of my hand. Dave turned away as if he did not see them. "Damn Vichy French," he muttered. "Probably a damn Nazi spy."

We stopped a little ways up the seawall. The burning ship was moving slowly away from the dock. Like a wounded creature, it crept away from the other ships and crawled with infinite slowness out into the sea. Our hearts were on the ship. Our chests were hollow pits of apprehension and helpless desire to be of help. Teeth clenched, nails digging into flesh, eyes damp, we moved heart-pounding inch by inch.

"The old man went down to take the ship out himself," said Dave. "So if it explodes it won't damage anything else." We thought of the admiral, in our club, drinking cocktails, having himself a time. We thought of the admiral now standing on the bridge of the burning ammunition ship. We thought of the crew. We thought of each man of the crew, smooth-cheeked youngsters in bell-bottomed trousers. The ship was out in the stream, and there was now only her faint red glow and steamy billows of smoke. Then there was only smoke settling peacefully, then thinner and thinner wisps blowing away.

We walked slowly toward the Stork Club. At the seawall a portable phonograph was blaring some frenzied rhythm, and beside it two Red Cross girls were dancing with two officers on the pavement, shouting and laughing. We crossed over and sat on the Stork Club steps.

"I guess we ought to get some sleep," said Dave.

"I guess so."

"Do you think you can sleep?"

"No."

"If they come back again I'll come right over," said Dave.

11
Comforts

A Cup of Coffee

We stood grouped around the snack bar counter, Gil, George, Liz, and I. At the counter too were three Frenchmen and an Arab, our newly hired snack bar crew, their dark skins glowing in contrast to their fresh white shirts, gazing in wonder at the water heating in the Silex coffeemaker on the gas burner. Their eyes were filled with disbelief. "Impossible," they had said. "If you don't put coffee into the water, then how will the water become coffee?" "All right, we will wait and see, but we know what we will see."

Little bubbles began to form, dance, and pop. Then agitated water heaved inside the glass, seeking escape. The watched pot boiled, water shot up a tube, and the heaving water met coffee again and again. We smelled its fragrance, and we licked our lips.

"Take it off the fire now, Maurice," said Gil. Maurice shrugged. His colleagues eyed him skeptically as he moved the coffeemaker to the unlit burner. With a slurp, the lovely mud-brown liquid eased down the column and rose in the glass carafe.

The Frenchmen and the Arab cocked their heads, bent over for a closer look at the coffeepot, then nodded and shook their heads. We had a coffee-tasting ceremony. Gil poured us each a cup, and we held it in our hands, inhaling the fragrance, intoxicated, the first pot of coffee in our own club. We sipped, keeping watch on one another. We rolled the liquid over our taste buds and smiled. It was good, the best coffee we had tasted since we had come overseas. *Our club will have the best coffee in North Africa,* we thought. We raised our cups. To victory. To the end of the war. The Frenchmen and the Arab bent down again, eyeing the coffeemaker. "Very good," they say. "America very good."

That afternoon the snack bar opened. There was grapefruit and tomato juice. There was fresh army bread, fresh butter from the navy, whole cheese, real ham, sardines and tongue, and raisins, and men stepped up and made their own sandwiches and took them to a table. There was cocoa and coffee. It was a treat even for us, but for the men coming in from outlying bivouacs and from Tunisia it was a delightful surprise. It was fun to stand among them at the counter or drop into a seat beside them at a table and hear their comments.

"I haven't seen cheese for, let's see, five months."

"I never knew I could feel this way about a can of sardines."

"Gosh, just to eat sitting down!"

"Well, I don't know whether I don't even prefer this coffee to that vino you get."

"This is something to write home about. It'll pass the censor, and you wouldn't run out of material to write about for weeks."

The snack bar became the hearthstone of the club, and we learned that the snack bar was always the heart of every club. To come in off the road, to get cleaned up, and then to have a cup of coffee and something to go with it. To be able to drink the coffee slowly, lounging at a table with legs stretched out. To watch other people, to linger and chat, to ease into a conversation. To have another cup of coffee perhaps, and another and another, and perhaps to meet a fellow from your outfit or someone who came over on the same ship or even sometimes someone you knew at home, maybe a friend, a brother, a cousin, maybe someone from your home town or state or part of the country.

"Come on, Edie, have a cup of coffee."

To sit across a table from an American girl. To be an individual man again. To talk to a woman as one human being to another. To think of a woman as a man thinks of his mother, his sister, his wife, his sweetheart, his daughter. For a few moments to be a single individual, to have someone to say hello to and good-bye to, someone to be remembered by. All this was a cup of coffee.

The Miracle of Ice Cream

It wasn't long before Gil achieved his greatest triumph. In the afternoon, along the Rue de la Paix, amid the jumble of street noises, the grinding of truck motors, the clip-clop of burros, the clomp of boots and slap of sandals, the cry of shoeshine boys and street hawkers, and the hubbub of voices, one might sometimes make out a new sound, a purring sort of putt-putt-putt. And then there would appear the three-wheeled delivery scooter, its Arab driver tall and stiff, red fez on head, eyes straight ahead, arms stretched taut, knuckles tight on handlebars, bouncing along at eight miles an hour with his precious cargo in the big box behind him. Perhaps by then the first man would be standing in line at the snack bar counter. As the scooter puttered to a stop in front of the club, one of the snack bar men would drop whatever he was doing and rush outside. By this time several more men would have joined the snack bar line.

In a moment the driver and snack bar man would come through the door, lugging a heavy copper cylinder. "Ice cream!" an officer would cry, springing to his feet. In the lounge the men's faces became suddenly animated, and they would rise in the middle of a sentence. Or they would awaken or lay down their cards, set down a checker, and suddenly the lounge would empty. Sheets of writing paper would flutter to the floor. A cigarette would smolder in an ashtray. And the ice-cream line would grow longer and longer and curl back into the lounge. The line always moved quickly. The snack bar men worked energetically, with great satisfaction, slapping huge slabs into bowls with their trowels. The ice cream lasted an hour or so, depending on the number of men in the club, and for a time there was a hush of quiet contentment as the officers spooned up their treat.

Spring

The weather grew beautiful in April. Now and then one or another of us would snatch a few moments to stand outdoors in front of the club on the corner we came to call Times Square, crossroads of the world. All you had to do was to stand there long enough and you would meet everyone you had ever known or see something that you had never seen before.

Peg was added to our staff temporarily, and we each took a day off a week, feeling the winter melt from our bones. Coughs went away, and we enjoyed languorous warmth and ease, the luxury of a day out of uniform, sleeping late, reading in bed, going up with a blanket to the Stork Club roof, lying in the sun there, having time to talk with other girls, reading, studying French, and sleeping some more, with gulls wheeling overhead and the sea peaceful and sunlit beneath the golden cliffs. We wrote letters home, had time to think and time not to think, and had time to do nothing, absolutely nothing. We lay in the sun and breathed and were alive and slept and enjoyed the sleep—reveled in it.

12
Honoring the Dead on Easter

Easter Sunday was cool and cloudy, but Peg and I changed to our tropical uniforms anyway and wore white shoes and gloves like most of the Red Cross girls in town, and we were the only ones in town who had new clothes to wear. We slept late, luxuriously, and two of the navy base boys came in and brought up coffee from the kitchen. We dawdled over coffee, and they went down for second cups, and we sat around, chatting idly, with the doors thrown open to the balcony and the gray and gusty sea. After a while Peg and I sauntered to the club.

The club was abloom with lilies, carnations, roses, and flowers whose names we did not know. We had ordered great quantities from the country, and, as usual, every one of the civilian staff who could lay hands on some flowers or greenery had brought some: the checkroom boy, one of the snack bar men, and Jeanne, and the Belgian artist, Frank. And Curtis the paratrooper, who was a mortician in civilian life, cut stems and arranged blossoms joyfully. There were few patrons in the club so Peg and I went visiting the other clubs to admire their decorations and bid everyone happy holidays. There were whole hard-boiled eggs for lunch and vegetable salad with real mayonnaise—real holiday food.

When we got back to the club, George said, "You and Peg are to be part of the Red Cross group at the cemetery today."

I didn't want to go. The dead were dead, and nobody could speak for them. Let them lie in peace, without big words and promises.

"Why don't you go?" I said to George. "I'll stay here."

He looked at me with troubled eyes and shook his head.

"I don't want to go," I said. "Why me?"

He shrugged, his mouth clamped tight.

"Okay."

The dead were my responsibility as much as anyone's. They lay in the ground I walked upon, and they had given their lives for the ground

I walked upon. I was alive and free to fight for freedom. I would go out and stand on the ground in which they lay.

A colonel gave us a lift in his lumbering car after the officers' truck had gone off without us. Even with the low-hanging clouds, in the brooding grayness, the countryside was lovely and beautiful on the way toward La Sénia: peaceful fields and vineyards and rolling hills. As we neared the airport a sign marked the turnoff to the cemetery, and we went more slowly along the narrow road, which was filled with jeeps and trucks and lined on either side by a silent, moving file of civilians walking at a weary pace.

High above a hill against the clouded sky a US flag waved in the breeze, and tall tops of cypresses swayed like mournful dancers. Peg and I walked up the hill amid the neat rows of plain white crosses interspersed with stars.

The earth was hard-packed, yellow-brown, and mounded into graves, on each of which had been laid a white lily and, here and there, other flowers. At the top of the hill a rough wooden platform had been built, and here sat chaplains and representatives of the Allies. Behind the platform, the French and British flags fluttered with the Stars and Stripes. To one side stood a mass of civilians, and on the other side nurses and officers sat in the few rows of chairs that had been set out, with a crowd of more officers and enlisted men standing behind them. In front of the platform, in formation, stood square ranks of representatives of the Allies in North Africa—American soldiers (Negro and white), American sailors, English soldiers, French soldiers, Zouaves, American Red Cross workers, a military band, and a color guard.[1]

We took our places, drawn up stiffly, trembling. There was a short and simple service, and the singing of the hymns was borne off by the wind to the tops of the cypresses. There was a silent presentation, the laying of wreaths of homage. And then from the crest of the hill rose the lonely cry of a bugle sounding taps, tremulous, like the anguished voice of the sorrowing earth itself. The sun broke through the clouds, and from the far side of the hill a second bugle echoed, lonely as the first.

Here on this hill in Africa we buried our dead. Here on the day of Resurrection. And these dead must rise again in a world of beauty, a world of peace and brotherhood.

1 "Zouave" was the title given to certain light infantry regiments in the French army, especially those serving in French North Africa between 1831 and 1962.

The sunlight lay pale and ghostly on the airport, on the great salt flats, on the hills and fields. Clouds darkened the height of Santa Cruz.

Here on this hill we buried our dead, our dead of Addis Ababa and Manchuria, of Jarama and Warsaw, of Bataan and El Alamein and Stalingrad. *O day of Resurrection,* I thought, *let the dead rise in the living and live in our zeal to banish fascism from the earth.*

We went back slowly to the car, walking among the graves. November 8. November 9. November 10. November 11. Name, organization, date of death. On some, a metal identification tag. On others, no marker at all.

There had been little resistance to the German invasion of North Africa, although the resistance had been stronger, more bitter, in Oran than in other places. Casualties had been light compared to invasions elsewhere. But for each who gave his life, they could not have been heavier.

O men who lie beneath this dry and barren earth, so pitifully strewn with wilting, fading flowers, who were you? What mothers bore you, what families nurtured you, what young girls loved you? We read the names, and my heart pounded in fear of reading a name I would know. But what matters that? There lay my brother Art, there as in every antifascist's grave.

These are our lives, I thought. *This we must do. O day of Resurrection.* Someday there must come a time of peace, not only for the dead but for the living too, for the living to live in a world without war, without fascism.

What could one do? One could do one's job the very best one could. That was all one could do. It was never enough, but that was all one could do. Somehow, somewhere, someone said, "Shoot." Or "Drive." Or cook or fly, or load or unload, or be a Red Cross girl. And that was how the war was to be won. Maybe if one had stopped to think about it, it would have been hard to see how what one was doing was going to win the war. But you didn't stop to think about it. You just kept going. You were part of it, and you felt part of it. There was nothing else but the war. There was nothing else but we and they.

You judged individuals by how well they did their jobs, how hard they worked, how much ingenuity they used to get things done, how they got along with others. You depended on each other, no matter how remote or how indirectly another's job affected you. No one could win unless everybody won. The home front was part of it too, but it was good to be overseas.

Map showing Edith Witt's American Red Cross Service in Italy and Algeria from 1943–1945. Courtesy of Ann Boykin

Edith Witt, 1914, age 3. Witt family collection

Edith, 1915, age 4. Witt family collection

Edith, 1916, age 5.
Witt family collection

Edith, with mother, Ida, father, Herman, and brother, Arthur, 1919. Witt family collection

Edith, grade 8 graduation, 1923. Witt family collection

Edith and mother, Camp Lincoln, Stormville, New York, 1928. Witt family collection

Edith and mother, Tucson, Arizona, 1942. Witt family collection

Edith in Red Cross uniform, January 1943. Witt family collection

Edith, Italy, 1944. Witt family collection

Edith, Italy, 1944. Witt family collection

Edith (far left in car), Italy, 1944. Witt family collection

LEGHORN, ITALY—Miss Edith Witt, 4511 Agnes Ave., North Hollywood, Calif., never thought too much about cooking before—not in such quantities anyway. Now in this war-blasted Italian port city she has 25 Italian cooks working under her and turns out 20,000 pastries daily for American Red Cross clubs in this area.

Edith at bakery, Leghorn, Italy, 1944. Picture from unknown newspaper, 1944

Edith, home on leave with mother, January 1945. Witt family collection

Edith (far left) on leave in New York with aunts (and their husbands) and mother (far right), January 1945. Witt family collection

It's a Woman's War

U. S. Coast Guard Photo

OUTNUMBERED, Coast Guardsman Daniel Miller retires behind gun as the girls take over. (L. to r.) Edith Witt, Red Cross, 44 E. 92d St.; Army Nurses Elizabeth T. Brooks, of Centre Moriches, L. I.; Rose M. Carluccio, Hoboken; Helen E. Selbert, Rochester; Elizabeth E. Knlock, Troy; Connie R. Tomselli, Utica; Elinore Bailey, Red Cross, Genesco; Ann Willburn, Wac, 1940 Bay Ave., Brooklyn, and Beulah Person, 60 E. 34th St.

Edith (far left, standing), *New York Post,* January 22, 1945

HEADQUARTERS

88TH INFANTRY DIVISION

APO 88, C/O POSTMASTER NEW YORK

OFFICE OF THE ASSISTANT DIVISION COMMANDER

15 November 1945

Miss Edith Witt
Area Club Office
ARC

Dear Miss Witt,

On the occasion of your departure from the Division, I should like to take this opportunity to express to you my personal appreciation for your outstanding services. You were with the 88th Division during our last campaign in Italy, and your help was a vital contribution to the morale of the men I commanded. I saw you on many occasions conscientiously performing your duties, and I know that the individual soldiers were deeply appreciative of your efforts. I wish to thank you personally and also on behalf of all members of the Division.

I realize that during redeployment your duties have been most difficult from a personal angle and have undoubtedly been very trying. Your consistently calm demeanor and conscientious efforts to improve recreational facilities has been a great contribution to the reorganization of the Division. We shall miss you in the future.

I am sure that the Division Commander will have written some similar letter in appreciation of your efforts, but I could not resist adding my own particular thanks. My sincere wishes go with you for a happy future wherever you may travel. You have earned a well deserved place in the history of this Division.

Sincerely,

J.C. Fry

J. C. FRY
Brigadier General, USA
Ass't Division Commander

Edith, letter of commendation, 1945. Witt family collection

Edith, San Francisco Human Rights Commission, 1966. Witt family collection

Edith's Greenbrae Boardwalk home. Witt family collection

Edith, San Francisco area, 1985. Witt family collection

Edith along the boardwalk, 1980s. Witt family collection

Edith blowing bubbles on Greenbrae Boardwalk, 1988. Witt family collection

Edith and brother Bert, 1991. Witt family collection

Peter Witt and wife Joyce Nies, with Edith, 1992. Witt family collection

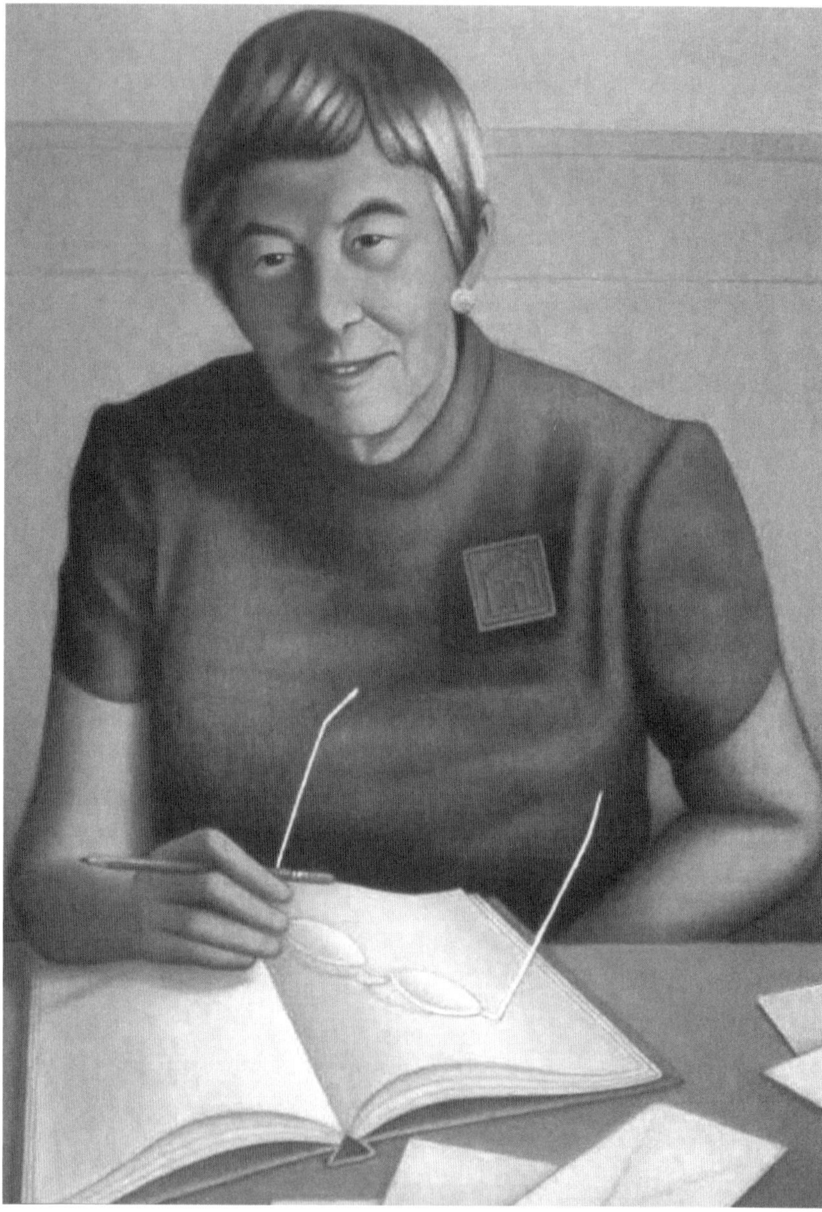

Portrait of Edith by Dana DeKalb, 2010. Courtesy of the artist

13

The End of the War in North Africa

A New Convoy Arrives

A few days later the Allies entered Tunis and Bizerte, and all day, back behind the rear, Oran was filled with rumor that the war in Africa was over.[1] A few days later the rumor were that the fighting in North Africa would be over in nine hours, but no one knew when the nine hours had begun. All of May was filled with rumors, and the one the GIs clung to longest was that President Roosevelt had made a speech in which he said that men who had received their April pay in North Africa would receive their August pay in the United States.

Day to day the air filled with rumors, and the streets filled with sailors, soldiers, merchant mariners, officers, and nurses as a new convoy unloaded and people found their way into town from their staging areas. From early morning until late at night the officers and nurses descended on the club, in dozens and in scores, even hundreds in at once, in and out, in and out, thousands in a day. They came with their fresh clean uniforms, suntans, and fresh clean faces, with their stateside smiles and energy, bursting with excitement and adventure. They were a bunch of tourists on a holiday, sightseeing and loaded down with souvenirs.

As they caught sight of people who had come over on the same ship with them, they screeched across the club and leaped into one another's arms. They couldn't get enough to drink and drank too much and made the round of all the bars and found their way back to the club to talk about it. They crowded us off the streets. They made long lines at our restaurants, PX, post office, finance office, and movie houses.

They turned the club into a madder madhouse than it had ever been, crowding us off into the corners, plucking at our sleeve, as we fought our

1 The Allies entered Tunis and Bizerte on May 7, 1943.

way through, to ask a million crazy questions, capturing the snack bar and holding it six deep, taking over the ice cream line, wanting to know where they could get a real good meal, real French cooking, and tossing aside our precious ancient magazines with the complaint that they had seen that issue way back in the States. Didn't we have any current ones? They had just come over, but they seemed to be falling to pieces. They needed everything repaired—shoes, watches, eyeglasses, fountain pens—and their laundry done and suits dry-cleaned. They got the plumbing of the club snafued, and George discovered at midnight, probably with a divining rod, that there was a water main out in the middle of the Rue de la Paix and got a barefoot crew together to dig up the street and lay a pipe between it and the club to increase our supply of water. We old ones huddled in a dim and gloomy corner and sorrowed.

"They don't even know there's a war on," we said.

"They probably haven't even been bitten by a flea yet," we said.

"You'd think they hadn't just been eating ice cream a week ago," we said. "Why didn't they bring their old magazines off the ship so we'd have something new to read?"

"You'd think they hadn't just been drinking real honest-to-goodness Scotch and bourbon a couple of weeks ago."

"They want to know where the drugstore is so they can get some aspirin." "What do they need aspirin for?" "They just came over."

"Remember the good old days when you could step up to the snack bar and get a cup of coffee and sit down at a table to drink it?"

Ah, we resented the new ones. This was the first convoy that made me feel like a veteran. I had been over less than three months, but it seemed I could not think back to a time when I had been anywhere else. We forgot. We denied that we had acted the same way when we had landed.

"Did we act that way when we came over?" we asked ourselves. "No," we answered. "We couldn't have."

But our bitterness toward these innocents was tempered by our seasoned wisdom. "Oh, let them have a little fun. They don't know what's ahead of them." "And they don't have much time before they begin finding out."

In a couple of days, as if something suddenly clicked, I was out of the swamp. The mobs were there, but I could take them. They swirled around me, but I held my footing and breathed. The crowds were part of the landscape, part of the day, part of my life. Liz said that the same thing had happened to her.

The sun came out, and it grew warm. It grew hot. It grew dusty. George battled the garbage disposal and had Ralph make him a swatter and went about the club happily killing flies and keeping score—fifty-one, fifty-two, fifty-three—as if he were carving notches in his belt.

Over the weekend we had four dances, almost one continuous dance, with the dance floor crushed into nightclub-size, the orchestras coming in shifts, but Liz and I danced with the old-timers and let the new nurses take care of the new men.

Reflecting after Long Days at the Club

After the club was closed and the hectic hordes had dissolved into the night, I walked home to the Stork Club, dull with weariness, with Dave or Carl, and we would lean against the seawall, on the other side of the monument to the dead of the last war, looking down on the hushed and dimmed activity of the docks. Night after night long lines of trucks inched up the port road, like a weekend traffic jam along the West Side Highway in New York. Sometimes they held human cargo, and sometimes they were loaded with equipment and supplies. The trucks had their headlights on, and here and there the signal beams of MP flashlights were visible, but the men in open trucks were in darkness, silhouettes of helmets and hunched shoulders and humps of gear. We watched them roll along the road below us, silent, we and they, Dave and I each thinking back to our own arrival, separate thoughts, and wondering what the men below were thinking, wanting to call down softly to them, "Hey, buddy," or lay a light, friendly hand upon their shoulder.

Directly down the seawall from the Stork Club was a broad expanse of flat sea-level land that the army had converted into a great outdoor assembly plant for jeeps and seemed to use also for unloading and other equipment operations. It was a fascinating place to watch, too far below for any details to be seen but a kaleidoscope of motion, sound, and color. We watched the moving shadows, strange and distorted under the great hooded spotlights, tiny figures of men bending, reaching, lifting, and carrying. Now and then a wide patch of darkness would come alive with the lovely blue of a welding torch. We listened to the sounds, the hum of an engine, the whine of a hoist, the terrible rending apart of a giant crate, the clang of steel on steel, the dull thud. The depot was an ant heap of purposeful activity, racing against time, as if a giant boot were poised above it, threatening it with oblivion before the last of its precious supplies were moved out and on and on up to the fighting front.[2]

Carl was a navy man, just come over with a transport jam-packed with men, casual replacements. He had light brown wavy hair and dark brown eyes, and his young face was already lined and weathered.

"Such waste," he said. "Such waste of men and lives. Such work and work and work. And all to nothing. All to be destroyed. All the things mankind might be doing, making, building, learning, creating. It's not going to be enough to win this war. A better world has got to come out of it to make it worth anything, the kind of world that will make up for all this insane destruction and death. Imagine all this same kind of energy and talent and imagination and science and knowledge and desire, mankind all over the world, working to build a decent world for everyone. Enough food, enough clothing and shelter, and then to live, to enjoy life and to live to enjoy it."

Chip took me out to the quiet of his bivouac area for supper when the long lines outside the Red Cross restaurant and the wall-deep crowds around the snack bar became impassable in the little time that we could spare in search of food. The rows of tents were neat on the bare earth where wheat had been worn off. The rough dirt road was screened off from the camp by high barbed wire fencing and pressed up close to it, on the other side, with others behind clamoring for a place, were Arab women and children, calling for soldiers or for anyone to negotiate concerning laundry and other deals and services of all kinds. But there was no one on the camp side of the wire, and I saw no one paying any attention to the calling of the women and the cavorting of the children. Chip's tent had four cots in it, each with its barracks bag and suitcase at the foot, its shoes lined up beneath, its clothes and Tommy gun slung up on nails, its mosquito bars, and canteen.

Above Chip's cot, a piece of the tent's bracing served as his personal

2 Oran was a major staging area used to supply military forces first in North Africa and then Sicily and Italy.

shelf, where he had his books, his pipe, a beaded Indian doll, and a porcelain dog with one leg missing. There were electric lights, a radio, and a phonograph. Outside the tent were a blowtorch, a rock, and half a gasoline drum for heating water for shaving.

"My bed, toy books, my good-luck charms, my pipe," said Chip. "I stand revealed."

Chow was served in mess kits—canned chicken curry, canned peas, canned string beans, fresh cabbage, bread and grape jelly, and water but no coffee to drink. There were many flies. For a few minutes we sat on the step of Chip's tent. A couple of fellows were playing catch with a baseball. Another was shaving. Here and there men called to one another, brushing off their spruced up clothes, going to town. It was good to be among the simple little things of a man's normal daily life. Chip borrowed a brush for me, and we both bent down and dusted off our shoes, and then we too went into town.

The Triumphant Return of the First Division

Then we learned that the First Division was coming back.[3] The First Division was on its way! The First Division was in Algiers! The First Division had torn up Algiers, busted it wide apart, overrun it, drunk all the wine, eaten all the food, and captured all the girls, in exuberant revelry. The combat infantry was coming to Oran! The war in Africa was over. Electric expectation filled the air. The whole town braced itself, waiting and watching in joyful, shiny-eyed anticipation, restless, as if drawn down the road by which the victorious combat men were coming.

On May 15 the army issued summer uniforms to the men stationed in the area, and the town blossomed. The next day, Sunday, Liz and George spent all morning with men on a hospital ship. They too had come back from victory. During the day advance officers of the First Division, in town to make arrangements for their men, began coming into the club. Even those who were under average height were giants.

3 The First Infantry Division, the Big Red One, was part of the II Corps of the US Army. The division landed in Oran on November 8, 1942, as part of Operation Torch and fought in North Africa until May 9, 1943. After this the First Infantry was part of the invasion of Sicily in July 1943 and part of the first wave of troops landing on Omaha Beach on D-Day. Society of the 1st Infantry Division, "History," Society of the 1st Infantry Division, https://www.1stid.org/historyindex.php.

Even those whose noses were too big, whose ears stuck out, whose chins were not squared off, were handsome, wonderful-looking guys. They were all big and strong. Their faces were tanned and lean and hardened, their eyes far-seeing and determined. They wore woolen olive drab, and the red 1 on their sleeve and the white 1 on their helmet liners was a proud insignia marking them apart from the summer-clad newcomers. They were a different breed. To think that we had been considering ourselves veterans.

I felt shy around them. They were here, but they came from another world I had no knowledge of, and that world was still with them. I looked at them from a distance and did not speak until I was spoken to, having no knowledge of their language although we used the same words. They were like men returned from the dead. I had thought that I would ask them, "What was it like?" But when I saw them I knew that one did not say those words aloud. There was so much I wanted to learn from them. But that was the first thing I learned. There is no way to tell another person what war is like. There is no way to tell another person what combat is like.

In the club, they looked for simple things. A shower first, a shoeshine with knife and brush and polish, a cigarette, a shave and haircut, a cup of coffee, music. They did not dance at first but stood and watched and listened.

Next day, all during the day, the First Division came into town. And with them came exhilaration that burst the lungs and that practically burst the air itself. Excitement raced along my nerves and hammered every pulse. The salt smack of the sea and the wafts of desert spring were fragrant with victory, and my tongue tasted victory. We were part of it: it was our victory. These were our men. The war in Africa was over. We had won. We! There was only Europe now, and we would all be home by Christmas.

The First Division men were conquerors. They were alive. They were alive on earth, and the earth was theirs. "We took this town," they said. "This town is ours. We took this building. We took this little piece I'm standing on. And now we've come back to take it over again. All these new people clogging up the streets, all dressed up in their fancy clothes, think they're something because they're overseas. They look at us out of their smug faces. Why, they don't even know there's a war on."

By evening the men had overrun the Empire Club. They took over the offices, leaned back in their chairs, stretched their feet up on the desks, smoked cigars, and answered the telephone. They took over the information desk, ate up the snack bar larder, bulged out of every room, and milled about the halls. Tex called me every little while to give me a report, her voice shrill with excitement.

The officers were more restrained. They were still intensely keyed-up, and they wanted to relax. But they had relaxed just enough so far to be completely exhausted. Outwardly they were calm and at ease, most of them, but we could sense the strain they still felt, their unreleased tension and unaddressed fatigue. They moved slowly, putting a cigarette to their lips or raising a cup of coffee, but there was an almost imperceptible tremor in their hands, and their eyes were feverishly bright.

It was a mad week. To a woman, the town seemed like a gold-rush mining town. There was no room on the sidewalks for pedestrians. There was no room on the streets for traffic. You elbowed your way wherever you went, stood in line, got pushed off the curb, and were engulfed by an overflowing tide of humanity.

More ships kept coming in. French soldiers began coming back from Tunisia with flowers on their bayonets and captured German guns. Ships poured out soldiers, merchant seamen, and sailors—the British ones in white shorts and knee-length socks, and the French with caps with red pompoms.

At the restaurant, men stood in line patiently all the way down the street and around the corner. One ate quickly to make a place for others and to get back to the club. At my right was a very young sailor who had come in on a mosquito boat during the November invasion. He was from a town in the mountains of North Carolina with a population of 380, he said. He held up a bite of the canned beef stew on his fork midway to his mouth. "I wouldn't trade a piece of North Carolina as big as this piece of meat for all of North Africa," he drawled, and then he plopped it into his mouth.

On my left was an infantryman. He had landed in Oran, flown to Bone [in northeastern Algeria], and gone on from there by train, with women all along the way coming down to the train with flowers and wine and kisses, and then gone on over the mountains by donkey. He had flown all the way back by hospital plane and had missed the flowers and wine and kisses.

Across the table from us sat a new boy. He listened to the

conversation, but he didn't seem to be hearing it, didn't ask any questions. Every so often he would say something, and it was always the same thing.

"I can't see why we're here," he would say. "I don't know what we're doing here." We would look at him each time in amazement.

Then one of us would say, "You'll find out, boy, you'll find out."

At the club the snack bar ran out of meat, ran out of cheese, ran out of bread, and then ran out of coffee. People ate handfuls of raisins and drank cocoa or powdered lemonade. Then we ran out of water. As soon as the army's water truck came around, a line would spring up in front of the Lister bag and out the door, and in half an hour the water would be gone for the rest of the morning or afternoon.

Another large contingent of Red Cross people arrived in one of the convoys, and the Stork Club was overrun. Extra cots were put into all the rooms, and they became a tangle of bedrolls, barracks bags, footlockers, suitcases, musette bags, and drying underwear. Old Red Cross people were coming into town on their way to new assignments or on supply missions or on leave, and each of us never could be sure we would not come home to find someone sleeping in our bed. We had to get home early. The broad, curving stairway to the second floor became a sitting room. Occasionally one would stumble around the sleeping figure of a soldier on the floor, one who had not quite made it back to camp.

The Refuge of the Seawall

For many of us the seawall became our refuge, where the dusk could wall us off from other seawall refugees and where the noises of the port below became a pleasant muffled roaring like the sea itself. There we might lean against the wall with chin on folded arms, with one another in close if fragmentary companionship, and look out to the sea, with the rose sky fading to dusk blue and the sea aglow and lavender. Or we might swing up on the wall itself, legs dangling down the cliff, watching the changing lights and the silhouettes and furrows of the hills toward Mers el Kebir, the lights on ships gently swaying and reflected in the water, the ant parade of vehicles up from the port, and the shadowy clumps of prisoners on the open flat ground in their barbed wire compound.

Or we might lounge on a bench along the path, back slumped and feet far out, head facing up to the sky, admiring the deepening and then dimming colors and noticing the first faint stars and an occasional signal flare of white or red from hill or sea, letting the day drain out of us. With sunset and twilight came soothing and peace.

Parked in front of the club was a First Division jeep called From Hell to Victory.[4]

Then, when there seemed there was not another inch of spare space, the Ninth Infantry Division began returning to Oran.[5] And somehow they found room and took their places in the crowd, with their scalloped red, white, and blue shoulder patches, and, like the First, their tanned, lean faces, wonderfully handsome and intent eyes, satisfied set of shoulders, and sure stride. There were differences too between the First and Ninth. For the first time we realized that there was something a man carried with him of his division—an aura, an attitude, a way of acting and thinking in the same way that men acquired different characteristics from the branch of service they were in. We likewise began to sense certain national characteristics and even regional characteristics that were not, of course, inborn, but became part of individuals in the same group. The First and the Ninth were both seasoned warriors, exalted with victory. The First had a bursting wildness in them and swaggered. But the Ninth was quieter, more contained. The Ninth's self-confidence was held deep within. We loved them both dearly, and each man we met or talked with or danced with or drank with was different from any other man and was all himself.

It was growing warmer and lovelier all the time. The evenings were balmy and caressing, and it was not yet dark at nine o'clock. In the beginning of the month there was a thin sliver of new moon, like

4 "The Long Motto Call" of the First Division: "From hell to victory / (Response) We are the fighting first! / No mission too difficult / (Response) No sacrifice too great! / Duty First / (Response) Victory!" *The Victory Standard: The BRO and Fort Riley Standards Book* (Fort Riley, Kansas, 2016), http://www.riley.army.mil/Portals/0/Docs/Units/1ID/TheVictoryStandard_2016.pdf.

5 The Ninth Infantry Division was among the first US combat units involved in ground operations during World War II. It landed in Algiers as part of Operation Torch in November 1942 and was involved in Tunisia beginning in February 1943. After the Allied victory in May 1943, the division landed in Palermo, Sicily in August 1943, and it landed on Utah Beach in France four days after the initial D-Day invasion of Europe. "Battle History," www.9thdivision.net, http://9thinfantrydivision.net/battle-history.

the curve of a barrage balloon catching the light, and all month we watched it grow, thinking that by the time the moon was full it should be warm enough to go swimming.[6]

Under Attack?

One of those evenings Dave walked me home from the club. As we went out the door into the softness and quiet of the air, there seemed something different about the night, and as we went slowly along the street a vague and almost unnoticed uneasiness edged along my nerves. About half a block down, Dave said, "Did you notice? Lights are out."

I hadn't noticed, but that was what was strange. Even the feeble dim-out lights along the street that usually stayed on till midnight were off that night, and the streets were uncommonly dark. We wondered about this but then walked on, without thinking about it anymore. In front of the Empire Club last groups of soldiers were climbing into their trucks with muttered oaths as they banged a shin or smashed a finger. Otherwise the streets were deserted, and the only sound after the grinding of the trucks, was that of our slow footfalls.

Suddenly the hoarse wail of a siren filled the night. We stopped. We looked around. The shattering sound was everywhere. It was the first siren I had heard overseas, and it sounded too real for it to occur to me that it might be a practice drill. Besides, as the harbor had filled up with ships, with material and men, we had talked about the Germans sending planes over and wondered why they hadn't up to then, until the idea of a raid was accepted as almost inevitable.

We walked on, and the siren died with a rattling sigh. Nothing happened.

"I guess that's why the lights are out," I said. I felt reassured to know why the lights were out.

"I don't think we're supposed to be on the streets," said Dave.

"Nothing's happening."

"I don't think they want us on the streets, though."

6 A barrage balloon, sometimes called a blimp, is a large balloon tethered with metal cables, used to defend against aircraft attack by damaging aircraft on collision with the cables or at least making the attacker's approach more difficult. David Wragg, *Historical Dictionary of Aviation* (London, England: Sutton Publishing, 2009).

"We'll be at the Stork Club pretty soon."

"How about going into the naval dispensary?"

"Okay."

I didn't feel it was necessary, but there was no one else outdoors and not even any vehicles. I didn't feel any alarm. I was sure that our anti-aircraft defenses would not let any planes through. It was only a matter of waiting for the all-clear to sound, and it was a good chance to see the inside of the naval hospital, an attractive three-story gray stone building that I passed every day on the way to work. Dave pulled open the screen door, and we went into a small lobby at the foot of stairs. All the lights were out, and dim figures, some with shaded flashlights, were moving about, up and down the steps and through the door off to the right. Dave asked if it was all right for us to stay until the all-clear. A tall shadow came forward, one of the doctors whom Dave knew, and clapped Dave's shoulder. "Let's go up on the roof," he said. He seemed quite excited. We'll have a swell view up there of the show if anything happens. With navy decorum, Dave presented him to me.

"Do you want to go up on the roof?" Dave asked me.

"Okay." I didn't like the doctor's using the word 'show,' but I would just as soon wait up on the roof as in the dark indoors.

"Come on," said the doctor, already a little out of breath. A couple of the other officers went up with us.

It was beautiful on the roof: a full moon, a soft haze across the sky, a few pale stars, a calm sea, and the dark, silent shapes of ships and docks. Perfect weather for them, someone said. Full moon and mist.

But I didn't believe it any more. It was such a beautiful night. The air was so soft, and the sky and the sea so lovely and peaceful. Then I heard the sound of a plane.

"Hear it?" someone said.

"Pretty close."

"Just one."

"Can't see it."

"No, can't see it."

There was no thought in my mind that it was not our plane. I had been told that you could recognize a German plane by its intermittent drone, but this was just a small steady hum making its way far up across the sky. Then the sound was directly overhead, but still no plane was visible.

Suddenly there was a tremendous burst of flame down at the docks. A jagged wall of fire with fantastic towers leaping in the dark to the sky. The whole world exploded into frenzied attack. Tracer bullets streamed in red and yellow intersecting arcs across the sky. Sky and sea and air and earth were noise, as if the planet had cut loose from its moorings and was banging away at all the other stars and planets.

I stood petrified. *It can't be. It isn't real. Human beings can't do this to one another.* Tremendous anger brought me back to life, anger swelling up. This is really it. *This is what I have read about it. This is what I have seen in pictures. This is really happening.* But I stood there, torn and battered by the noise, staring at the fire, at the docks and the lethal sky.

And then fear came. *I am not afraid,* I thought, *because there is no sense being afraid.* But my legs were limp and trembling, my heart pounded, my throat was tight, and my hands were wet with sweat. I stooped, half-crouching, not yet able to move. A few feet from me I saw Dave half-bending too. It was a comforting thing to do, as if it made one less conspicuous then standing erect on the top of a tall roof.

A strained voice said, "Guess we better go inside." The voice released us from immobility. I saw two figures hurtle headfirst through the door and then another, upright, moving slowly.

"Come on," said Dave.

It was terribly dark inside by contrast, and we groped our way down one flight of steps and stood, backs pressed against the landing wall, weak and quivering, panting. I found Dave's hand, hung limply from his arm, like mine, and took it, moist palm to quivering palm, without the strength to clasp it tightly. A million guns were shooting off inside of me, their noise beating me to pulp. The desire to rush outside again was almost overpowering: to see, to find out, to know what was going on.

If we moved over away from the wall we could see a piece of sky outside the stairwell window, an unreal world of tracer bullets. When our breathing had calmed somewhat we decided to go down to join the others. Dave put his hand up to his head. "My hat," he exclaimed. "It's on the roof."

"Oh, well," I said.

"I better get it."

"You don't want to get it," I said.

"Yes," he said. "Wait here. Be right down."

In a few moments I heard him coming back.

"Find it?"

"Yes."

He was quite pleased.

14
Visiting Mr. Reeves

Mr. Reeves, the engineer on one of the Liberty transports still in dock, invited me to his ship for lunch.[1] We walked down the port road, down the long wooden flight of steps to water level, across the railroad tracks, and out along the pier. Mr. Reeves was a tall, middle-aged gentleman, of medium build, stiff with humorless formality, and it was hard for me to temper the wild excitement mounting in me as we approached the ship. As I felt the gangplank quiver beneath my foot it seemed a bridge that would lead me to the United States, and as I set foot on the deck itself, it was as if I had come home for the holidays. American ship, American crew, American voices, American steel, American paint. The ship had recently touched the United States and would soon, with luck, touch its shores again. There was the fragrance of America about her, in the smell of her steel and her paint, her tar and her grease. I breathed in deeply, breathed in the crisp, coppery, raw, wet, salty, piney, lilac, honeysuckle, rain-rich air that I remembered.

Mr. Reeves led me down into the depths of the ship, and we climbed up and down ladders and along catwalks as he tried to make me understand the workings of the turbines, boilers, shafts, motors, valves, and gauges that I wished I knew something about. How wonderful, I thought, to be the master of such power, to learn and understand and control it and bring a ship across the ocean—instead of playing Ping-Pong. It seemed more wonderful that Mr. Reeves could do this and yet not be a giant of a man but just a man, of no greater genius than other

1 During World War II, 2,711 Liberty ships were built, with the first one, the SS *Patrick Henry*, launched on September 27, 1941. The ship was 441 feet long and 56 feet wide and powered by a steam engine. Later in the war, a new class of faster Victory ships was built. "Liberty Ships Built by the United States Maritime Commission in World War II," *American Merchant Marine at War*, http://www.usmm.org/libertyships.html.

men. But why not women, then? Why should such knowledge and such work be kept from women?

"An awful lot of stuff," I said, shaking my head in rebellious ignorance.

"It is—an awful lot of stuff," said Mr. Reeves. "I got twenty hours of sleep in the fifteen days coming over."

Mr. Reeves ordered lunch brought into his quarters. The steward set the table—white tablecloth, silver creamer, silver sugar bowl. It was a tiny cabin, trim and tidy, with everything in its place: bunk, shelves, locker, table, and two chairs.

In the wall to the left of the table was a half-open doorway through which I caught a glimpse of what looked like a shower curtain. I found myself losing track of the conversation, my attention shifting more and more to what might be a shower curtain, until I was staring at it in silent concentration. If it was in truth a shower curtain there might be in truth a shower behind it. Mr. Reeves noticed my increasingly restless inattention, and he broke off in the middle of some polite conversational phrase, nonplussed.

"Is that a shower?" I blurted.

Mr. Reeves's kindly face remained puzzled. "Why, yes," he said.

"Could I use it?"

The moment the words were out I realized how startling this simple request appeared to Mr. Reeves. The expression on his face even made me feel uncomfortable for a moment, remembering how it would be back home if I were having dinner in the apartment of a man I hardly knew and asked to take a shower. But I could not give up the thought of such a luxurious delight so close within my grasp. I plunged on.

"I could take one before the food comes," I said, getting up and edging my way around the table. "I bet there's hot water too," I said, getting out of my shoes and jacket.

"Here's a towel," gulped Mr. Reeves.

I closed the bathroom door as if it were the gateway to a promised land—with me inside. Ah, wondrous warmth of water, making skin come alive, relaxed, and warming through and through to my marrow. And the warm mist, like breath, and muscles eased, and the splash and splatter that sets the throat to singing, and the little pool collecting for the feet to wallow in, turning them from numbness into flesh again.

It was only when I emerged, beaming with the great adventure, that I could take time to explain to Mr. Reeves. The food had been brought, but the white tablecloth, silver creamer, sugar bowl, and even the real butter and bowl of salad could not compete with the shower for excitement.

"You see," I said, "I haven't had a bath or shower since we landed—more than a month now. A couple of the girls have met men in town with bathtubs, but I haven't come across one yet. And even when they have a tub in their apartment, hot water's rationed, so they only have it maybe two hours every week, and then there's four or five of them to use it and all their friends. I had a chance once to go along with some of the other girls, but I couldn't get away from the club just then."

"Of course we wash," I hastened to say. "We even get a helmet of hot water now and then when there's time while the gas is on—but you can only get one foot into a helmet at a time."

Mr. Reeves was amazed.

And then there were apples for dessert. I couldn't remember back to when I'd had an apple last. I held one in my hand, cool and firm against the warmth of my skin from showering, letting the fragrance rise into the air I breathed, remembering rough, gnarled trees and the feel of bark, pulling oneself up, and the uneven grassy earth beneath them. The rich tang and the feel of a ripe apple kicked in.

"Aren't you going to eat it?"

"I think I'll save it, if I may, take it with me."

"We can get some more for you to take."

"No, I couldn't do that—they're for the ship."

"But we have bushels of them."

I left the ship with my pockets full and all the space between my shirt and sweater bulging with apples. I never knew how heavy apples were until I dragged myself across the railroad tracks and climbed the long, long stairway from the port.

15

The Hospital Train

The sun had come out, and I got back to the club hot and tired.

"Do you want to go down to meet a hospital train?" George asked.

"Sure."

"About half an hour. Go over to the Empire Club to meet the other girls."

I finished taking the apples out of my clothing as if they were stones or crumpled balls of paper, and I made conversation with Liz—telling her that I'd had a shower—as she went out to grab a bite of lunch before I had to leave. But I was thinking one thing: *hospital train*. I walked about the club, looking silently at the men, trying not to be drawn into conversation, emptying ashtrays, straightening magazines, tidying books and games, and grew more and more uneasy as the half hour went by. What was it like on a hospital train? What did one say to a face on a litter? How did one smile to a man who had lost a leg? I ridiculed myself, remembering how I had thought six hundred miles was close to war. What did I know of war?

There were six of us—Bunny and Tex from the Empire Club, Peg from the Allied Club, two of the new girls awaiting assignment, and I. Joe, the program director of the Empire Club, had driven us down in a weapons carrier with cartons of stuff we would distribute. We stood in front of the little old redbrick railroad station, making motions at helping Joe get things ready. The train stood before us on the track, about seven cars long, weather-beaten wood with faded red crosses on its sides and roof. The train was quiet, and the long row of dull windows stared vacantly back at us.

We turned our backs and bent over our supplies, sorting stationery, pencils, washcloths, decks of cards, books of matches, old magazines, handkerchiefs, cigarettes, combs, comic books, and razor blades onto the wooden cookie trays we would use to take them on the train. We felt the train behind us, a pull on our backs, and we moved slowly, dreading the moment we should be ready, fumbling, impatient, with tension tightening and twisting within us.

The pavement had not been swept, and little gusts of wind raised the grit and cinders and scraps of paper there, swirled them in the air, and laid them down to rest again. We whispered to one another nervously: "What do you say?" "What do you do?" "How can you offer them washcloths?" "It isn't the stuff that counts," we whispered. "It's just coming down, just being with them for a couple of minutes, just talking." "But what do you talk about?" "It'll be all right once we get on the train. They're fellows just like any others." "Just act natural," we told each other, with our hearts beating in our throats and our lips dry. For how can one act naturally with men in war? How can one accept as natural the tearing, maiming, bleeding, shredding, mangling, crushing of the beautiful, young, strong human body with a life of work and love before it? How can one accept that one is whole but a soldier disabled in the fight, a fight as much for me as for him. Ah, you have lost a leg, my lad, but it is little to lose for what will be gained, the safety of your family, the safety of your country, human dignity, the defeat of slavery and horror—but it is your leg and not mine that has been lost.

"Just be cheerful," we whispered to one another, "be normally cheerful." "Why are we whispering?"

Our trays were ready, but we continued to delay. Someone found she had too many of something, another found she had to rearrange her things, another wanted more of something, and someone else wanted a better assortment of colors of something.

Joe understood what was going on.

"Why don't you go in pairs?" he said. "And each one take a couple of cars. They'll be glad to see you," he added firmly.

"Okay," we said. We grouped ourselves in twos. I was with Peg, and we turned and faced the train and took a few steps forward, slowly, raising our shoulders and filling our lungs. The girls in front stopped. We conferred. We turned back to Joe.

"Don't you think we ought to check with someone before we go on?" we said. "An officer or someone? Maybe they don't want us yet."

Joe shrugged, looking up and down the platform. "Doesn't seem anyone is around in authority," he said.

But by this time we had been sighted from the train, and here and there a curious head was trying to figure out who we were besides being women.

"Go on," grinned Joe. "They're waiting for you."

We walked along the platform, still hesitant, the war beside us on the track, deciding which car each pair of us would enter. On one of the car vestibules a tall blond fellow on crutches stood with a short dark boy who had his arm in a sling.

"Say," the tall boy said as we went by, "you know when they're bringing up the chow?"

Peg looked up and down the deserted station. "There's no one around," she said. "Maybe that's where they are. I guess maybe they've gone to get the chow."

A fellow came rushing up the platform from the front of the train. His long, ungainly overcoat was flapping and he was grinning broadly, waving his hand in a high arc, exuberant. "Hi!" he shouted, clasping my free left hand in both of his and pumping my arm up and down despite the tray in my right. "Remember the *Flossie?*" he boomed. I *did* remember him from the *Flossie*. "They say I'm loco," he laughed. "They're sending me home. I don't want to go home yet. Hell, I only been over a few months. If only I'd kept my mouth shut," he laughed. "They're sending me home because I'm nuts. All because I kept spouting my big mouth off. Hell, I don't want to go. Oh, excuse me. I mean, heck, I don't want to go home yet. I just got here. Well, good luck," he said and raced on down along the train.

Peg and I walked on down another car. There was no one here in the vestibule and no one looking out the windows. We looked at one another with little spirit-boosting smiles and climbed aboard. The car was like many old coaches, with two rows of double redwood seats. The passengers on this car, however, were all males, and all were dressed in olive drab. As we came in the car was quiet. The men, some of them half dozing, some holding a magazine or comic book in their lap or glancing at it, were silent, in a sort of relaxed numbness, with masks of waiting and resignation. As if a sudden wind had stirred a field of drowsy grass, the car came rippling to life with fellows straightening up, smiling, drawing their legs in from the aisle, smoothing their clothing, brushing back their hair.

And then the questions came: What were our names? Where we were from? How long had we been over? What was the name of this town? What did we have on those trays? Where was the chow? When was the train going to start again? Where was it going? Did we think they were being sent home to the States? If you got to the States did they put you in a hospital near your home? How were we doing at the front?

Most of these questions we could not answer, but the conversation did not lag. We moved slowly up the aisle, stopping every couple of seats, slow on our feet but quick with a comeback and a smile, our dread, fears, and fumbling gone, naturally. What guys! What wonderful guys! To put us at ease like that. So tough and sweet. The warm understanding and sympathy of human beings for one another, reaching out, hand to hand. The touching, the mingling of emotions.

They wanted anything we had. That washcloth? It was just what they had been dreaming of. The handkerchief? "I imagined that handkerchief!" And: "Look-a here, Joe, cigarettes, and you won't be having to get yourself all those germs—no more smoking every other puff of mine. And matches too. Now don't they just think of everything!" "Look at these cards, Slim. Bet there's fifty-two in every pack and all the same design on the back of every one. And a comb! Just watch this. You think I forgot how to comb my hair just because I got a busted arm. You got a mirror in your powder case? Just let me see that mirror—say, it ain't even turned gray yet, and me an old man."

Of the walking wounded, some had visible bandages and some had casts and braces, but some had no signs of injury that could be seen. One boy, I had noticed, had not joined in any of the bantering and had not asked for any of our supplies. He sat alone on a double seat, looking down at his hands. I leaned close to him.

"Hello," I said.

"Hello," he said, not looking up.

"Would you like something to read?" He shook his head.

"How about a pack of cigarettes—or matches?" He shook his head.

"Do you need a comb or a handkerchief or washcloth? Do you chew gum?"

I tried a different tack. "I'm from New York," I said. "Where are you from?" He shrank back in his seat and turned his head to the window.

I rejoined Peg. "What! Nobody from Texas?" a man called out.

"Sure," we told him. "There's always someone from Texas. She's behind us, she'll be coming through."

We went on to the next car. "Thanks!" they called after us. "Come back again!" "Stay on the train with us till Casa [Casablanca]!"

Ann and I stopped short. The next one was a litter car, with double tiers of litters on either side. But heads were raised, bodies shifted, necks craned, and the car burst into incredulous delight at our appearance. We spent more time in here, talking with each man, quietly, beneath the boisterous crisscross of brave laughter and raillery.

"Look at Mac there. He's so full of lead, they're going to put him in the scrap drive when we get home."

Quentin's arm was partially paralyzed. "We got a farm in Pennsylvania. Strawberries mostly, and some cows. Yeah, strawberries are nice," he smiled, "the smell of them when you're picking. But I don't know," he said, "there's just Mom and Dad and me, and I don't know about this arm, I don't know if I'm going to be able to work the farm, and Dad's getting older all the time, and I don't know about this arm. They say it's only partly paralyzed, but I don't know what that means. I don't know if I'll be able to work the farm. I wish I knew. Say, isn't this Oran? We took this town. But you can have it. And when you're through with it, give it back to the Ay-rabs—with our love."

Tony cried, "You got a pen? I want your autograph!" And he threw the blanket back so we could add our names to all the scrawls and flourishes already on the two casts on his stumps where his legs had been taken off. Tony said, "I didn't write my mother or my girl about my legs. I think I ought to write them so they'd sort of be prepared when I get home. Don't you think so? Yeah, I think I ought to write them but I'm not so good at writing. I just hate to write letters. If I give you their names and addresses, would you write them for me? Just tell them—You want to see their pictures? My mother. And my girl."

And Bob said: "There were times we prayed for help to come. Just two divisions fighting this war. Some of those prisoners are just like us, just like American boys, especially the Italians, but even some of the Germans, fellows just like us. But the Germans are sure cocky. They thought they were something. They still had creases in their pants. I used to think they'd never get me, not me. My buddy said 'Watch out!' and I never knew what hit me. I want to show you something—my daughter. Pretty cute, huh? She was six weeks old when that picture was taken, but she's a year old now. Nancy." He chuckled to himself.

"So where's the chow? We haven't eaten since six o'clock this morning. Say, why don't you girls scoot back to town and get us a couple of bottles of vino, huh? That's real nourishing stuff. Full of vitamins."

Carl lay flat on his top bunk, not moving. "I never thought I'd go home like this," he said. If I could only just walk off the boat. I never knew what hit me. I never knew—"

We stayed so long that Tex and Bonnie came in from the cars behind, and the joshing and joking started all over again. Then Betty and Pat came in from the cars ahead. Their eyes were wide with shock.

"Have you been in the car ahead?" they whispered.

"We're just going now," I beamed.

"It's," said Pat, and she turned away.

There was no stirring when we went into the next car. It was another litter car, but here there were no faces turned, no calling out, and no grins or wisecracks.

From the windows of the car we saw groups of GIs bringing big containers of food. We walked softly down the aisle and stopped beside each bed and spoke softly, saying hello and noting that chow was coming, and here and there a blood-drained face would try a feeble smile or murmur "Hi."

Toward the front end of the car there was a lower litter on which lay war itself. It was a nonhuman thing one knew had been a man not long before, a youth of clear, fresh skin that had delighted in the feel of sun and wind and rain. A growing young man, proud, eager, with expanding chest, knotting biceps, running, jumping, swaggering, dancing, trying a man's work. A clean-cut young man, whose eyes now—whose mouth—whose lips—bore no relation to anything human. Circumstances forced us to recognize that this charred crust of thing was a living human soldier. Where the ears had been were two jagged holes in the crust. Where the eyes had been, two sockets. Where there had been a nose, two slits. Where the mouth had been there was a gape with no lips. And there was another body like this on the adjacent bunk.

The food was frankfurters and sauerkraut and tea, as unappetizing a menu as I could imagine. There was soup in two canteens for the two burned boys, and Ann and Bonnie volunteered to feed them.

There was a great mix-up about forks and spoons, tin plates, mess kits, and canteen cups, for few of the fellows on the train had any, and the cooks had hardly brought enough or had enough to bring. So the rest of us raced up and down, between the cooks and passengers and up and down the cars, trying to pair up a container and utensil, serving food, washing ones that had already been used, helping fellows who had difficulty, and racing back for seconds. The men ate the food as efficiently as possible and made no complaints.

We stood on the platform to see them off. Another train had come in on the second track. It was longer than the hospital train, and men swarmed about it, youngsters, tanned and lusty, swearing, shouting, laughing, loading on their gear, and climbing on after it. They did not pay any attention to the hospital train or to us. They were replacements, moving up to the front.

16

Ministering to the Troops

A Guest for Dinner

That evening I got out of the club late for supper and wondered if I would still be able to get anything to eat at the Quantin. As I turned the corner, the figure of a youth emerged in the dim light. He was dressed in civilian clothes, pants and work jacket.

"Red Cross," he said. "Can you tell me where I can get something to eat?"

I hesitated. I didn't like to take a chance on taking him along to the Quantin and then finding it closed or out of food. Since civilian restaurants were off limits to us, I didn't know of any, and there were no other authorized places to eat in town besides the Quantin. I told him this.

"Would you have dinner with me?" he said. "I know a place where we can eat."

His face was luminous in the dimness and very young, and his voice was young and earnest in the flat, clipped accents of Boston. We turned and walked in the direction he had been going when we met, and I realized that he, as happened often, had stopped me for information that he didn't need as an excuse to talk to an American girl. The restaurant was a small basement room down a flight of flagstone steps, with marble-topped round tables, noisy with wine-gay American soldiers, calling and visiting from one table to another in carefree fellowship. There were omelets and lentils to eat, served with an easy clatter, and a giraffe-necked bottle of cool red wine. Dennis had rich black hair, wavy, and bright blue eyes the color of the sea with the sun full on it. The line of his jaw from ear to chin was strong, and he was not yet eighteen.

"Two years," he said, "I spent hanging on street corners, not doing anything, not being part of anything. I saw an ad to join the merchant marine, and I had to get my mother's consent. We went to a notary public, and he said it was the best thing in the world for me, and my mother signed. And he was right. I've been all over and done all kinds of things. It's like I got into the world. I didn't want to stand on a corner all my life watching the cars go by."

Dennis had found his place in the world and was a man. What his world had offered him was a youth of depression and a manhood of war. This was his first job, war.

"I like to hear you speak," I said. "I like the way people from Boston talk."

"Why?" said Dennis. "Do they talk any different from anyone else?"

Some of his buddies from the ship came in as we were finishing our meal and ready to leave. They had an empty wine bottle and were making the rounds trying to buy a refill. They kept arguing good-naturedly with the proprietor.

"I cannot, I cannot," he kept telling them in English. "No, no, no. It is you who make the regulations, and it is you who want me to break them."

Suddenly one of the group ended the argument. "Okay, Mac," he said. "It's okay. Take it easy. Forget it. Never mind." The proprietor shrugged and stamped off.

"Say, Boston," the seaman said to Dennis. "Are you sure you're through with that wine there? The bottle was more than half full, and we were leaving." "Okay," the seaman said. "We'll just make a slight exchange." One fellow slipped their empty bottle onto our table, and another slipped our half-full one into his jacket. They clapped one another on the shoulder in congratulation, laughing and chuckling. "We've been doing that all evening," they laughed, and then they waved good-bye.

Dance Interactions

The dance that night was mad and drunken. A member of the band we had arranged for had called that morning to say that it couldn't come, after which we made a long string of calls before finally engaging a French civilian band. But the first-invited band came after all, so there were two bands, one at each end of the room, crowding the dancers and whipping one another up to frenzied rhythms, and the club packed with all those from the last convoy who by now had learned one way or another how to get into town. A large contingent of these included nurses who had been deposited on a barren, tent-less dust heap that they called Goat Hill. The music shut out the sounds of bombs and shells and tanks. It shut out the sound of train wheels and the sound of men and women and children crying out. It shut out thought itself.

The room grew hot and thick with smoke. The walls and ceiling seemed to press in on the crowd as cymbals crashed and drumbeats jolted our hearts and the bray of trombones, saxophones, clarinets pierced our flesh.

I danced with Dick, and Dick said, "Ah, how do you beat off all these wolves?" And I said, "They're nice, Dick. People are nice. There's nothing nicer than people. They're not wolves. There's such good in people, Dick. They're such wonderful people, decent."

I danced with Cotton, and he waved a folded *Stars and Stripes* high above his head. "I have a daughter. It says so in *Stars and Stripes*. Her name is Margaret. I have a daughter. It says so right here."

I danced with Hardy, somewhat the worse and somewhat the better for a bottle of Scotch he had bought from a British sailor, handsome in his freshly pressed pinks and garrison jacket bedecked with ribbons. And Hardy said, "I want to get to the front. I want to get this damn war over with. What good am I doing here? Sitting in an office—is that the way to fight a war? I'm going to ask 'em—send me up to the front. You don't believe me. You think I'm drunk. You think I don't know what I'm saying. I know what I'm saying. You think I don't mean it. I won't be here long."

I danced with Lee, dark eyes large and burning in his twitching face, uniform hanging like loose flesh on skinny bones. "They're going to send me home," said Lee. "I'm all washed up. Sniper got me. Bullet through my chest. I had to hide out in a shell-hole full of water. Got pneumonia. Bullet wouldn't have been so bad if I hadn't got pneumonia. I'd like to go back up. I've got a brother over here. I found out he's been wounded too, but I can't find out where he is. No, no, that's all right. I'll find out. I think I've got a way to find out. No, I don't want you to try."

I danced with Winslow, six foot four and a giant-shouldered surgeon, who danced with gracious calm, who moved serenely and gracefully through the turbulence, his arms around me lightly, delicately, a protecting circle of calm, dancing as if the floor were smooth, the music soft, the lights low, unhurried, unruffled, making polite conversation as if he were at a tea. "Have you ever contemplated the beautiful sound of a flush toilet?" said Winslow. "The glorious magic of the sound?" "After you have been out on Goat Hill a while," Winslow started, and then he trailed off. "Boone and I were downstairs before. We were utterly fascinated. We pressed the little lever again and again—the wonderful sound of civilization!"

I danced with Jory, who could buy me a fountain pen on his ship for the boy who had asked Tex to find him one. "I have a ranch near Spokane, Washington," Jory said. "Wheat and cattle. My father's running it till I get back. The tractors down at the port keep reminding me of home. I came in at Casablanca with the amphibian troops. Gee, I was scared. Three days back and forth, and at night the search lights right on us. Our boats on the rocks, and up to our chins in water, and the fellows getting it right and left. What a mess. All I want is to get on a horse again, a horse going up into the mountains. I want to raise wheat, that's what I'm for. That's what the Earth's for. I see these Arabs down at the docks, not even half alive, and I think of the wheat I could raise. My wife's a city girl, and she's back home on the ranch with my mother. I don't know how long she's going to be able to hold out away from the city. I can understand."

Jory reached into his pocket for his wallet, and drew it out among the arms and elbows in the way. We stood for a moment, with the bodies bouncing off of us, while I looked at the picture from the wallet. "I'd fight fifteen wars for that," said Jory. It was a snapshot of a little girl with a small red wagon. Jory flipped the wallet shut and poked it back into his pocket. We danced again. The French orchestra was playing "Stardust." "All I want," said Jory, "is to get back into overalls."

In a brief moment between one band and another, Bob edged his way through the dance floor mass. "There's someone in the office to see you," he said.

It was Spike, in leather jacket and dusty, stained pants, and worn boots. He was tanned and happy. "My nose has peeled seventeen times," he said.

"Come and dance." I said.

But he shied back. "Oh, no, I'm not dressed. I can't dance in these boots. I'm not dressed properly. I can't go in there." But finally he came, and we danced at the edge of the floor in deep-dipping, fancy maneuvers from Brooklyn. But he was still ill at ease in his work clothes. "I want to write some letters," he said, and for the rest of the dance he sat on the sidelines, his GI boots stepped on and stumbled over, and wrote on his lap, pages and pages and pages of letters.

When the dance was over, the last lingering chess players had gone, and the club was locked, with its phantom creaking and sighing, Spike drove me out to his bivouac area. The jeep bumped softly on the dirt road and came to a stop beneath bright and far-flung stars. Quiet and dark and peaceful. The fresh, green smell of grass. To our right were the proud spires of tents thrust to the sky, and from them came the sounds of dogs barking and howling and the voices of men talking, shouting, and laughing. We inhaled deeply the sanity of sky and grass and peace and the joy at being alive.

"Pinch me," said Spike. "I'm supposed to be dead. All the way back we kept hearing the story of how our outfit was wiped out."

He reached down out of the jeep, pulled a blade of grass, put it in his mouth, and chewed.

"Want one?" he said.

"Please."

He reached down again and got me one.

PART THREE

Reflections

17
Time to Go Home

In January 1944, Edith was transferred from Oran to Italy, via Sicily. She would remain in Italy until she eventually went home in December 1945. Edith did not write many accounts of the time she spent in Italy, like she had done for the early months she spent in Oran. However, we do know from letters she wrote home while in Italy she helped open a club in an empty art gallery in Naples, worked at a villa on the sea at Agropoli that the Red Cross used to host soldiers on R&R (rest and recovery), and worked at a club at the railroad station in Florence. She also worked at tent camps north of Florence and ran cookie bakeries in Livorno and Bologna.

The final surrender of Axis troops in Europe took place on May 8, 1945, which became known as VE (Victory in Europe) Day. Japan surrendered on September 2. Of course, the job for the Allied troops was not complete. They continued to serve in Italy and throughout Europe and the Pacific for a number of months (in some cases years). Thus, even after VE Day, Edith continued her assignment in Italy. Edith had now been overseas for almost two and a half years, and her thoughts increasingly turned toward returning home. In her first letter home to her mother after VE Day, dated May 12, she discussed her excitement about being able to relate her location and other information that had previously been deleted for security reasons by censors. She wrote home again after that date, but it was not until August 19 that she fully started expressing her feelings about being ready to come home. She would not arrive home until December 1945.

12 May 1945[1]
Dear Mother:
I don't know how I'm going to be able to manage to write an uncensored letter. Even the idea of it feels awfully strange. It

1 In Edith's collection of World War II materials were several V-mail letters, with the full salutation and signature. The ones from 1945 are included in their entirety in this chapter.

would be so much easier to say I am now where I came to from the place I was in last, but instead, I can just go ahead and plain say, I am in Bolzano. It certainly is an incentive for writing—I feel just like writing to just everyone I know just to be able to write, I am in Bolzano. You can imagine the novelty of it, after more than two years, and the strain it is to get over the inhibition of not saying it, and the kick it is to say it—I am in a town called Bolzano. Bozen, in German. It's about 40 miles south of the Brenner Pass, up from Verona, the town where Juliet stood on the balcony [in Shakespeare's Romeo and Juliet]. Bolzano was Austrian until after the last war and most of the signs around town are in German, first from civilian days, and then from the German Army. So just at the point where I'm able to say a couple things in Italian, bingo, it gets to be German and where am I? You go into a store here and you don't know whether the people are going to speak Italian or German or you say Buongiorno [good morning], they say Bruess or whatever it is.

So my birthday [May 11] turned out to be the finest day it could be—the war in Europe was over and I rejoined my outfit. I'm sure you must have read about my outfit—the 88th Infantry Division, the Blue Devils, they who crossed the Po and went right on up.[2] As they say, every time you see the word "spearhead" in the papers, that was the 88th. Now they've got the job of rounding up all the German soldiers that are all over the place. And they are all over the place. I just got here last night and it's still very strange to see them everywhere around. My feeling toward them sure hasn't changed with the war over here.

Coming up, the road was full of Czech soldiers going down—they'd been captured by the Germans and forced into labor battalions. Now they're on their way home by anything they can get hold of—on foot, bicycles, German horses and wagons. And at one point one of the MPs asked us if we had room to give a lift to two Danish soldiers who were going north, heading home.

2 The Battle of the Po Valley took place from April 5 to May 8, 1945. The Eighty-Eighth Infantry arrived in Naples, Italy, in February 1944, and became the first draftee division to enter a combat zone during World War II. They were also the first all-draftee division to enter Rome in June 1944. Jami Bryan, "The 88th Infantry Division in Italy," Army Historical Foundation, January 20, 2015, https://armyhistory.org/the-88th-infantry-division-in-italy.

The other day the MPs asked us to put up a woman and a little boy about four years old at our billet in Bologna. She had walked through the Brenner Pass from Dresden [Germany], was going to look for her relatives right outside Bologna.

What am I doing here in Bolzano? (I had to think very hard not to put down "in this town.") Together with the field director, I am trying to resurrect the swimming pool. It must have been a nifty joint once—a tremendous pool, beside a good-sized one for kids and even a wading pool for toddlers. It's got hundreds of dressing rooms and lots of terraces and a place that used to be a restaurant that could be our snack bar. But you really ought to see it now. Once it had lots and lots and lots of windows and all kinds of indirect lighting, even in the swimming pool, but after we got through bombing around it—railroad yards and bridges and such, there wasn't a piece of glass more than an inch square anywhere, but truckloads under an inch strewn all over the place. Then the Germans lived in the place and when they left they left a place that looked like a million pigsties had all been strung together. And besides that they burned part of it out and they and the Italians or both ripped out light and plumbing fixtures, I don't know why, and ripped off wooden doors to use as firewood to keep warm with last winter. There's also a thousand pound bomb still reposing out in the open with a neat sign in German stating that it is as yet unexploded. But I don't think we'll keep that around much longer. We got a crew of Italians to begin cleaning it out today with shovels and brooms. It really will be something if we get it into shape again. It's in a beautiful spot, ringed round with mountains with a breeze blowing through the place.

Last time I wrote you I was talking about how cold it was. The weather turned suddenly all over, from winter to summer and it's been very hot everywhere. Strangely enough these towns in the Alps are hot as the dickens, even though here and there are still patches of snow still to be seen on the tops of mountains. But the towns are set in hollows with the mountains all around to keep the cool away. So we really have powerful incentive to get a swimming pool in shape.

I got your birthday card in the mail that was brought to me today. This is one time when everyone's birthday wishes really did come true—the war here ended before my birthday. I remember last year my birthday was the night of the push out of Cassino and Anzio, and the year before that was just about the end of the fighting in Africa. I don't know though about next year and the Japs.

The handkerchief is very nice and it was a nice surprise to find it in the card. I can't think of anything I need. I was hurting for some Kleenex, about the only thing I lacked, but somewhere along the line we came into a whole case of it and my share was a good sized handful that will last a while now. I guess what I want more than anything is mail, and from people also to whom I don't get a chance to write. I'll have to make these family letters most of the time and hope you get the news around and that I get answers.

I got a letter from Ned [a cousin] recently that I enjoyed receiving with swell news about Richard [another cousin] which was good to hear. Got a letter from Em [an aunt] today too—hope they keep on writing, got one from Birdie [another aunt] too and news about Bert [Edith's brother] from yours too. That sure is a crazy thing and I was especially sorry it was an Army vehicle. I do hope he is well on the mend and turning it into an opportunity for a much deserved rest. I will certainly try to make time to write to him [Bert's injury was not serious, and he soon returned to active duty].

Life is still crazy and mixed up here. Bit by bit we begin to realize that the war in Europe is over. But more and more we realize that Japan is yet to be defeated.

Certainly this will be the best Mother's Day for many mothers for many a year. I hope your day personally was very pleasant.

With best wishes and best regards and love to everyone, and much love for you.

Edith

P.S. I do want some 620 film

After months of trying to find a way to visit her brother Bert, who was with the 291st Infantry Regiment, Seventy-Fifth Infantry Division, Edith finally got a pass and soon after VE Day went to Spain, where he had been. From there Edith traveled to meet up with Bert, whose unit was now in France. Many decades later, in a 2010 letter to a friend, Bert recalled:

> *After VE-Day when my outfit was finally pulled out of Germany to France where we thought we could relax, we started training instead for the expected invasion of Japan. Morale was low. We had thought we were going home. One day a runner came to tell me that I had a visitor. It was Edith. Somehow she had managed to breach the almost impenetrable wall between the Italian Theater and the European Theater—and there she was, her beautiful self in her beautiful Red Cross uniform. I was so popular that evening! Officers I didn't even know from companies in other battalions were stopping by to see their "old buddy!"—and, as casually as they could manage, to ogle Edith and wangle an introduction.*

On September 12, 1945, Edith wrote home from Cividale del Friuli, Italy:

> From the story on officers' demobilization in *S&S* [*Stars and Stripes*] it looks like Bert ought to be home before the end of the year.[3] As for me, I don't know. Italy is being taken over by ETO [European Theater Operations] on Dec 1 and I sure hope to be going home around that time, if not before. No one's been encouraging about it yet, however. But I don't think they're right. I think it's time for me to go home. I'm not even interested any more in seeing any new places. Yesterday came news that the 34th Division is going home and the 86th will take over occupation here. I will have seen practically every Division go home from Africa on up.

3 First Lieutenant Bert Witt in fact arrived by Victory ship in Newport News at the end of November 1945. On December 3 he was assigned command of a troop train containing about 475 men. The train arrived at Fort MacArthur, San Pedro, California, on December 10, 1945, and he was reunited with his wife, Ellen, and two-year-old son, Peter. In January 1946, Bert was promoted to captain, and on February 13, 1946, he was honorably discharged and assigned to the Southern California Officer Reserve Corps.

On September 17 she wrote to her mother from Verona:

> People at home seem to think that because the war's over it's all over and overnight the world has returned to peace and plenty, or at least normal living. [Japan had surrendered on September 2]. But it will take decades just to clear the rubble, thousands more lives before the mines become harmless, generations before a decent life is achieved, and I don't know what before the political problems are solved. All the clamor at home for discharging all men with blue eyes, all men with brown eyes, all men with two eyes, all men with one eye, all men, is just as if it were all a football game and now it's over and our side won so let's all go home and listen to the news on the radio.
>
> Yes, I'd like a rest when I do get home, in a quiet beautiful spot somewhere.
>
> How lucky you are to be able to walk down a street where the buildings are all standing.
>
> 26 September 1945
> Dear Mother:
> Please note the change in address—as of October 6th. The 34th Division is going home and the 88th men are moving in and the 83rd Division is taking over as the occupation division in Italy. Our Red Cross operation is being taken over by the 88th as it is and we go right on operating during the shift and then become an 88th Division installation. Sometime shortly thereafter our Verona headquarters will close up, and since we will then be far away from any Red Cross headquarters, we had better get our mail right through Division.
>
> I don't know any more about my going home. I've sent a letter of resignation asking to go home in November, but as of today there's still a ruling that would mean I'm supposed to stay until March.[4] But I'm still hoping the ruling will be changed—I don't see how it can stick.
>
> The weather suddenly changed to winter here. Other day we went through a snow storm coming through the mountains.

4 By March 1946, Edith would have completed over three years of service overseas.

Today it's clear, but cold. We're already wearing most of our clothes and wondering what we're going to do when it really gets cold.

We've had two swell USO shows here—The Roxy Revue and the Shuffle Along—both of which I've managed to see. I had a swell break this weekend. I have another Red Cross gal as assistant now, which is why I have any time at all to write this note.

Hope you are all well and in good condition.

I wish the people at home would realize that it isn't all over here or in Japan. There's as much of a job to do now as there was in getting the shooting over. I'd hate to see the war lost now.

with love –
Edith

■ ■ ■

3 October 1945
Dear Mom:
Well, it's OK now. I'm going to get to go home. When, I don't know exactly. Naples wrote they'd try to get me transportation home in November, so it just depends on shipping space. I hope it will be no later than December and I hope it is November, but there's no telling yet. In fact, until you're actually on the ship and the ship has pulled out you're not really sure.

But anyway, I know I'm going home. I know it, but once again I just don't realize it. This time it's for good—or for a long time at any rate. Really finito. I can't really picture it—but I do keep thinking of Arizona and California—winter months of sun and warmth—a country untouched by war. And every so often the tunes start going through my head—California here I come, and When It's Springtime in the Rockies, and Make San Fernando Valley My Home. I don't know how I'll be coming out—train or plane or car. I'll spend a couple of weeks in New York, see what's what, take care of whatever business that is necessary, look up a slew of people. I'd like a place to stay, of course, when I get out to California. But after I've been in North Hollywood [where her mother Ida was living and near where Bert and his family would be living] a while, I think I might want to go to one of the sea towns. But, gosh I really don't know what I want to do. I may not be able to let you know exactly when I'll be coming home, but I'll try to keep you as closely posted as I can. But you know by now how uncertain such things are.

At any rate, the man who is going to replace me came up today. I'm writing this from Verona where I'm taking care of division business before this headquarters closes down. Tomorrow I'm going back up and start handing things over. The clubs are going full blast. The gals are having farewell parties for the 34th men who are leaving and then getting up (or staying up) to serve them doughnuts and coffee as the trucks pull out at 4 a.m. And then they're having welcome parties for the 88th men coming in. It's tough going, but they're a swell bunch of girls and their spirit stays up. I'm going to be one of the few people going home who will have the good satisfaction of knowing that the work I've done will go on for a long time, for while we've been building in the occupation area, other areas have been closing down.

With love—Edith

---

10 October 1945

Dear Mother:

Just got the news that I am definitely scheduled to go home some time in November. That means that Bert and I should be back in the States about the same time. And it means also that we should be able to spend Xmas together in California—as civilians.

I can write this all right, but I sure can't realize it.

By now it seems like I've been away from home for three years straight. That leave at home was all too fast for it really to sink in.[5] I guess this time it will take about a year for me to get to understand that for me it is all over.

I wish it were all over for everybody. We were talking about it the other night, trying to imagine how it is for the people over

5 Edith did get a leave and came back to the United States in late December 1944 for a few weeks. Her mother was able to travel east from California, and they spent some time together in New York City and Connecticut.

here who don't have the States to go to home to. Or the WAAF [Women's Auxiliary Air Force] I met the other night who applied for a six months extension over here when it was time for her to go home because she felt the winter in England would be even tougher this year than it would be here.[6]

I know this news will make you happy—but hardly as happy as it makes me, I just hope I have time to pack and get ready before it's time for me to go—we've been working like everything.
Much love to everyone.
Edith

■ ■ ■

16 October 1944
Dear Mother:
It is very hard for one over here to read about anti-Semitism at home, to be told of its increase. But it is not frightening. For the millions of men in our armed forces will quash it like they would a louse. There is no anti-Semitism in the Army—or in Red Cross for that matter—or any other organization over here. This is really one that our boys have discarded. I remember one young kid in the infantry who worked at one of our clubs for a few days while his outfit was there. He was a sweet tough Italian kid from Pittsburgh. He had seen his buddy killed next to him in action, and he told me about him one day, "I feel lost without him," he said. "We were buddies for two years. He was the best morale-builder in the Army. He was a Jewish boy from Brooklyn. Whenever I was feeling low, he'd sing that song. He could make a joke out of anything. And he was good fighter. All the Jewish boys in our outfit sure were good fighters. They knew what they were fighting for. I don't look like I would cry, do I? I couldn't help it then."

I sent Em [aunt] a clipping from a copy of Stars and Stripes recently that told how the people of Rome acted toward the Jews when the Germans were there. How a Catholic church was made available to Jews for holding their services, how Catholic women

6 The Women's Auxiliary Air Force was an auxiliary of the Royal Air Force.

made unleavened bread and gave it to the Jews for Passover, how Catholic nuns made it possible for Jewish children to study at school—I don't remember all the incidents.

In our Army, arrangements are made to facilitate the possibility of every Jewish soldier to attend services regularly and for all the holy days. Last Passover there were matzos in the foxholes and wine was flown from Africa and hardboiled eggs were gotten from somewhere and Seders were held under the boom of German artillery. In this town and in another one I went through there is a Jewish soldiers club where Jewish soldiers from all the Allied armies can meet one another.[7]

In the Army itself the camaraderie that grows out of common danger and common hardship and common hopes is deeper than any differences of nationality or religion. So far as the job goes, a man stands on his merits as a fighter or a worker. So far as community life goes a man stands on his merits as a decent social human being.

I read a book over here called Delilah, which is the story of a destroyer.[8] There's a passage in that about a Jewish Navy captain of a ship—something goes wrong with the ship in the harbor—it's a submarine—and there are the thoughts of the people watching, this Jew, what will he do, he is not made for moments like this, traces of anti-Semitic prejudice. But he acts like any man would act in that situation—with desperate courage, hidden fortitude. It's an intense passage, and a moving exposition of how one's own experience wipes out prejudice.

I have met up with boys from the Middlewest who have told me that they had never seen a Jew before they came into the Army, had strange ideas about what Jews were like, were amazed

7 The Red Cross operated a number of clubs intended to serve Jewish soldiers. Like the situation with black soldiers, Jewish soldiers were not excluded from any of the Red Cross clubs. Which club they attended was a matter of preference based on where they might feel most welcome and comfortable. George Korson, *At His Side: The Story of the American Red Cross Overseas in World War II* (New York: Coward-McCann, 1945).

8 *Delilah* by Marcus Goodrich was published in 1941 (New York: Farrar & Rinehart). The novel told the story of a fictional US Navy destroyer, the USS *Delilah*, and epic struggles of her crew in the Philippines in 1916–17. The author was the first husband of Olivia de Havilland.

when they discovered that the fellow who slept next to them was a Jew.

When our men finally do get home they will leave behind them the crosses row on row, and mingled with the crosses, the six point
stars. And the men who get home one day will never forget the men who stay behind—will remember them as men.[9]

Much love –

Edith

■ ■ ■

9 During the 1920s and 1930s, antisemitism increased in the United States, driven largely by religious and business leader demagogues who held Jews responsible for the Great Depression. One in particular had a tremendous following. Father Charles Coughlin's radio broadcasts and publications reached millions and extolled the anti-Jewish policies of Adolf Hitler and questioned the character and patriotism of the American Jews. In many American cities Jews faced physical dangers through personal and property attacks. While President Roosevelt did appoint numerous Jews to senior positions in his administration, including the nomination of Justice Felix Frankfurter to the Supreme Court, these appointments in some instances only heightened public expressions of antisemitism.

With the rise of Hitler, the US government and public were slow to respond to the horrific consequences of Nazi policies toward the Jews in Germany and Europe. The United States did not increase the quotas for immigration of Jews from Europe as they tried to flee Nazi oppression and eventually the Holocaust. With strong support from people like Father Coughlin, Henry Ford, and Charles Lindbergh, the American First Committee, formed in 1940, advocated for the United States to stay out of the war in Europe. However, the Japanese attack on Pearl Harbor in 1941 ended talk of US non-involvement in what now was a worldwide conflict. Leonard Dinnerstein, *Antisemitism in America* (New York: Oxford University Press, 1994).

With the onset of World War II, 550,000 American Jews fought in the US military. Solomon Grayzel, *A History of the Jews: From the Babylonian Exile to the Present* (Philadelphia: Jewish Publication Society, 1968). Jewish solders served with distinction during the war. Jewish scientists (many exiled from Germany) also played key roles in the Manhattan Project that produced the atomic weapons that helped end the war with Japan. "*The Manhattan Project: Making the Atomic Bomb,*" AtomicArchive.com, http://www.atomicarchive.com/History/mp, adapted from F. G. Gosling, *The Manhattan Project: Making the Atomic Bomb* (Washington, DC: History Division, Dept. of Energy, 1999).

However, antisemitism was still evident in American society and the military. And for many Americans, strong anti-immigrant, anti-Jewish sentiment existed despite evidence of the slaughter that was taking place at the hands of the Nazis. However, after the war, with the creation of Israel in 1948, and with increased economic prosperity in the United States, antisemitism declined in the United States, and there was renewed optimism in the Jewish community about their social, cultural, and economic future in America. Dinnerstein, *Antisemitism in America.*

10/17 [from Trieste].

I've moved from Cividale to Gorizia with Division Headquarters but today I came down here to stay overnight with the girls at the club and get some rest. I wanted to go skiing this afternoon but they told me a mine went off close to the shore this morning so I lost my enthusiasm. It's still warm here during the day and the hills are beautiful in autumn colors, brilliantly red. The sea is soft blue, and lovely . . .

I have just about turned everything over to my successor. We're having a meeting Fri to make the official announcement to all the club directors. I was recommended for another promotion as of yesterday, so if you ever get a check with an additional $25 don't be surprised. Even at that, the man who is taking my place is a regional Assistant Club Supervisor, which is about two grades above me.

And I'm supposed to teach him the ropes. I guess you can definitely count on my coming out to California somewhere around the middle of Dec. What's the car-buying situation out there? Just got a letter from Bert saying his outfit would start moving about now on its way to being processed for home, so I imagine he'll beat me back by a little. I sure will be glad to get back to the States. I think then I'll really be able to realize the war is over. The next one is not inevitable but it sure will take a lot of doing to see it isn't.

■ ■ ■

Edith was scheduled to begin her trip home to New York beginning November 28, 1945, from Capodichino near Naples, Italy, but her plane was canceled. On November 29 she took a ship to Rome, and then she caught a plane to Casablanca, Morocco, the next day. After a several-day layover at the Hotel Majestic, Edith flew out on December 2, arriving first in San Maria in the Azores, then Harmon Field in Stephenville, Newfoundland, Canada, and finally arriving at LaGuardia Field in New York City at 7:45 a.m. on December 3, 1945. For Edith, she was home. She would now go through debriefing and exit processing with the Red Cross and then begin her transition to everyday civilian life.

From her autobiography Edith picks up the story in the following paragraphs.

Early in 1946 I flew over the beautiful earth to visit my family in Los Angeles. I shared the room my mother rented and ate with her at her sister Lillie's family house across the street. Every day I wrote stories about the war on the same typewriter I am using now. Some were published in good small magazines that were discontinued soon after.

The sweet relationship with my mother and my family, the process of writing, the loveliness of California, and the absence of war gradually healed me.

I needed a car, but cars were scarce. I heard about a man who was selling his Ford for $500 at a nearby gas station on his way out of town. Should I take a chance? The car looked okay. Were the tires stuffed with newspapers? He looked okay. Should I trust him? I was used to trusting everybody (on our side). I gave him the cash, and he signed the pink slip and gave me the keys, and I drove it home. It was a fine car for many years.

A Red Cross friend looked me up, and we drove north one weekend to see San Francisco. Oh, San Francisco! It felt like home. Soon I moved up there.

18

Think We'll Forget?

Edith wrote this gripping, fast-paced account of everyday Red Cross club life after returning from the war. In it we hear the voices of men searching for information, an understanding ear, and interaction with an American girl from home. Men enter and leave the club, connections are made, and what seems trivial on the surface reveals fears, hopes, and the impact of being in a war zone. Dorie, the Red Cross girl at the front desk, fields questions, provides information, and engages the soldiers as they approach the desk. At the same time Dorie deals with her own thoughts about Blake, a soldier with whom she has interacted in the past: Where is he? What's become of him? Is he okay?

A wet North African winter wind came in with the men as they thrust aside the blackout curtains at the front door of the club. They blinked their eyes at the sudden change from dark to light and glanced around the packed lobby at the chance there might be someone there they knew. As their eyes fell on Dorie's Red Cross uniform at the information desk, they brushed their wilted OD caps quickly off their heads.

The air was thick with male voices. Weaving in and out, in rain-streaked leather jackets or dark raincoats, men headed to and from the other quarters of the club. Some strode straight through to get an early seat for the movie in the lounge. Dorie heard the sudden shuffle up the stairs that meant the snack bar had just opened. She looked up at a lanky kid with bright red hair above a thin, beaked nose.

"Evening, Sunshine," the fellow said, handing her his travel orders for a bed. "What's the quickest way to get drunk in this town?"

There were two names on the travel orders for a three-day leave. "Both of you?" asked Dorie.

"The first one's me. The other guy is dead. You want to see my dog tags? Here, have a look. No charge."

Dorie pulled up on the chain around his neck. He grabbed her hand and held it while she read the tag.

"Los Angeles," she said.

"Where are you from?"

"Connecticut."

"Well, after the war you come out to California, I'll show you what God's country's like." She handed him his billet slip. "Listen," he said. "After the war, I'm going to have my nose straightened. Will you date me then?"

"You're all right, Red, the way you are," said Dorie.

"My girl back home doesn't think so. I'm going to get stinking drunk and tear this town apart." His bright red hair moved quickly through the crowd.

Dorie took the travel orders of three air corps boys. "To the United States," she read. The paper trembled in her hand.

"Let me touch you for good luck," she said. She put a finger lightly on each wet leather sleeve in turn. "Why, you'll be home for Christmas," she said softly.

"Maybe you will too," said one.

"They're giving even money in London," said another.

"What year?" said Dorie.

"We don't believe it either," said the short dark boy. "It's just that when you're going home yourself—"

The next man was somewhere in his thirties, tall and thin, his face deep-lined and pale, his voice restrained.

"Someday," he said. From somewhere, it seemed the very center of her skull, Dorie heard the bells again. She heard the ringing of the bells that she had heard that morning. And then she thought of Blake and wondered if he was alive that night. She always saw Blake wandering in the darkness through the mud, alone and lost, the tall, broad height of him against the sky.

"Do you think that we'll forget?" the soldier said. His travel orders read that he was on his way back from the hospital. "When we get home, I mean. When it's all over."

A sailor came and planted himself beside the older man. He slapped a hand down on the counter. "Red Cross," he said. "I have a complaint to make. Is this the place to make it?"

"Okay," said Dorie. "What's the matter?"

"Now this is serious," he said. "I gave a dollar to the Red Cross last year. I want my money's worth. I've walked around this town all afternoon. Into all the dirty alleys, up the hills. I looked under every 'off limits' sign. And still I couldn't find her."

"Who?"

"Hedy Lamarr [movie actress], of course," the sailor said.

"Of course you'll get your dollar back," said Dorie.

"Have you ever seen a man's face blown off?" the older soldier said. Dorie watched the sailor cross the lobby to his buddy and look back at her and laugh.

Oh, Blake, she thought, and saw him stride against the stormy sky.

"One minute he's right there next to you," the man went on. Each finger of his hand trembled separately. "I've got two sons," he said and fumbled for the snapshots in his wallet.

Two little boys were standing in the grass. Two little boys were sitting on the front stoop with their mother. Two little boys were on a swing. In all the pictures, the bells were ringing. It was back in the States, and Blake was pulling on the rope that rang the bells, and she was waking up to know that it was true.

"They're wonderful kids," she said. "I don't think that we'll forget." The man smiled slowly.

"I haven't had a letter for two months," he said.

"I hope there's mail waiting at the outfit." He noticed the two Negro boys waiting with their barracks bags behind him. "It sure was good to talk to you," he said. "It's the first time in a long while that I've talked so much to anyone. All right if I take some stationery?"

The taller of the Negro boys came over first.

"Can we get a place to sleep?" he said. He handed over their orders and their dog tags.

"Hartford," said Dorie. "That's my hometown too." The boy's eyes lighted up.

"Well, just imagine that," he said.

"That's a good town," Dorie said.

"Sure is."

Then neither of them spoke. *If he were any other boy,* thought Dorie, *I'd ask him now, Where'd you hang out, whom do you know, where did you used to go to eat, where did you dance?*

They took their billet slips and swung their bags up on their shoulders.

"See you in Hartford," Dorie suddenly called after them.

The lobby was quite clear, except for moving traffic, now that the show had started in the lounge. A scowling, stocky fellow was at the telephone, yelling, "Daylight! I want to get Daylight! Yes, Daylight!"

At the other end of the information desk was a sailor Dorie realized must have been standing there like that for half an hour, his arms resting on it, his face staring into space.

One of the men she knew breezed in, his raincoat dripping.

"Say, Dorie, what's the show?" he said.

"Hello, Freddie. It's *Holiday Inn*."

"That's the one that has 'White Christmas.' Come in and see it with me." She shook her head, smiling. "I'll hold your hand," he said, "just like back home."

"Hello, Daylight?" the boy at the telephone yelled.

"Get me Dynamite. Yes, Dynamite!"

A great big soldier came in. The rain ran off him like rivers down a mountain.

"Must be pouring," Dorie said to him.

"It's a little damp," he conceded, wiping a huge hand across his face. "Is there a message here for me? The name's Gale Edwards."

Dorie looked through the E's twice. "I'm sorry," she said. "There isn't any message."

"I was supposed to meet my brother here," he said. "I just came in from Italy. He was supposed to get here today."

"Where's he coming from?"

"Casablanca. He just came over. He was a kid last time I saw him. He was just a little boy."

"I'll phone out to the airport. See if they know anything about his plane. Soon as the phone is free."

The boy at the telephone shouted, "Dynamite? Is this Dynamite? Give me Darling Red, please. Yes, Darling Red."

Dorie went down to the other end of the counter. "Hi," she said and smiled into the sailor's staring face. "You've been here quite a while."

"All right if I stand here?"

"Sure," said Dorie. "I just thought you might be waiting for something."

"Just standing here," he said.

"My name's Dorie."

"Marsh Paley." He looked at Dorie, but his eyes still stared at something far away, and he spoke softly. "You load your ship with soldiers and you get to know them like your friends," he said. "And then you take them to a beach and dump them there, and then you go away. You leave them on the beach, your friends. You never know what happens to them after that."

And there was Blake again, plowing through a dark wind at night, alone.

"They're wonderful guys," said Dorie. "All of them."

"Yes, they are," said Marsh.

"I have to go back to the telephone," she said. "I hope I get a chance to talk to you some more."

"I'll come and say good-bye to you before I go," he said.

And then you go away and leave them, Dorie thought, and she went back to the telephone.

A tall, thin boy was at the phone, struggling through dim memories of high school French. "*Est-ce que je peux venir chez vous ce soir?*" [Can I come see you tonight?] He said each syllable distinctly until it did not sound like what it was. A wispy man she hadn't seen before reached over the counter and touched her sleeve.

"Good evening, Miss Red Cross," he said. Dorie looked up and smiled. "That's good," he said. "That's very good. I've been watching you all evening, and you don't smile enough. My name is Gus. "

"My name's Dorie."

"I'm from Milwaukee."

"I'm from Connecticut."

"Well, now we know each other. But don't forget to smile. I'll be around again."

Gale Edwards was still standing there, looking toward the door. The thin boy at the phone shrugged his shoulders and turned to Dorie.

"Say, do you speak French? I say it just like the book, and she can't understand me." He handed her the phone.

"She says you can't come over tonight because her parents aren't home. She says to come tomorrow."

"My aching back," he said. "I don't get it. I won't be here tomorrow, anyway." He took the phone. "Well, I'll be—She hung up."

"I'm sorry," Dorie said. "Maybe she wondered who I was."

Four paratroopers stood waiting, a little distance from the counter, while they let the raindrops stream down their jackets. "Bullfrog," said Dorie into the phone. An infantryman whom Dorie did not know came up.

"I just wanted to thank you," he said. "Thank you very much."

"Please, ma'am," said a soft southern voice. "May I have a guest card for my friend?" He nodded toward the French soldier who was with him. "I'm attached to his outfit."

"Sure." She wrote out billeting slips for the paratroopers. "It's the Parker House," she said. "Up on the fifth floor."

"I'd like the bridal suite myself," said one.

"Yourself?" another asked.

"My wife's going to meet me here," he said. "'Make it the Parker House, Honey,' she said. Coincidence, isn't it?"

"Do you speak French?" the Frenchman asked. "A little," she said. "Extension 53," she said into the phone.

The Frenchman's words spilled over, his voice intense, his gestures quick and sharp. He had just come from France, five days across the Pyrenees, seven months in and out of Spanish jails, across to Casablanca and then on to here. He had expected to get right into an invasion boat for France. Another month would be too late. The strength of the French people was being turned to water with the waiting. Starvation they could stand, and beatings, prison, torture, cold. But not the waiting. Why don't the ships set forth?

The little wispy man was back again. His hair fell on his forehead in thin yellow strands. He peered over the edge of the counter like an elf.

"You understand all that?" asked the southern boy.

Dorie nodded. That's what all of them were waiting for. The summer before last and through the fall and even through the winter when they knew that it was scarcely possible.

And then last spring and through another summer and now, day after day, although another winter had begun.

The plane the Edwards boy was likely to be on had not been heard from since it had taken off from Casablanca early in the morning.

"I don't understand his lingo," said the southern boy. "But I know what he means. The Russians from one side and us from the other." He smashed his fists together. "I want to get this over with. I want to go back to South Carolina."

Dorie heard the bells again, the shattering sound that had awakened her that morning. Her heart pounded as if the hammers of the bells were beating on it.

"They don't know anything out there," she said to Edwards. "They'll call me back if they find out. Why don't you go upstairs and get some rest? I'll know where you are then if your brother comes in."

"Don't worry so," the elfin Gus was whispering. "You'll stay young longer, if you live. But I'll be back."

A powerfully built sailor they called Sampson shuffled up and took her hands in his. Dorie had never seen him sober.

"I know I'm disgusting, Dorie," he said softly. "I'll stop drinking when they put me on another ship."

"You're okay," Dorie said.

"Then have a drink." He reached down clumsily and pulled a bottle up from inside his shirt. The sound of voices filled the lobby once again. The snack bar had just closed.

Outside, the first trucks taking soldiers back to camp were warming up. Sampson leaned over her, his huge bulk swaying.

"Come on, Dorie, have a drink," he said. "All these guys bothering you. You need a drink. I want to cheer you up."

Dorie took his hands and the bottle slid down back into his shirt. Freddie came out of the lounge.

"Dorie," he said, "come on in for a minute. They're going to sing 'White Christmas' now."

"I can't leave yet."

"Well, then I'll sing it for you," Freddie said.

Marsh Paley touched her arm. She heard Freddie's voice, singing low beneath the crisscross of men's voices.

"I just wanted to say good night," Marsh Paley said. "If I get liberty tomorrow I'll come to see you again."

"Good night, Marsh," she said. She saw him walking down the dark hill to the docks. And she saw Blake again, but now Blake looked like all the others who had come and gone.

"I held on to him all the time, Dorie," Sampson said. "But when they picked us up they told me he was dead. He must have been dead when I first grabbed him in the water."

"I'm dreaming of a white Christmas," sang Freddie softly.

The men were streaming through the lobby from the lounge, out to the trucks. Some of them called good night as they went by. She caught a flash of bright red hair above a beaked nose.

"Thanks, Freddie. That was nice," she said.

"Time for me to go?" said Sampson.

"Yes. You go back to the base now, Sampson. I'll see you tomorrow." He lumbered off.

Red waited till the crowd had gone and then came over.

"Why, Red," she said. "I thought you—"

"Ah, I'm sick and tired of getting drunk."

The blackout curtain through which all of them had gone flapped wildly with a sudden gust of wind. The place was strangely quiet. Only the lamp on the information desk was lit. As Dorie turned to get her coat, the siren tore the night apart, died down, and then ripped it into shreds again.

"I'll wait with you until the all-clear sounds," said Red.

She came around the counter and they leaned their elbows on it, facing toward the blackout curtain at the door.

"This morning when I woke up, there were so many church bells ringing," Dorie said, "I thought the war was over."

They laughed together softly, waiting for the all-clear shriek to pierce the night.

19

Race Relations after the War

Although more than a million African Americans served in the United States military during World War II, they were organized into segregated units and were most often assigned to support roles. Many of these units fought with distinction (e.g., the Tuskegee Airmen and the 751st Tank Battalion). However, there was backlash against the military's segregation practices, which led the black press in the United States to adopt the Double V campaign, which advocated one V for victory over fascism abroad and another V for victory over discrimination at home. At home African American leaders demanded an end to discriminatory employment practices, particularly in industries that received military contracts to supply the materials needed to fight the war overseas. Protests led to President Roosevelt issuing Executive Order 8802, which banned employment discrimination in the defense industry and government.[1]

When Edith came back from the war, she was optimistic that race relations would be improved. She expressed that hope several times in her letters and in the narratives she wrote about her experiences. However, the realities of postwar America were quite different. Segregation, and often violent attempts to maintain it, continued. In response, President Truman ordered full integration of the military. However, black Americans and an increasing number of whites became involved in the civil rights movement of the 1950s and 60s, which was necessary to further advance the cause of racial equality.[2]

1 Brett Pike, "Discrimination against African American Soldiers in World War II: Racial Policies and the March to Desegregation," https://www.scribd.com/document/165853187/Pike-discrimination-Against-African-American-Soldiers-in-Wwii; Henry Louis Gates Jr. "What Was Black America's Double War?" *Root*, May 24, 2013, http://www.theroot.com/articles/history/2013/05/double_v_campaign_during_world_war_ii_what_was_it.html.

2 Michael C. C. Adams, *The Best War Ever: America and World War II*, 2nd ed. (Baltimore: Johns Hopkins University Press, 2015).

Seeing the struggles that African Americans faced when they came home from the war, Edith wrote a short story that captured some of her disappointments about race relations. Edith's concerns followed through on her efforts before the war to counter racial prejudice and injustice and foretold her continuing efforts in the coming decades to achieve the second of the two V's, Victory over discrimination at home. The story presented below is as published in the journal Common Ground.[3] *Edith's story portrays the battles that soldiers had to fight even when the war was over.*

Hunting

The cabin rested in the stretch of woods that lay between the highway and the river about twelve miles from town. The only way to find the place would be to stumble on it or to know exactly where it was. It had been built years back by some old man named Higby, but after he had died, it was unused and gradually forgotten.

As the September sky grew lighter grey, the early morning light filtered through the trees and brushed against the open windows of the cabin. Inside, the young man in the narrow iron bed turned over on his back. He heard the calling of the birds and felt the light against his eyes. He kept them closed and sighed and stretched contentedly. He loved this moment of awakening every day when he could decide whether he would get up or go to sleep again. He pulled the blanket over his head as if to wrap himself securely in his dream.

The Higby cabin had become a dream to Bradford Lee through three years of the war. He was a kid when he first came upon it once when he had gone off hunting by himself. Then in the Army, and especially overseas, when men around him thought aloud of the time their fighting job was through, it was sometimes Bradford Lee who said, 'I'm going out to a place I know. Hunting and fishing and lying in the sun.

3 Edith Witt, "Hunting," *Common Ground* 7, no. 2 (1947): 74–80, http://www.unz.org/Pub/CommonGround-1947q4–00074. "Hunting" was Edith's first published article for which she was paid. She received $5 per page according to a letter from its editor Margaret Anderson to Edith Witt, September 5, 1946. Princeton University Press published *Common Ground* between 1940 and 1949 for the Common Council for American Unity, with funding from the Carnegie Corporation. It was one of the first American periodicals focusing on ethnic and intercultural issues. "Common Ground (magazine)," *Densho Encyclopedia*, http://encyclopedia.densho.org/Common_Ground_(magazine).

It's in the woods. . . ." Out of the dreamy silence then, someone would say, "Woods going to be full of ex-soldiers trying to get away from each other after the war."

When he first got back to the States and was discharged, Bradford Lee did not think of Higby's place at all. It was exciting just to be back where the lights were bright and girls were freshly washed and gaily dressed, where buildings weren't half knocked out and roads were smooth and cars moved fast, where there was good cold beer and shops that overflowed with a million different kinds of things. It was a thrilling joy to walk around his own home town, stand on the corner of Main and Fifth, look, listen, breathe it in.

There came the time that he was through with looking on. His feet grew restless of walking on the edge. He wanted to break through into the human stream that passed him by on Main. He tried. He couldn't lay his hand on peace or freedom, on jobs for all or decent homes. He could not touch the promise of atomic energy for an abundant life. He reached out toward the postwar world that he had fought to find.

Instead, the shadow of a world he did not want hung over him. It was a New Year's eve balloon, inflated with the profits made on war, black market manipulations, blown up by speculation, fat with shortages, swollen on wage reductions, lay-offs, bulging, bursting, ready for the pinprick. The people crawling on it were riding high. They cut the tapes that held it to the ground. They yelled down to those left behind: Blow hard, use all your breath. Their teeth knocked together as their fingers slipped. They babbled about Negroes, Jews, Catholics, Yankees, foreigners, Reds. They spluttered about Negro vets who tried to vote, Negro workers who tried to keep their jobs. They chattered nervously, scrambling to plug the leaks. They gibbered of another war. They were not people whom he knew, or even saw, and yet the air seemed thick with them.

The seven days that he had been at Higby's cabin were a precious time. A thing like that could never stop. Fishing, hunting, lying in the sun. Sleep when he wanted to, eat when he wanted to, chop wood or play his guitar; no one to bother him. He decided to get up.

He lay quiet for a moment, listening. The strange sound that he heard must have been there all the while, the rhythmic breathing of a man asleep. He pushed the blanket down and slowly turned his head.

The man lay curled in the middle of the floor inside the door. He had his back toward Bradford and the collar of his Army field jacket was pulled up over his head. There wasn't much of him to see, but he seemed young and deep in sleep. *He must have been so tired,* Bradford thought, *when he had come upon the place that he had just about crawled in the door and gone to sleep.* Bradford chuckled. Another vet trying to get away from it all. They always said they would be bumping into one another in the woods. He looked forward to the other fellow's waking up. They would enjoy the joke together.

He sat up carefully, not to make a sound, and swung his feet down to the floor. The bedsprings creaked. The fellow on the floor leaped to his feet. He doubled over, as if caught in pain, then straightened slowly.

"Oh," he said. "I didn't know anyone was living here." He began backing toward the door.

"Wait," said Bradford. He was surprised to find the fellow was a Negro. Yet his surprise did not overcome the bond he had already established in his mind. He was a little taller and thinner than Bradford, about the same age. He had a narrow face, a short straight nose, a square blunt chin. One eye was badly swollen and his lips seemed cut.

"I didn't know anyone was here," he said. "I better go." Although he didn't move, he looked as if he were about to run.

"As a matter of fact," said Bradford slowly, still sitting on the bed, "you have as much right being here as I have. I couldn't find anyone to pay rent to. I just moved in. Although," he smiled, "I did get here first."

"I better go," the man said once more.

"Where are you going?" Bradford said. This time the fellow put his hand up on the door.

"I don't know," he said. He let his hand fall to his side.

"Say, are you sick?" said Bradford.

The fellow shook his head. "Just a little stiff."

"You ought to have something to eat. I'm going to fry some cornmeal I cooked yesterday. There's enough for both of us."

The other man looked out the window and then back at Bradford.

"Anybody ever come around here?" he asked.

"No. Nobody even knows I'm here. You're the first person I've seen since I came out a week ago. Say, you in trouble?"

"Trouble? Most people got trouble, one way or another."

"Trouble with a girl?"

"No. I didn't kill anybody. I didn't steal anything. I didn't even hurt anyone, although maybe I should have."

Bradford went over to the stove and squatted down to start a fire. "Well, it's your business," he said, without turning around. "But if you're in trouble, no sense running away. Got to face it and fight back to lick it."

"Why are you out here in the woods?" the fellow said.

Bradford stood up and turned around. They looked squarely at each other for a moment. Then Bradford laughed.

"Say, my name's Brad," he said.

"Mine's Sam."

When they sat down at the table, Bradford remembered back to the first time he had eaten at the same table with a Negro. He had taken his cake and coffee from the counter in the Red Cross club and sat down before he noticed one of the soldiers at the table was a Negro. His muscles tightened to get up, but it occurred to him that if he hadn't noticed it, it couldn't matter very much.

"What outfit were you in?" he asked Sam now.

"Aircorps engineers. In the Pacific."

"I read about the things you did out there. I was in the 36th Division—infantry."

"I heard of them," said Sam.

"I'm sure glad it's over," Bradford said. He poured the coffee.

"I used to look forward to it being over, too," said Sam. "This here's good coffee."

"It's not GI," laughed Bradford. "We always used to say how the whole Army would be wandering in the woods after the war, trying to be alone."

"I'm lucky it was a guy like you I walked in on."

"You're welcome to stay as long as you like," said Bradford.

"A thing like this can't last too long."

"I don't think about that," said Bradford shortly. He poured them each another cup of coffee. "Listen," he said. "I can go into town today. I can go in and look around and find out how things are."

Sam grasped the table tightly with both hands. "I thought you didn't go into town," he said.

"I meant to find out things for you," said Bradford.

Sam put his hands down in his lap. "You think if you went into town I'd still be here when you got back?"

"Damn it," said Bradford. He got up, banging against the table. "What kind of guy do you think I am? Why do you think I came out here?"

"I tell you one thing," Sam said slowly. "You go into town again, you're never coming back out here."

"What do you mean by that?"

"I mean you try to come back out here, you're going to take the town back with you."

"I don't care what's going on in town," cried Bradford. "I'll stay out here forever."

"Sit down," said Sam. "Let me tell you how it happened to me." He began to clear the dishes off the table.

"Just dump them in the basin there," Bradford said. "I save them up and wash them all at night. And don't think you have to talk. I don't really care."

"I'm twenty-one this year," said Sam. "So I thought I'd like to vote." Bradford went over to straighten out the bed and Sam took the broom and began to sweep the floor. "No one in my family's ever voted before. Oh, yes, way back right after the Civil War they did. But not since then. I thought it would be a good thing to start it going again." He leaned on the broom and looked toward Bradford, who sat down on the bed. "You know, being part of the war, you get to thinking about such things." He brushed the sweepings to the door and opened it and swept them out. "So, yesterday, I went around to the registration place to get myself put down as a voter." He put the broom back in the corner and walked a little closer toward the bed.

"Listen, Sam. I don't want to hear about it," Bradford said. He lay down on the bed.

"O.K.," said Sam. "I just thought you might feel better if you knew you weren't in the same room with some kind of fiend that ought to be strung up."

"I'm not worried," Bradford said. "I just think you have the wrong idea. We're not all like that. You couldn't find more decent people anywhere than in this town. You think they'd let a few crazy goons—?"

"I didn't get to register for voting," Sam said simply.

"Wait till people find out. Don't you think there are any people in this town who remember what the war was all about? They're not going to let—"

"They must be the ones who are out fishing," Sam said quietly.

Bradford got up and walked across the room and out the door. In a few minutes Sam heard the sound, back of the house, of someone chopping wood. He went out.

"Let me have a hand at that," he said.

"Go inside and get some sleep. I think better when I'm chopping wood."

"I couldn't fall asleep."

"Get some rest. You couldn't have had much last night. You can keep track of me by the sound of the axe." Sam laughed and went inside.

The two men came up suddenly. Bradford gripped the handle of the axe and stared at them.

"You live here?" the dark stocky one called out.

"Yes."

"This the Higby place?"

"Guess so."

They had come closer now. They both wore badges and had guns in holsters on their hip. There was an air of uneasiness about them, although they spoke as if they had stopped just to pass the time of day.

"Didn't know anyone was living here," the stocky fellow said. His head was too big for his body.

The other man was slightly built, with pale, thin hair. He said, "Have you s-s-seen a nigger hereabouts?"

"No,"

"W-w-we're looking for a n-n-nigger."

"Nobody around here," Bradford said. "How come you looking here?"

"Somebody thought of the Higby place," the stocky fellow said, "and sent us out. You been here long?"

"About a week. I just got out of the Army."

"They w-wouldn't take me," the blond boy said. "N-nerves, they said." Bradford looked at the gun the fellow carried.

"Why you looking out here?"

"N-nigger r-r-raped a white g-girl."

"No," the other man said. "He tried to register to vote."

"That's what the p-paper said. But I know d-d-different."

"But why did you come out here? Why don't you go down to Swamp Hollow?"

"N-not much left of S-swamp Hollow after 1-1-last night,"

"They told us to come out here. We were the only ones at the plant to volunteer. None of the other boys would take it on, imagine that."

"None of the other men would volunteer?" said Bradford.

"No. Vets and all. I don't know what's the matter with them. Bunch of Reds. They don't care if the niggers take their jobs away."

"I thought the plant laid off all the Negroes since the end of the war."

"Some of the white men, too. You got to keep those niggers in their place. They never should have let them in the Army."

"Maybe you'd like to take the place of one of them who died in uniform," said Bradford.

"We better be getting back," the other fellow said to his companion.

"W-we'd smell a nigger if he was a m-m-mile from here."

"We better go. Have you got a gun, in case he turns up tonight? You know this cabin was a hideout for a lot of them after the last war."

"I'll be all right," said Bradford.

"I guess they'll put deputies on the road tonight, if you need help." He turned to the blond boy, "Come on, Lughead," he said.

Bradford watched them until they were out of sight. He took a few whacks with the axe, and then he went inside.

"Want to play cards till it gets dark?" he said to Sam.

They made a rabbit stew for supper.

They kept on playing cards until the stew was done. By the time the dishes were washed it was good and dark.

"I'll take you through the woods about three miles and put you on a trail that you can follow into Lion County," Bradford said. "Maybe from there it will be all right for you to take a train."

"You don't have to bother doing that. I'll find my way."

"Hell," said Bradford. "There you go again."

"I just don't want to get you into trouble."

"You won't. I'll take my gun. And you can carry it, if you don't trust me."

"You'll carry it," said Sam.

It was a dark night but Bradford knew this stretch of country. They didn't talk. When they got to the trail, Sam said briefly, "I sure do want to thank you, Brad. It was worth meeting up with you."

"Nothing to thank me for," Bradford said. "I hope you make it."

"Hope you make it, too," said Sam.

Bradford, starting back, wondered what Sam meant. He cut across the woods and jumped down the embankment to the road to take the short way back. It was quite dark. The only sounds, besides his own footfalls, were of the woods. The air was clear and fresh. The stars shone through the branches of the trees. He'd make a fire when he got back, do some mending on his fishing gear before he went to bed.

As he approached turn point where he should cut back through the woods again, he walked more slowly, watching for the large old sycamore that marked the spot. For a moment he was on night patrol again, nerves trigger-sharp against the enemy, stalking freedom on a mine-strewn earth, aching in his bones to feel the rest of the platoon around him. He saw the outline of the sycamore, made for it eagerly.

Out of the shadows of the tree, he heard a harsh voice cry, "Look out, he's got a gun." He heard a bullet whine go by his cheek. He felt a crack against his skull. Two men leaped on him and then a third. He thrashed his legs and kicked his feet. He struck out with his arms, heaved his body, twisted, turned. He heard another voice, "He's white. Hold it. He's white." A flashlight shone into his face. He heard their panting, heavy breath. He felt hands try to pull him up. He pushed them off. The men were talking in low worried tones.

"Is he hurt bad?"

"He's breathing all right."

"He's the f-f-fellow who l-lives in Higby's p-place."

"Lughead," he said. He brushed them away and got to his feet. He didn't know the other men. The stocky fellow wasn't there. He was breathing hard and he felt groggy. He leaned against the sycamore, pulled at a loose strip of bark. It would be good to be able to lie down now and go to sleep, to sleep until the world got straightened out.

"It's his own fault," he heard the tall man say. "What's he doing, wandering around in the dark for, anyway? What's he doing, hiding out at Higby's place? We better take him in."

"He ain't no deputy," the man with the flashlight said. "He ain't one of us, for sure. He turned the light on Bradford's battered face. They stood back, some distance off.

"What you doing way out in the woods this time of dark and

carrying a gun?" the tall man said.

Bradford breathed in deeply, looked down at his rifle lying on the ground and tightened up his hands.

"Hunting," he said.

The tall man laughed. "What you doing all alone out here? Where you going all alone?"

"I'm not alone," said Bradford. "I'm just the advance patrol. There's a column of men coming up the road. Listen. You hear their feet? They're all in step. Hear 'em? They're singing now. Here they come. They're going to pass you right on by."

The flashlight suddenly clicked off. The three men stirred uneasily,

"You're crazy, boy," the tall man said. His voice rose, quavering, uncertain. "We're going to take you in."

Bradford heard them stumble in the dark. They shuffled through the last year's leaves. He saw their ghostly shadows closing in on him.

His fist hit out against the darkness with the strength of many men. The crack of bone against his knuckles split the night. The three men staggered backwards, gulping in their breath.

"I don't need anyone to take me in," said Bradford, picking up his rifle. He glanced at the lonely dimness where the cabin lay. Then, "I got to catch up with those guys," he said, and swung his legs out on the road for town.

We'll make it, Sam, he thought. We've won before.

His footsteps rang out like a column marching.

PART FOUR

The Postwar Years

20

My Life after the War

The Levering Oath

In the late 1940s I worked briefly as a junior probation officer. As a City of San Francisco employee, I had taken the oath to uphold and defend the Constitution of California and of the United States. Then in 1950 Assemblyman Harold Levering introduced a bill in the state legislature to require public workers to take another oath that they were not members, had not been for the past five years, and wouldn't become members of any organization that wanted to overthrow the government of the United States or the state of California by force and violence. We organized to defeat the bill; we held meetings, wrote letters, spoke on the radio, and visited legislators. But the bill passed.

It was the beginning of the era of the Cold War, the Korean War, the McCarthyism blight on the Bill of Rights. The fruits of victory of World War II were rotting in the earth.

The people I worked with were good, sweet, gentle, sensitive, intelligent, considerate, friendly, helpful people. I spoke to them about the Levering oath. They understood why I would not sign it, even though I could truthfully have done so. But they were married, they had a family, they had children, they had elderly parents, they had nine or thirteen years invested in their jobs, and they would be dependent on their pensions. Besides, what difference did it make just to sign a piece of paper?

We stood in a close circle while our very nice supervisor explained that we should repeat the phrases of the oath after him, which later we would sign. Sometimes, I thought, you have to act as if many people are acting with you. I stepped back from the circle and stated briefly why, having watched such oaths Nazify Germany, I could not take that oath. The supervisor nodded and proceeded.

In 1957 the California Supreme Court declared the Levering oath unconstitutional.

The bill containing the Levering Act was passed on October 3, 1950. State, city, county, and University of California employees were given thirty days to sign the oath or lose their jobs. Edith was among thirty-one City of San Francisco employees who refused to sign the oath and were fired. Another five resigned rather than sign.[1]

Work in the Fifties

During the 1950s and early 1960s, Edith continued to live in San Francisco and worked for several different survey research and consulting companies, including Kellogg and Associates and Hal Dunleavy and Associates. She also did some private consulting work. For example, in 1958 she undertook a survey, for the William Babcock Memorial Endowment, of individuals who had received assistance from the endowment to help pay medical bills.[2] *She also wrote occasional pieces for advertising trade publications. One piece painted a whimsical picture of an individual who became a "personal adman," who helped others with consumer decision making and financial planning.*[3]

Edith also reported that:

> at the same time, I was exploring the city—the beach, the park, neighborhoods, streets. I went swimming in the public pools, including wonderful giant Fleishhacker. Outside the city I went hiking and camping, on nature walks and rafting trips with the Sierra Club and with friends.
>
> From time to time I felt the welling up of the religious feeling of oneness with the universe. At other times I asked myself, "Oneness with destruction by earthquake, tornado, flood and drought?"

1 "Consigners among S. F. Employees," *San Francisco Chronicle*, November 4, 1950.

2 "Babcock Medical Fund Reports Operation Success," *Daily Independent Journal* (San Rafael, CA), August 28, 1958.

3 Edith Witt. "The Personal Adman," *The Reporter*, May 14, 1959, 36–37.

Edith also continued to write short stories for publication in literary magazines. In one of her 1959 stories, she told a fable about the animals, plants, and trees in the forest holding a convention to discuss how humankind was destroying the environment and their worries about the potential of humans to destroy the earth through atomic warfare. Some participants in the convention were in favor of destroying humans, but the elephant responded: "You sound like a convention of men, discussing how to save the world by destroying it! How to have peace by making war." The elephant continued, saying, "If man destroys himself with atomic war, he destroys us. But if we destroy man, we destroy ourselves. Extermination is the problem—not the solution to the problem."[4] *"The Convention" was written at the height of the Cold War, a time when there was real fear about the use of atomic weapons. Edith was clearly worried, as were many Americans and people around the world, about the ability of humans to destroy life on earth as we know it.*

Edith was also an occasional writer of letters to the editor dealing with war and the environment. In a November 2, 1961, letter to the San Francisco Chronicle, *she expressed the need to both protect the environment and save the human race from communal suicide. Having visited Fort Funston, a picturesque site of a former military installation on the coast near San Francisco, Edith commented:* "Surely Ft. Funston must be a park for all the people to enjoy. But surely, too, the whole earth must be saved. . . . There must be an end to testing and making bombs, to digging and blasting the earth into a common tomb for all of us, and for a beginning of disarmament and peace."[5]

Edith published "The Convention" *under the name Ede Witt. In a 1991 letter to me, she noted that the magazine to which she had submitted the story did not seem to publish works by female authors, so she adopted a gender-ambivalent name. She also indicated that this was the only time she did this for one of her stories.*[6]

4 Ede Witt, "The Convention," *Fantastic* 8, no. 5 (May 1959): 74–84.

5 Edith Witt, "Communal Peace," *San Francisco Chronicle,* November 2, 1961.

6 Eric Leif Davin has done an extensive study of articles published in science fiction magazines from the 1920s through 1965. He goes to great lengths to disprove the common perception that women authors were not published in science fiction outlets. However, what is not clear is whether the work of women authors was more routinely rejected when manuscripts were submitted and whether a woman would have reason to perceive that works by women authors were not published as often in science fiction outlets. With regard to the

The Sixties

In 1962, Edith completed a master's degree in social science from San Francisco State University, specializing in housing, so she would have a better chance of enhanced employment related to housing and urban redevelopment. Her thesis provided a detailed critique of the filtering theory, which proposed that the best way to meet the housing needs of society was to build new dwellings primarily for upper-income individuals on the assumption that individuals of moderate and lower incomes would then "filter up" into the vacated housing. In other words, according to this theory, individuals buying high-end housing will pass down less-desirable housing that has deteriorated or is now in neighborhoods that have become less desirable, but lower-income individuals will benefit since housing stock they previously couldn't afford will become available.[7] *The theory sharply contrasted with an approach that advocated building new housing for people of all income levels.*

Edith's paper carefully analyzed each of the assumptions underlying filtering theory (e.g., housing quality decline is accompanied by a decline in value; a decline in housing value is accompanied by a change in occupancy; and changes in housing value are downward only) and discussed a number of factors that didn't appear to be accounted for by the theory (e.g., population growth, changes in population characteristics, and the concentration of population through urbanization). After careful analysis Edith concluded, "The filtering theory is so hedged with implicit assumptions and limiting conditions which impair the logic of its argument and which do not correspond to the reality it offers to explain that, in my opinion, it is not a reasonable or useful theory."[8]

Around 1960, Hal Dunleavy and Associates, a real estate research company, employed Edith to undertake a feasibility study for St. Francis Square (an integrated housing development in the Western Addition area of San

specific publication to which Edith submitted her manuscript, according to tabulations done by Davin only a small number of women authors appeared in the magazine from its founding in 1952 through the time that Edith would have submitted her manuscript in late 1958 or early 1959. Eric Leif Davin, *Partners in Wonder: Women and the Birth of Science Fiction 1926–1965* (Lanham, MD: Lexington Books, 2006).

7 Edith Witt, "The Filtering Theory and the Social Structure" (master's thesis, San Francisco State University, 1962).

8 Ibid., 62.

Francisco). In the 1950s considerable redevelopment had taken place in this area, which led to the construction of luxury high-rise apartments and the displacement of families and businesses from the area.[9] *In 1960, the San Francisco Redevelopment Agency set aside three square blocks for affordable garden apartments, which eventually would become the St. Francis Square Cooperative. The project was sponsored by the International Longshore and Warehouse Union (ILWU) and Pacific Maritime Association. The ILWU was willing to invest some of its pension fund monies in the project.*

Dunleavy and Associates also involved Edith in a feasibility study that led to sale of land in the Western Addition to the ILWU Longshore Redevelopment Corporation in the early 1960s. The original vision was to build affordable housing that could be controlled by the residents and represent all races and groups in the community. Construction of co-op units began in 1962 and was completed near the end of 1963. Today three hundred affordable housing units comprise the development.

Edith's studies at San Francisco State, her thesis, and the consulting and other work she had been doing provided a springboard for what became the most important job Edith held during her career, housing representative for the San Francisco Human Rights Commission.

Edith wrote of the times, "The 1960s was a decade of assassinations, the Vietnam War and the struggle for peace, and of the civil rights movement. I walked and marched and sang and sat at meetings and collected signatures on petitions and wrote letters and walked and marched. As in New York City, my shoes left imprints in the pavements of San Francisco (like the handprints of movie folk in Hollywood)."

Edith covers significant events of the 1960s in just one paragraph. During this decade President John F. Kennedy, Malcolm X, Medgar Evers, Martin Luther King, and Robert Kennedy were assassinated. The civil rights movement was in full force, with the Freedom Rides, the March on Washington (with Martin Luther King's immortal "I Have a Dream" speech), church bombings, the Selma–Montgomery March, and the subsequent Voting Rights Act. In addition, the United States became involved in the war in Vietnam, which prompted huge protests on college campuses and across America. Edith's activism in the sixties was rooted in her deep concerns for

9 Carol Cuenod, "Redevelopment A-1 and Origin of St. Francis Square," *Found SF,* http://foundsf.org/index.php?title=Redevelopment_A-1_and_Origin_of_St._Francis_Square.

social justice and the very survival of the human race that are evidenced in her involvement in social causes dating back to the 1930s.

Edith's autobiographical description of her involvement in the Selma to Montgomery March was very brief, but she also left us a vivid description of her participation in days four and five of the march in a letter she wrote to her family after she returned to San Francisco.

In 1965 a friend and I went to Montgomery, Alabama, to march with people from all over the country, led by Dr. Martin Luther King, to the state capitol (with its Confederate flag) in support of the passage of the Voting Rights Act.[10] It was intensely educational and tremendously moving. It was also very scary.

A call had gone out from Martin Luther King Jr. for people of conscience to come to Montgomery in support of the fifty-one-mile march to Selma along US Route 80. Well over three thousand marchers began the march in Selma on March 21, 1965, but by court order only three hundred people were allowed to march on days two through four. Edith, along with several other people from San Francisco, arrived in Montgomery on March 24, 1965, and along with the marchers and thousands of supporters stayed overnight at Camp Site Four at the St. Jude's Educational Institute. The next day they participated in the final march into Selma, and Edith flew home on March 26. A few days after she returned home from Montgomery, Edith wrote a six-page, single-spaced letter to her brother Bert and his family about her experiences.

> We had a couple of hours waitover at the Atlanta airport and we sat in the Delta waiting room, rather forlorn and uneasy with our knapsacks and sleeping bags under the stares of the other people. Until suddenly a gay and excited group of Negro and white people appeared, well-dressed, with suitcases, who looked like New Yorkers, like celebrities, like entertainers. The first one any of us recognized was Floyd Patterson, then Shelley Winters, James Baldwin, Leonard Bernstein, Peter, Paul, and

10 The Voting Rights Act was designed to prohibit racial discrimination against people registering to vote and to enforce voting rights guaranteed by the Fourteenth and Fifteenth Amendments.

> Mary, and lots of others. Our spirits changed from apprehension to triumph; we all got on the plane. At the Montgomery airport there was a whole crowd to meet them, television cameras and much gaiety, with Harry Belafonte in charge.

Edith and the small group she was traveling with from San Francisco were met by volunteers, who directed them to buses that would take them to the campsite that marchers had reached at the end of day four. In her letter she writes,

> A clergyman and a young white girl approached us and told us a bus was waiting, to be sure it was marked Special. We were the only ones on the bus and it pulled out onto Highway 80; we felt like sitting targets in the lighted bus on the dark highway. Soon we were turning in to St Jude's; there were groups of soldiers with guns on their shoulders and thousands of people streaming in through the gate from all directions. St Jude's is a Catholic institution established in 1931 to serve Negroes; it is in a Negro section; has a school and children's hospital, church and nunnery; and great massive grounds between the arch of brick buildings and the road. Ironically, one of the women who works there told me that the school and office are now integrated; White people from the nearby Army base wanted to send their children to school there for a long time (I presume Catholics) and in the last two years the State finally gave them permission to do so; also in the last few years white people have applied for jobs in the office, which was formerly all Negro, and some have been hired. A kind of reverse integration, we agreed.

Edith describes the concert that evening, where she and others sat on the ground that had been turned to mud by heavy rains over the previous couple of days. She found a place to sleep in the St. Jude's gym, but all the women were soon rousted and sent to sleep in the girl's locker room by a Catholic priest who thought it was wrong for women to be sleeping in the same area as men.

Finally the show was over and we slogged through the mud to the stage. Some people went off in buses, mainly to Negro churches to sleep. Our group was asked, "Do you want to sleep in the gym?" This was right there and was fine; all we wanted was a place out of the mud to stretch out. It is a tremendous and new gym; we took our muddy shoes off at the door; in a few minutes the whole floor was covered with the bodies of hundreds of men, and the stage was covered with about fifty women. It felt wonderful to lie down, to have most of the lights out. Suddenly a voice in a thick Scottish brogue announced, "No girls in here." It was a priest from St. Jude's in a fancy embroidered robe. One of the girls sat up and said, "Surely you're kidding!" "I am not," he said. "No girls in here!" Conferences ensued between him and the monitors and others. Decision—the girls must go. Back into our muddy shoes. About two o'clock. Some slept, right outside. We slept in a girls locker room down the hall, creaking door, lights on and off, as girls came into the lavatory. When I woke, people were getting up. I looked at my watch: 5:30. Funny, I thought, my watch must have stopped. But it was 5:30.

The next morning Edith had a conversation with a black woman, about forty, who was poorly dressed, had a few teeth missing, and had slept on her coat.

"Where are you from?" I asked. "Selma. A little ways outside of Selma." We asked her questions and she said, "When they tear-gassed and clubbed us, I was there. When they drove us off the courthouse steps, I was there. A policeman jabbed his club into my stomach. I said, 'Don't you jab your club into my stomach,' so he grabbed me by the hair and he drug me down the steps. And we marched across the bridge on Sunday. I was there."

She has never voted, but now she has her card (the equivalent of an application to register), and she will keep on trying. Someone asked her, "What's going to happen when the march is over and all of us go home? Isn't it going to be worse for you?" "They'll call me a name," she said, "but they've called me a name before."

Edith then described lining up with a group under a California state flag and waiting patiently for the march to begin. People were singing, and they were reminded that this was to be a nonviolent march. "Don't speak to anyone along the march. If anyone speaks to you, don't answer back. If anyone attacks you, don't touch anybody."

For a long, long time we walked along the fence around the grounds, sloshing through the mud, until we went through the gate, an exciting moment. Negroes were on their porches and on the street, waving and calling. All the houses were very tiny, and many were sagging and crooked, propped up on bricks, unpainted. Now and then we had to run for half a block or so to keep the lines closed up, with our forty-degree clothes in the seventy-five-degree heat, the college prof still wearing his thermal underwear. He said later, not because of the underwear, that it had reminded him of going into combat in World War II. A school bus of little Negro girls was parked along the street, and they all put their hands out the windows to touch our hands. Six abreast and taking up the whole street, the line wound through the streets of a Negro district.

At one uphill part we could see the people ahead of us to the horizon like a moving river. We passed a brick school called the Loveless School; the windows were black with children calling "Freedom! Freedom!" Along a curb a nursery-school class stood with their teachers, the children all dressed up, with US flags, saying "Freedom! Freedom!"

Then we swung into downtown, the Jefferson Davis Hotel, and a large Confederate flag on one of the office buildings. No new buildings, a poor town. White faces and Negro faces in the windows of the buildings, the Negroes waving and the marchers waving back. I wondered who the whites thought we were waving to. Some white men along the street, no white women. If they said anything, I didn't hear them; the marchers drowned them out. One man standing grimly with a Confederate flag in his hand.

Suddenly the sight of the capitol, a great concourse leading up to it, filled with people; the Capitol a white building of lovely architecture, two long, low wings and the dome in the center. On the dome, the state flag of red bars and below it the Confederate flag. No US flag in sight. The speakers' stand below the steps, a line of soldiers on the steps, ranks of state police above them. Government buildings on either side, soldiers on their steps, soldiers on the street, a strange, strange sight.

Preparing to hear speeches, Edith's group sat down a couple hundred yards from the capitol grounds, directly in front of the Dexter Avenue Baptist Church, the church where Dr. Marin Luther King had been pastor from 1954 to 1960. The church would be renamed the Dexter Avenue King Memorial Baptist Church in 1978. After the speeches, including a rousing talk by Dr. King, the crowd dispersed, and Edith went into the church to get something to eat. There she encountered a young woman from Chicago who said, according to Edith's letter, "I wish they could come with helicopters and take all the people out of Selma." To this "an intense Chicago Negro woman" responded, "No. We have to bring more love in. That's what we have to do, bring more love into Selma."

That night Edith found a place to sleep on the floor at the Dexter Avenue Baptist Church.

Next day's Montgomery newspaper editorialized on the "Nobelians," a new term like "beatnik," "Communist," and "outside agitator." The paper also reported how Governor Wallace was eating a good meal of roast beef floating in ketchup as the march came up the street. It struck me later that this was like the report of the prisoner's last meal. Then he went up to his secretary's office to peek through the Venetian blinds (his office windows have bars on them, so you can't see so well). A reporter said to him, "Looks like an inauguration parade." Another reporter joked, "Looks like an inauguration parade a couple of years from now." Said Governor Wallace, "Don't talk like that."

Also, since there weren't enough windows for the state legislature to watch, they appointed an official reporter with field glasses. The only thing he reported that was recorded: "There's a lot of people out there."

In a few sentences Edith described her feelings about the march and what would come next.

A triumphal march. A wonderful, exultant feeling of jubilation. Fifty miles. Three miles the last day. Only three miles. Only the beginning. And many, many miles ahead.

And then it was time to go home.

We called a cab. "You called a Negro cab?" a staff worker asked me. As soon as he could get out of downtown he drove on back streets in the Negro section and then inevitably on Highway 80. He said the company had taken the cabs off the streets the night before.

"It's going to change," I said.

"I hope it do," he said.

My Mother's Passing

My mother had her own apartment in Los Angeles and her own interests and activities until she had a heart attack. I stayed with her for a month. My brother Bert and I discussed possibilities for her future, but there were no good solutions (and there are no better ones today). We need to change the aim of our society from making lots of money to taking care of one another.[11]

One day my mother and I got annoyed at each other about some small thing. Suddenly my mother said, "Edith, what do you want me to do? I'd do anything to make you happy." Without thinking, I heard myself say, "Just accept me as I am." That was immediately followed by the thought, *Then I should accept her as she is, not only as my mother but also as a person.* The tension between us drained away for good. I wished I had realized this much earlier in my life.[12]

11 Edith and Bert were able to arrange for Ida to move into a group home in Los Angeles where she had her own room and could share cultural interests and receive nutritious meals and other assistance.

12 Ida died of congestive heart failure on August 28, 1963.

21

Working for the San Francisco Human Rights Commission

In 1963, San Francisco, like most large US cities, was in the midst of the civil rights movement. Demonstrations were held against hotels, supermarkets, drive-in restaurants, automobile showrooms, and automobile repair shops that were discriminating in their service to and employment of African Americans. Minorities were also being discriminated against in the rental and purchasing of housing. In early 1964, Mayor John F. Shelley appointed the Interim Committee on Human Relations, which subsequently recommended to the city's board of supervisors that a permanent human rights commission be established. In July 1964, the board of supervisors passed the recommendation, and Mayor Shelley signed an ordinance establishing the Human Rights Commission.[1]

The official announcement of Edith's appointment as the first housing representative hired by the Human Rights Commission (HRC) appeared in the San Francisco Chronicle *on April 21, 1966. The article noted that Edith had helped prepare the feasibility study for St. Francis Square, the integrated housing development in the Western Addition. Frank Quinn, the director of the HRC, said that Edith's experience would be "an invaluable aid" since the commission was "especially concerned about the maintenance and development of integrated neighborhoods."*[2]

Over the next ten years Edith made important contributions to the work of the commission and was widely recognized as a powerful force in creating positive solutions to the many housing issues that arose due to continued

1 San Francisco Human Rights Commission, *Annual Report 2014* (San Francisco: Human Rights Commission).

2 "San Francisco Human Rights Post," *San Francisco Chronicle*, April 21, 1966.

development throughout San Francisco and the implications of that development for low-income individuals and those who would be displaced by "urban renewal."

It is typical of Edith that in her autobiography written for the family history she said very little about her experiences with the Human Rights Commission. Edith was modest and self-effacing. Even her friends knew little about the work she did for the commission.

In 1966 I was hired for the new staff job of housing representative for the San Francisco Human Rights Commission. I knew of no other job I would rather have had. It seemed the culmination of my working life, where all my experience, information, and skills came together and stretched my brain and determination and energy to try to get done everything there was to be done. Six months, I thought. In six months we will have worked ourselves out of our jobs. I worked there ten years until retirement.

We worked like fury to try to gain a quarter of a mile toward human rights, and maybe gained a sixteenth of an inch. And we learned that even with advancement, nothing is ever done, nothing is ever won for good. All the work I did was not only for us but also for the children and their children and their children who would come after us.

■ ■ ■

Although Edith didn't provide much detail about her work with the Human Rights Commission, her contributions are worth recounting because of the issues she dealt with and the esteem others had for her work. The following summary of several of Edith's major accomplishments during her ten years with the commission is based on minutes and annual reports from the commission, books and articles that discuss development and housing issues in San Francisco during this period, and interviews with several people who worked with Edith during those years.

Two major areas represent Edith's distinguished work with the commission: her work with the Fair Housing Planning Committee and her work on the Fair Housing for Children Ordinance.

In 1972, the San Francisco board of supervisors established a thirty-five-member Fair Housing Planning Committee (FHPC) to make recommendations to improve the racial, ethnic, and economic integration of neighborhoods.[3] *The need for such a committee arose from concerns about whether several major redevelopment efforts in San Francisco were leading to racial ghettos and economic segregation. Ten city agencies, along with twenty-five private groups with interests in housing in San Francisco, were represented on the committee. Edith, then sixty-one years old, was asked by the mayor's office to provide staff support for the committee. Mayor Joseph Alioto appointed Calvin Welch, then in his late twenties, as the presiding officer of the committee. Welch was already known for his work as a community activist.*

According to Welch, Edith provided tremendous leadership for the committee, although officially she was in a staff support role. In a 2015 interview, Welch indicated that it was Edith who had convinced the mayor that such a committee was needed.[4]*Edith suggested ("handpicked" was the term Welch used) the committee members. It was evident to Welch that Edith was the motivating force and the one with a vision. Welch felt that Edith "had a clear mastery of the subject, knowledge of the people appointed to the committee, and was able to relate to the different agendas and constituencies they represented. Edith had clarity of thought around issues of social justice that helped guide the committee through its work."*

Welch described Edith as "extraordinarily fair and even-tempered." She was "an Eleanor Roosevelt type," he said, "educated, well-read, deeply committed to vulnerable people" but "not condescending in any way . . . a true people-oriented individual." Welch noted that Edith was "adept and skilled at getting the best out of people, to move them collectively toward a coherent report." He was in awe of Edith's ability in working with the committee. He saw her as fundamentally a decent person who could get the best out of people without manipulation.

According to Welch, the committee work was a matter of horse trading and bringing together disparate viewpoints, while weaving together a coherent, comprehensive, and detailed report with doable recommendations. Edith was largely responsible for keeping people focused on the task and moving the effort forward.

3 Jerry Burns, "Supervisors Set Up Fair Housing Unit," *San Francisco Chronicle*, November 14, 1972.

4 Calvin Welch (community activist), in discussion with Peter A. Witt, November 9, 2015.

Eleven months after the committee was appointed it issued its report, which contained eighteen recommendations for policies that it said the city council should adopt, including the establishment of a rehabilitation assistance program; creation of zoning classifications to preserve and expand neighborhood integration and housing opportunities; consideration of civil rights impacts in environmental impact reports; and establishment of a development incentives program.[5] Welch was convinced that the report wouldn't have happened without Edith's leadership. Getting a large committee to agree on its substance in under a year was amazing.

Welch saw Edith as a rare individual who was known for her good works rather than for bragging or promoting her own accomplishments. She was "studiously invisible," by choice. She saw herself as a staff member and allowed the accolades for what was accomplished to go to the committee and others.

Edith was inspirational. Summing up, Welch said: "There are a few times in one's life that you meet extraordinary people. . . . Edith was one of those people. She had a sense of social justice and a desire to create better places for us all to live. At the same time, she had a sense of humility and a dignity about how one goes about doing that . . . she rejoiced in empowering others."

From the work on the committee, Welch developed a relationship with Edith that lasted into Edith's retirement. He noted that the lessons he learned from watching Edith work with the committee informed his own interactions with people over the rest of his career.

A second area that typified Edith's work entailed her efforts to promote the passage of a controversial Fair Housing for Children Ordinance by the San Francisco board of supervisors. The ordinance was designed to stop landlords from refusing to rent to families with children. The rationale for it was based on the large exodus of families with children from the city due to the lack of available housing. The ordinance was opposed by landlords who wanted the right to choose their tenants and by senior citizens who wanted to be able to live free from the noise and other perceived problems of living in buildings that allowed children.[6]

5 San Francisco Fair Housing Planning Committee, *One City or Two? Report of the San Francisco Fair Housing Planning Committee for the Racial, Ethnic and Economic Integration of Residential Neighborhoods in San Francisco* (San Francisco: Fair Housing Planning Committee, 1973).

6 "S.F. Landlords Must Rent to Families with Children," *Santa Cruz Sentinel*, June 19, 1975.

Edith became the public face for advocacy work on behalf of the ordinance. She talked passionately before the HRC in support of the ordinance, was often quoted in newspaper articles arguing for its passage, and worked behind the scenes to move it forward. When the ordinance came before the board of supervisors, after much discussion it was passed, but then it was vetoed by Mayor Alioto. Eventually, however, the board of supervisors overrode the mayor's veto and the ordinance came into force. Within a few years, a test case for enforcing the ordinance was brought before the courts, and the city prevailed.

A letter to the editor in the California Living Magazine *shortly after Edith retired indicated the important role that Edith played in getting ordinance passed: "It was through her efforts that a coalition of more than eighty organizations, religious groups and agencies . . . was formed. That coalition was called Fair Housing for Children and is still actively engaged in making certain the spirit and letter of the ordinance are being observed."*[7]

Over time there continued to be reports of landlords refusing to rent to families with children, but Edith's work had brought recognition to the problem of families leaving the city due to lack of affordable family rental housing.

Although most of the old guard had passed on by the time this book was being written, a few individuals, like Calvin Welch, were young enough in the 1970s to still be around and able to provide a perspective about Edith and her work. David Prowler was another person who worked with Edith during that period. Edith hired him as an assistant when he was only twenty years old, and Prowler shared a small office with Edith during her final year at the HRC. When discussing his interactions with Edith, the only negative Prowler could think of was that in those days she was a chain smoker and that the office reeked of smoke.

Despite the smoking, Edith inspired Prowler. He described her as a heroic individual. He saw her as outspoken, politically astute, and knowledgeable about housing issues at a time when housing policy in San Francisco was very controversial. Prowler viewed her as a leader and a role model at a time when it was more difficult than it is now for women to be seen as independent and capable. Prowler described Edith as "an elder who had people's backs. She was a good translator of ideas into practical solutions that others

7 Rita Semel, "More on Crusaders," *California Living Magazine*, March 14, 1976, 39.

could understand." Prowler indicated that Edith gave strength to those around her. He considered her a mentor.[8]

During the time that Prowler worked with Edith they both played a significant role in efforts to prevent the displacement of a largely Filipino American population from the International Hotel (I-Hotel) to enable development of the area. The I-Hotel was almost all that was left of Manilatown, the heavily Filipino area of San Francisco. For years after the first eviction notices were served in 1968, many individuals were involved in the long fight that took place on the streets, in courtrooms, and in the everyday lives of the I-Hotel and Manilatown residents. As housing representative for the HRC, Edith was deeply involved in trying to retain the living space for the residents or insure that acceptable alternative housing would be supplied. In 1977, after Edith retired, evictions took place. The I-Hotel effort was typical of several efforts Edith was involved in to find adequate housing for people being displaced by rampant urban development projects. Many of these efforts led to wider recognition of problems caused by displacement and in some cases led to development that included more equitable housing solutions.

Edith also had great insights about the interconnections of poverty, race, and being a single parent. During hearings for a 1975 study on women and housing, Edith was able to capture the interconnection of issues facing many women living under these circumstances. As a 1976 report of the National Council of Negro Women put it, "The woman alone with the child or children really has the worst time of all because of the entanglement of all kinds of discrimination, the layers of discrimination. And if the woman is of a minority group it adds another layer . . . and if she's 'on welfare,' it adds another layer, [and] if she [has] a large family, it adds another; it becomes impossible."[9]

Thus, Edith noted that women in San Francisco found it advantageous to work collaboratively across community and neighborhood groups to find solutions rather than adopt a competitive, go-it-alone strategy.

8 David Prowler (consulting firm owner) in discussion with Peter A. Witt, November 5, 2015.

9 National Council of Negro Women, *Women and Housing: A Report on Sex Discrimination in Five American Cities* (Washington, DC: US Department of Housing and Urban Development, 1976), 83.

When Edith retired from the HRC, she requested that there be no formal luncheon or banquet or resolution. However, a letter signed by Victor Medearis Sr., chair, and Grant S. Mickins III, director of the commission, was read at her final meeting on December 18, 1975:

> Quite literally, you have been the housing voice of not only this commission, but, in many instances, of this community. The commission's reputation as a spokesperson for decent, integrated, low-and-moderate-income, nondiscriminatory housing goals in the City stems directly from your initiative, your deep personal and professional dedication, and your leadership.
>
> We think you are irreplaceable, but we will move on in this aspect of our commitment to human rights in this city, and we can do so with the object lesson of your work as our guide.
>
> There are bonds of comradeship, professional association, and affection that tie all of us,—Commissioners and staff, collectedly and individually, whether those now serving or those with whom you have worked in the past ten years,—to you.
>
> We wish you great happiness in your new life, and we thank you for the extraordinary gift of your work.[10]

Reinforcing Edith's many contributions to the efforts of the Human Rights Commission, the following assessment was contained in a 1976 "sunset" review of the HRC.[11]

> It should be noted that one staff member who recently retired, Edith Witt, came to symbolize for many community groups and minority and low-income residents, the kind of devoted and forceful service that the Human Rights Commission should offer San Franciscans. Partly because of her work, and partly because the Commissioners are highly representative, the HRC

10 "Minutes, Human Rights Commission," December 18, 1975, 4, Edith Witt papers.

11 In some cities and states, agencies are scheduled for periodic review to determine if they are meeting their stated purposes, and an agency can be dissolved or "sunset" or have its functions modified based on the review outcomes.

> does enjoy a degree of respect and appreciation in the community which is rare for a City agency.[12]

Even after Edith retired she still contributed to community discussion through opinion pieces published in the San Francisco Chronicle *about code enforcement and rent control. Her ongoing commitment to fair housing policy was abundantly clear in a February 1976 editorial on code enforcement: "I retired in December after ten years as housing representative for the Human Rights Commission, but I'm still worried and angry about the people living in unsafe and unhealthy apartments and hotels in San Francisco."*[13]

The op-ed provided a how-to primer for how to get housing codes enforced.

Likewise in a 1977 editorial Edith provided a detailed history of rent control efforts in San Francisco, with the conclusion that lack of rent control had considerably hurt the ability of people to be able to afford to live in the city.[14]

12 "Human Rights Commission, Annual Report," 1976, https://archive.org/stream/annualreport19751981huma/annualreport19751981huma_djvu.txt.

13 Edith Witt, "Ideas on Code Enforcement," *San Francisco Sunday Examiner and Chronicle*, February 29, 1976.

14 Edith Witt, "Remember Rent Control?," *San Francisco Sunday Examiner and Chronicle*, September 18, 1977.

22

Living on the Greenbrae Boardwalk

In about 1968, Edith moved across the Golden Gate Bridge to live at a home on the Greenbrae Boardwalk in Marin County. Ann McCorry owned the 787-square foot house. Edith and Ann had known each other since the 1950s. They lived together at the Marin County house until 1975 when Ann moved out, agreeing to let Edith continue to stay, although Ann would continue to own the house.

The Greenbrae Boardwalk is a small community of forty-nine water-front houses built over marshland that is only reachable by a boardwalk that juts out into Corte Madera Creek, near where the creek runs into the San Francisco Bay. The history of the boardwalk can be traced to an initial ark, a floating house, in 1903. Beginning in the 1920s and 1930s, the houses on barges began to transition to houses on posts that kept them above the high-tide line.[1]

Residents access their homes by foot or bicycle from a wooden, raised walkway only a few feet above the marsh. The water level under the houses rises and falls with tides. Below Edith describes her life there.

With the great glass windows and large deck of this house, I live as a family of one both indoors and outdoors at once. Witness the sunrise, witness the sunset, watch the clouds move and change, see the planets and the stars appear, stretch with the big sky over the marsh, know the tides of the creek each day, behold the path of the moon on the bay, see Mount Tamalpais and Ring Mountain. Know the cycle of the birds throughout the year, and the trees and flowers.

Forty-nine households depend on one another for maintenance of the boardwalk, the water pipes, the fire hoses, and the parking lot, for

1 Larkspur Smart Station Area Plan: Existing Conditions Report (Larkspur, CA: City of Larkspur, 2012), http://www.ci.larkspur.ca.us/DocumentCenter/View/2239.

emergencies and defending ourselves from development and encroachment. We are all kinds of people, but we are neighbors. We are a community.

In her autobiography, Edith describes the wonderful years she spent on the boardwalk after finishing her work with the Human Rights Commission.

Retirement was a delight. I was tired and burned out, but the sap began to rise again. The last year at work, I kept making a list of what I wanted to do when I retired.

I quit smoking. I read books. I swam. I made a kayak and paddled quietly on the creek, into the sloughs, under the freeway. I relearned to play on a neighbor's piano. I studied meditation, self-hypnosis, yoga, and t'ai chi at the community college; relaxation at the hospital; sail boating with the Recreation Department; dancing at the senior center; knitting with a neighbor. I learned how to fly a kite. I went out every week with a small birding group to marshes, beaches, woods, hills, refuges, sewage ponds, and dumps. I learned more about gardening and nurtured my garbage into the miracle of compost.

Friends and family also remember that when they went to visit Edith at her boardwalk home she would often invite them to join her in blowing bubbles. This playful side of Edith's personality became a trademark of sorts, and blowing bubbles became part of birthday celebrations and other events.

Edith also continued her lifelong passion for protecting the environment and making sure that development was done in a responsible and respectful manner.

I was active in the Boardwalk Improvement Club (BIC). I continued political activity for the earth and the life upon it. I helped people I knew who needed help. I saw people I hadn't seen enough before. I didn't have time to do all I wanted to do. I wondered how I ever had time to work before. But people asked me, "Retired? But what do you do?"

From the time Edith moved to the boardwalk, she was involved in an effort to mitigate the impact of building a ferry terminal nearby. Plans for a ferry linking Marin County to San Francisco began in the late 1960s.[2] *Ultimately the Marin terminal was placed near the boardwalk, with the first ferry service beginning in 1976. Boardwalk residents were concerned that placing the terminal so close to their community would create backwash and thus erosion problems for the environmentally sensitive marsh area their houses occupied. Problems arose almost immediately after the ferry service was launched.*

Edith took the lead on behalf of the BIC in lobbying the Golden Gate Bridge, Highway and Transportation District to reduce the speed of the ferries as they neared the terminal area (thus reducing the backwash) and to build some kind of a protective barrier that would mitigate the impact of the backwash created by the ferries. She worked with the BIC to develop lobbying efforts, wrote letters on the BIC's behalf, and spoke at hearings. Several current and past residents of the boardwalk community credit Edith's ability to work with governmental entities, her dedication to preservation efforts, and her leadership with helping to reach a successful outcome for the residents.

Reducing the speed of the ferries as they entered and left the terminal area was accomplished in a few years. However, it took until 1988 to reach an agreement to install and monitor the impact of rock riprap to provide wave and surge protection and prevent shoreline erosion along the boardwalk.[3] *Monitoring of the impact of the mitigation efforts was to occur every five years for a twenty-five year period.*

As Edith got older, she felt herself slowing.

I knew I was getting old when my activity became slower and slower, and more and more restricted. I read recently that on his ninetieth birthday the poet John Hall Wheelock said, "In old age things get more poignant—so many associations—everything reverberating with everything else. You don't feel you are any older, but suddenly you realize you are. But instead of life getting dimmer and duller, it gets so poignant, it's

2 "History of Golden Gate Ferry Service," Golden Gate Bridge, Highway and Transportation District, http://goldengateferry.org/researchlibrary/history.php.

3 "Calendar Item C12, State Lands Commission, April 12, 1988," California State Lands Commission, http://archives.slc.ca.gov/Meeting_Summaries/1988_Documents/04–12–88/Voting_Record.pdf.

unbearable. Like looking at the sun." That's the way I feel, as if I'm living my whole past together with the present.

In 1994, living alone and under the unique circumstances of the boardwalk community took its toll, and Edith moved to a nearby small group home in San Rafael. In the first few years, friends from the boardwalk, people she had known during her time living and working in San Francisco, and various family members came to visit, sometimes taking Edith out to one of her favorite restaurants for a meal or for drive to a nearby nature area. However, over time Edith became more confused about who people were and communication became difficult.

Edith died on February 23, 2000. That spring a small group of family, friends, and former coworkers gathered in a meeting room at a hotel near the boardwalk. People sat in a circle and recalled favorite stories about Edith. Many people at the gathering were meeting for the first time, having been part of Edith's life at different times or in different circumstances. Edith had kept much of her life compartmentalized. During her life, when she was with family members, coworkers, or friends, she focused on the individual or individuals there with her and did not talk about the others. This was one way Edith had for making each person feel special. Few in the room knew the details of her life beyond the particular relationship they had with her. But what emerged from all was a story of courage, someone who deeply cared about the environment, someone dedicated to issues of social justice, and someone whom everyone had wished they had gotten to know better during her life. And everyone could agree that Edith was a remarkable woman.

In the autobiography she contributed to our family history, Edith mentioned living most of her life as a family of one. After reading what Edith wrote about her life, her nephew Paul Witt asked Edith about this. Her reply in 1991 was illuminating about her philosophy of life.

In the 1950s I went to a weekend retreat held by the [American] Friends Service Committee. It was fine. What I remember most was, as we sat around the large round table, about 25 people, being asked various questions by the discussion leader. I remember only one. He asked, What do you want on your tombstone? The answers were very interesting and diverse. I had never thought of that before—I'm not going to have a tombstone—but the phrase that jumped into my mind was "She lived one life."

And that has been a comforting motto ever since. I feel I've lived a full and satisfying life—although life and the universe are more of a mystery than ever—but there are a dozen or two dozen or a hundred different lives I might have lived that would have been as full and satisfying. At the moment, however, I feel, of course, that my life is the only one I could have lived.

23

Honoring Edith

After Edith's death, two efforts were undertaken to commemorate her many contributions to insuring a better life for others. The first was the creation of an internship to honor her commitment to social justice and the concerns for working people. The second was the naming of a senior living center in San Francisco to honor her championing of fair housing policy during her distinguished service as a staff member of the San Francisco Human Rights Commission.

The PRRAC Internship

In 2000, family and friends contributed to funding the Edith Witt Internship through the Poverty and Race Research Action Council (PRRAC) to help develop a new generation of community activists. Each year from 2000 to 2009, PRRAC supported an intern hired by a grassroots community group to work on social justice issues.

For example, in 2003 an intern with the TransAfrica Forum in Washington, DC, worked with the TransAfrica Youth and Student Network to help build a national network to support on-campus organizing, facilitate cross-campus communication, and provide organizer training. In 2007 it was fitting that the internship grant went to the Manilatown Heritage Foundation to support its efforts to assist individuals applying to live at the new International Hotel Senior Housing Building. The building was the result of an effort of more than thirty years to develop affordable senior housing as a replacement for San Francisco's I-Hotel. Edith had been involved in the unsuccessful 1960s and 1970s efforts to help I-Hotel residents maintain their apartments in the face of developer efforts to have the building torn down for commercial redevelopment.

The Edith Witt Senior Living Community

The second action honoring Edith took a lot longer to realize. After Edith's death, several people who admired her work with the Human Rights Commission sought to honor her leadership and advocacy efforts during her decade on the commission. It took over ten years for their goal to be accomplished, but in 2010 the Edith Witt Senior Living Community at 66 Ninth Street in San Francisco was dedicated. Victor Honig, a San Francisco community activist and Human Rights Commission member, was instrumental in having the building named in Edith's honor.[1] The eleven-story facility, operated by Mercy Housing, California, features 107 affordable apartments for seniors (age sixty-two and older), with a clinic, health center, computer lab, and four thousand square feet of secure, landscaped outdoor space.

Material distributed at the dedication ceremony noted that Edith had played an important role in more than one struggle between the most and least powerful in the city. Edith was remembered "for her work in raising the consciousness of the people of San Francisco to the need for safe, quality affordable housing, in which people with low incomes could live with dignity; and for her work in bringing recognition to the concept that people must be provided with acceptable relocation housing before redevelopment of neighborhoods occurs."[2]

> *Specifically, it was noted that Edith had contributed by:*
>
> *Supporting San Francisco residents working to make the city's development policies accountable to the affordable housing* needs of *working families, the poor and the elderly;*

1 Victor Honig's obituary noted, "Victor made his mark in San Francisco as a fierce advocate for social justice, including a commitment to working for low-income housing, peace, and civil rights. As an accountant, he used his expertise to hold those in power accountable, regularly scrutinizing the city, state and federal budgets. He was a cofounder of Accountants for the Public Interest and offered his skills to numerous non-profit social change organizations, as their pro-bono accountant or as a board member teaching them the importance of diligent financial management. Though he owned and managed commercial real estate in San Francisco, and was an astute businessman, he often advocated for positions that were contrary to his personal benefit. "Victor Honig obituary," Legacy.com, http://www.legacy.com/obituaries/sfgate/obituary.aspx?pid=163233535.

2 Sarah Karpman, information sheet distributed at October 10, 2010, dedication ceremony for the Edith Witt Senior Living Community, in possession of Peter A. Witt.

> *Serving as a valuable resource for San Francisco neighborhood community groups working to preserve and expand affordable housing;*
>
> *Assisting community organizations working to prevent illegal evictions and advocating for fair and affordable housing for the residents of areas being redeveloped; and*
>
> *Bringing official recognition to the problem of sweatshops, forced labor and sub-human working conditions in San Francisco's Chinatown."*[3]

Among the speakers at the dedication ceremony was Edith's former assistant, David Prowler. David ended his comments about Edith by producing a bottle of suds and proceeding to blow bubbles in Edith's honor. Edith would have been happy.[4]

3 Ibid.

4 David Prowler discussion with Peter A. Witt, November 5, 2015.

24
Conclusion

Edith Witt lived a life of substance, meaning, and impact. She left a significant legacy to her family, friends, coworkers, and those who never knew her but benefited from her service to others. She was a strong, courageous, yet reserved woman. She never boasted of her accomplishments and would be surprised that people would find her accounts of life interesting and compelling. During her life, however, she was a role model and was respected and admired by those who knew her, and her life story continues to inspire the efforts of her descendants.

Edith came from humble beginnings. Her father never achieved his goal of being a lawyer; instead he worked in the shadows as a clerk in a large New York law firm. Her mother's life was devoted to raising her children during a time when perceptions of the proper role for women in society thwarted the possibility of accomplishments outside the home. However, through their love of reading and their appreciation for the value of good writing and verbal expression, Edith's parents inspired not just their sons but also their daughter to become educated. Edith and her brothers each graduated from college, with Edith and her brother Bert both achieving master's degrees in later life. Most importantly, Edith's parents did not block the efforts of their children as they each became involved in social, economic, and political movements aroused by the Depression and World War II.

At every stage of her life, Edith tried to make a difference in the lives of others, through her

- *involvements with Depression-era efforts to improve the lives of individuals deeply impacted by a shattered economy;*
- *devotion to soldiers during her three years with the Red Cross Club Service during World War II;*

- *participation in the Selma-to-Montgomery march to support the struggle for civil rights;*
- *dedication to ameliorate the impacts of urban renewal on those displaced from their homes during the time she served on the staff of the San Francisco Human Rights Commission; and*
- *involvement in local actions to protect environmentally sensitive communities.*

Edith lived a life that mattered—a life that her Human Rights Commission colleagues honored after her passing with the naming of the Edith Witt Senior Living Community in San Francisco. In addition, an internship program was named in her honor to further work in areas of social justice that Edith would have supported. Edith would have suggested that these honors go to others, but her colleagues, friends, and family knew that Edith deserved this recognition and hoped that Edith's story would inspire others.

Edith's stories about her World War II American Red Cross experiences are also significant. They are unique in the literature that has emerged from the letters and writings of other women who served. Edith's accounts provide a vivid record of the day-to-day impact of the experience of war from the point of view of the Red Cross personnel who worked so tirelessly to bring comfort and transplant a bit of home for the soldiers during their off-duty hours. She was indeed an American "girl" who made a difference during the war. By supplying integrated accounts, Edith provided an in-depth understanding of the value of the Red Cross clubs to the service members who were fighting to defeat the Axis powers. In several of her accounts she also reflects on the problems that servicemen had to face when they returned home.

Edith's autobiography and World War II narratives are unique in another important way. Due to social circumstances, a large part of Edith's life was hidden from public view. She grew up in an era when the questions she may have had about her own sexual orientation were not open to public acknowledgment or discussion. We see in her autobiography hints of her struggles to find her place in a world that was not ready to acknowledge or support lesbian relationships. Edith's relationships were not discussed within her family, and she struggled to achieve acceptance and understanding from her mother. In later life she lived alone, without full acknowledgment by herself and others of a significant part of her life and story.

Pulling together the materials for this book has been a privilege and an honor. Edith's autobiography has been available to her family since 1990, but the World War II materials only were revealed in the spring of 2015. Subsequent research uncovered more of Edith's writings and other materials related to her life, enabling a more complete understanding of the significant events in Edith's life and her many contributions to improving the lives of others as well as her efforts to take responsibility for the physical environment in which she lived. Edith's story also informs our understanding of what it means to take responsibility for social justice and change.

For those reading this book, I hope that Edith's story will inspire reflection and, more importantly, thoughtful action. Edith's was a life well lived, and her story inspires each of us to consider: Am I only passing through, or can I make a positive difference during my journey?

Bibliography

Acker, James R. *Scottsboro and its Legacy: The Cases that Challenged American Legal and Social Justice*. Westport, CT: Praeger, 2008.

Adams, Michael C. C. *The Best War Ever: America and World War II*. 2nd ed. Baltimore: John Hopkins University Press, 2015.

American Red Cross. *General Guide for Selecting Staff Assistants*. ARC 828. Washington, DC: American Red Cross, 1942.

———. *Red Cross Service Record: Accomplishments of Seven Years, 1939–1946*. Washington, DC: American Red Cross, Office of Program Research, 1946.

———. *WWII Services to the Armed Forces*. American Red Cross. https://web.archive.org/web/20160301150808/http://www.redcross.org/about-us/history/red-cross-american-history/WWII/SAF.

Atkinson, Rick. *An Army at Dawn: The War in North Africa, 1942–1943*. New York: Henry Holt, 2002.

"Battle History." www9thdivision.net. http://9thinfantrydivision.net/battle-history.

Berube, Allan. *Coming Out under Fire: The History of Gay Men and Women in World War Two*. New York: Free Press, 1990.

Bork, William. "Massacre at Republic Steel." *Chicago Labor & Arts Festival Blog*. https://web.archive.org/web/20160303224737/http://www.illinoislaborhistory.org/articles/267-massacre-at-republic-steel.html.

Bryan, Jami. "The 88th Infantry Division in Italy." Army Historical Foundation, January 20, 2015. https://armyhistory.org/the-88th-infantry-division-in-italy.

Bryson, Rhett. "The Bunins: Meet the Bunins, Hope and Morey." *Great Foodini*. http://drama2014.furman.edu/FoodiniWeb/FoodiniBunins.html.

Carter, Dan T. *Scottsboro: A Tragedy of the American South*. Rev ed. Baton Rouge: Louisiana State University Press, 1984.

Cohen, Robert. *When the Old Left Was Young: Student Radicals and America's First Mass Student Movement, 1929–1941*. New York: Oxford University Press, 1993.

"Common Ground (magazine)." *Densho Encyclopedia*. http://encyclopedia.densho.org/Common_Ground_(magazine).

Cuenod, Carol. "Redevelopment A-1 and Origin of St. Francis Square." *Found SF*. http://foundsf.org/index.php?title=Redevelopment_A-1_and_Origin_of_St._Francis_Square.

Davin, Eric Leif. *Partners in Wonder: Women and the Birth of Science Fiction 1926–1965*. Lanham, MD: Lexington Books, 2006.

Dinnerstein, Leonard. *Antisemitism in America*. New York: Oxford University Press, 1994.

Dulles, Foster Rhea. *The American Red Cross: A History*. New York: Harper & Brothers, 1950.

Final Report on the WPA Program, 1935–1943. Washington, DC: Government Printing Office, 1946. http://lccn.loc.gov/47032199.

Frankfurter, Felix. "The Case of Sacco and Vanzetti." *Atlantic Monthly*, March 1927. http://www.theatlantic.com/past/unbound/flashbks/oj/frankff.htm.

Gates, Henry Louis, Jr. "What Was Black America's Double War?" *Root*, May 24, 2013. http://www.theroot.com/what-was-black-americas-double-war-1790896568.

Goodrich, Marcus. *Delilah*. New York: Farrar & Rinehart, 1941.

Grayzel, Solomon. *A History of the Jews: From the Babylonian Exile to the Present*. Philadelphia: Jewish Publication Society, 1968.

Hansan, John E. "The Works Progress Administration." Social Welfare History Project, Virginia Commonwealth University Libraries. http://www.socialwelfarehistory.com/eras/great-depression/wpa-the-works-progress-administration.

"History of Golden Gate Ferry Service." Golden Gate Bridge, Highway & Transportation District. http://goldengateferry.org/researchlibrary/history.php.

"Human Rights Commission, Annual Report 1975 to 1976." San Francisco Human Rights Commission. https://archive.org/stream/annualreport19751981huma/annualreport19751981huma_djvu.txt.

Korson, George. *At His Side: The Story of the American Red Cross Overseas in World War II*. New York: Coward-McCann, 1945.

Larkspur Smart Station Area Plan: Existing Conditions Report. Larkspur, CA: City of Larkspur, 2012. http://www.ci.larkspur.ca.us/DocumentCenter/View/2239.

"Liberty Ships Built by the United States Maritime Commission in World War II." *American Merchant Marine at War*. http://www.usmm.org/libertyships.html.

"Louis Wirth." American Sociological Association. http://www.asanet.org/about/presidents/Louis_Wirth.cfm.

"The Manhattan Project: Making the Atomic Bomb." AtomicArchive.com. http://www.atomicarchive.com/History/mp. Adapted from F. G. Gosling, *The Manhattan*

Project: Making the Atomic Bomb (Washington, DC: History Division, Dept. of Energy, 1999).

Meyer, Leisa D. *Creating GI Jane: Sexuality and Power in the Women's Army Air Corps during World War II*. New York: Columbia University Press, 1996.

Murray, Robert Keith. *A Study of American Public Opinion on the American Red Cross from Newspapers and Periodicals, 1881–1948*. Monograph 30. Washington, DC: Privately printed, 1950.

Murray, Williamson. "Operation Torch: Allied Invasion of North Africa." *World War II*, November 2002. http://www.historynet.com/operation-torch-allied-invasion-of-north-africa.htm.

National Council of Negro Women. *Women and Housing: A Report on Sex Discrimination in Five American Cities*. Washington, DC: US Department of Housing and Urban Development, 1976.

Norwalk, Rosemary. *Dearest Ones: A True World War II Love Story*. New York: John Wiley & Sons, 1999.

Orchayon, Sheryl. "The Jews of Algeria, Morocco and Tunisia." *Teaching the Legacy* (Yad Vashem e-newsletter) 25 (October 2011). http://www.yadvashem.org/yv/en/education/newsletter/25/algeria_marocco.asp.

Pike, Brett. "Discrimination against African American Soldiers in World War II: Racial Policies and the March to Desegregation." https://www.scribd.com/document/165853187/Pike-discrimination-Against-African-American-Soldiers-in-Wwii.

Prowler, David. Interview with Peter A. Witt, November 5, 2015.

Ramsey, Julia A. "'Girls' in Name Only: A Study of American Red Cross Volunteers on the Frontlines of World War II." Master's thesis, Auburn University, 2011.

San Francisco Fair Housing Planning Committee. *One City or Two? Report of the San Francisco Fair Housing Planning Committee for the Racial, Ethnic and Economic Integration of Residential Neighborhoods in San Francisco*. San Francisco: Fair Housing Planning Committee, 1973.

San Francisco Human Rights Commission. *Annual Report 2014*. San Francisco: Human Rights Commission, 2014.

Sargent, Mary Thomas. *Runway towards Orion: The True Adventures of a Red Cross Girl on a B-29 Air Base in World War II India*. Grand Rapids, MI: Triumph Press, 1984.

Semel, Rita. "More on Crusaders." *California Living Magazine*, March 14, 1976, 39.

Shealy, Gwendolyn C. *A Critical History of the American Red Cross, 1882–1945*. Lewiston, NY: Edwin Mellen Press, 2003.

Society of the 1st Infantry Division. "History." Society of the 1st Infantry Division. https://www.1stid.org/historyindex.php.

Special Services Division, Army Service Forces, United States Army. *A Pocket Guide to North Africa*. Washington, DC: War and Navy Departments, 1943. http://www.ibiblio.org/pha/world/Pocket-Guide-to-North-Africa.pdf.

Stevens, Michael E., and Ellen D. Goldlust, *Women Remember the War 1941–1945*. Madison: State Historical Society of Wisconsin, 1993.

Taylor, Nick. *American-Made: The Enduring Legacy of the WPA, When FDR Put the Nation to Work*. New York: Bantam Books, 2009.

"Venereal Disease and Treatment during WWII." WW2 US Medical Research Centre. https://www.med-dept.com/articles/venereal-disease-and-treatment-during-ww2.

Victor Honig obituary. Legacy.com. http://www.legacy.com/obituaries/sfgate/obituary.aspx?pid=163233535.

The Victory Standard: The BRO and Fort Riley Standards Book. Fort Riley, Kansas, 2016. http://www.riley.army.mil/Portals/0/Docs/Units/1ID/TheVictoryStandard_2016.pdf.

Vuic, Kara Dixon. *The Girls Next Door: American Women and Military Entertainment* Cambridge, MA: Harvard University Press, forthcoming.

Weatherford, Doris. *American Women during World War II*. Edison, NJ: Castlebooks, 2008.

Welch, Calvin. Interview by Peter A. Witt, November 9, 2015.

Witt, Edith. "The Artist." *The Comet* 9, no. 2 (June 1927): 54.

———. "The Convention." By Ede Witt. *Fantastic* 8, no. 5 (May 1959): 74–84.

———. "The Filtering Theory and the Social Structure." Master's thesis, San Francisco State University, 1962.

———. "Hunting." *Common Ground* 7, no. 2 (1947): 74–80.

———. "The Personal Adman." *The Reporter*, May 14, 1959, 36–37.

Wragg, David. *Historical Dictionary of Aviation*. London, England: Sutton Publishing, 2009.

Index

Page numbers in *italic* refer to illustrations.